21
68

51-82
92

Theories of labour market segmentation

A critique

Theories of labour market segmentation

A critique

R. Loveridge

Professor of Manpower Management
University of Aston, Birmingham

and

A.L. Mok

Professor of Sociology
University of Antwerp

Martinus Nijhoff Social Sciences Division
The Hague/Boston/London 1979

Distributors for North America
Kluwer Boston Inc.
160 Old Derby Street
Hingham, MA 02043 USA

ISBN 90.207.0859.7

Preface

The objectives of this book are: to review and develop a framework of key analytical concepts in the field of labour market segmentation; to develop and test these concepts against available data; to indicate weaknesses in the data in the light of the analysis; to offer a critique of manpower policies in some European countries in the light of the foregoing analysis; and to indicate areas of further research. The authors hope that this survey of the literature and the comments that accompany it will prove useful to policy makers and students alike.

The authors would like to acknowledge the role of the Directorate-General for Social Affairs of the European Community, Brussels, in initiating and supporting the production of this volume of criticism and discussion. We have especially appreciated the role of David White, on whose advice we came to rely in directing our critique upon the application of segmental theory to matters of labour market policy. Others whose help and advice we have relied on are John Morley, also of the European Community, Peta Small, who typed the several drafts, and our respective wives and families whose encouragement and discreet silences enabled us to get past the nth draft.

Birmingham/Antwerp   April 1978

Contents

8. The labour market as an arena / 173

1. Overview of the subject

The marginal worker as a source of concern

From the classical notion of the labour theory of value to the neo-classical concepts of consumer preference and marginal utility the development of economic ideas was heavily influenced by current problems within the political economy. In seeking to explain the sources of these problems and to influence their outcomes economic theorists have tended to mirror the dominant ideologies of their day. Indeed economic theory may be said to have actively reinforced prevailing moral values by expressing them in a 'neutral' way. But from time to time in the history of the last two hundred years the emergence of large scale long-term unemployment and the revelation of poverty and economic disadvantage of hitherto unrealized proportions has undermined both the credibility of political regimes and the confidence that economists display in the viability of their conceptual tools.

During the 1960s the sequence of revelatory experiences was reversed. A fragmented but uniformly motivated movement for economic and social emancipation grew up among disadvantaged minority groups within the Western democracies. Largely as a result of this political pressure anti-discriminatory, and even counter-discriminatory, legislation was enacted by many Western governments. For a number of reasons a world-wide crisis of economic confidence followed these events; a crisis from which investors and, perhaps, consumers, have yet to emerge.

The pattern of long-term unemployment that has resulted during the 1970s has reaffirmed, rather than disproved, the continuance of differential career opportunities based on discriminatory employment practices. The seriousness of this pattern of discrimination is to be seen in its institutionalization and perpetuation in the investment and employment policies of major national and multi-national companies. It is hardly surprising therefore that the current focus of the theoretical critique of orthodox, neo-classical, labour economics should be upon its almost

total disregard of the firm as the architect as well as the creator of
employment opportunities and the most important source of training in
work skills as well as the principal allocator of rewards in society.

The marginal worker in theory

The marginal worker has often been connected with a phenomenon
known in the literature as *under-employment*. Whereas unemployment is
always defined from the 'people' point of view (as a phenomenon
whereby people temporarily do not belong to the work force but may be
activated), under-employment is concerned with 'jobs' as well as
'people'. First and foremost with jobs: jobs are left unfilled for a certain
period of time and gradually become involved in a process of marginalization. But 'people' can also be under-employed, when their qualifications, skills and capabilities are only used to a limited extent—as is often
the case with marginal workers.

The prevalence of under-employment over a long period has been
attributed to numerous causes. One's choice of explanations depends
very much on the theoretical perspective adopted. Neo-classical
economists are inclined to believe in the self equilibriating nature of the
economic system in which the price of labour is flexible in the face of
changing consumer demand and changes in the production process.
Unemployment or increased poverty is a purely temporary phenomenon
for at least so long as the level of real wages remains flexible. Keynesians
return to the classical (Malthusian) concept of aggregate demand to
explain long-term unemployment by reference to a low or falling propensity to invest among entrepreneurs. One of the weaknesses of post-
Keynesian economists is the disregard shown for the relative efficiency
of labour (its productivity) as against that of capital. Keynesian theory
(as distinct from Beveridge pragmatism) has little to say on differential
employment opportunities or the under-employment of labour. On the
other hand the continued existence of comparatively impoverished
sectors of employment are central to the Marxian analysis of capitalism.
In a state of monopsony such groups drive down the exchange value of
labour and enable larger profits to be made for reinvestment. The need
for a 'reserve army' is seen by Marxists to grow greater as the ownership
of capital becomes more monopolistic and the pace of technological
innovation (and therefore the need for investment) grows faster.

Institutional economists have pointed to the advantages to be gained by employers facing variable product market conditions in establishing a core of 'permanent' workers to which a variable number of temporary workers may be added for short periods. The term marginal worker has come to be applied to any temporary or part-time employee who is the last to be taken on in time of high demand and the first to be dismissed when trade falls off. As such he or she must necessarily be 'available' for short-term employment: this usually implies that his work should require little knowledge or training in special skills. Potential workers belonging to this external 'pool' may do so from choice, but more often their status is determined by their lack of characteristics that are *generally* sought after by all or most employers in their local labour market. One has of course to differentiate between the market positions of the peripatetic subcontracting tradesman or secretary/typist or nurse, all of whom are selling their skills at a high economic 'rent', and others such as the 'twilight shift' assembly worker or hotel porter who have little or no control over their employment opportunities.

Even so in neo-classical economics only a monopsonist (sole employer) should be able to secure marginal workers at less than the going average rate for a given grade of labour. One has therefore to explain the gap in earnings and working conditions between groups whose work is of a temporary nature and those of more permanent workers. It is obvious that monetary rewards are not the only form of returns from work. Adam Smith recognized in 1776 the idiosyncratic nature of job satisfactions when he suggested that each worker made a balance of net advantages in the job which was personal to him or her. Mill's response was to point out 'The more revolting the occupation, the more certain it is to receive the minimum of remuneration, because it devolves upon the most helpless and degraded, on those who from squalid poverty, or from want of skill and education, are rejected from all other employments' (1840: 372).

In this passage Mill rejects the orthodox economists belief in the individual's freedom and ability to make a rational choice between jobs and careers, a belief which remains central to modern manpower planning. More lately the concept of investment in education, training, and work experience, has been resurrected (again from Smith) to explain differences in wages and salaries as being differential returns to outlays on human capital. Formal job qualifications lead to enhanced but deferred rewards for personal abstinence as well as for higher produc-

tion. The expected correlation between earnings and formal qualifications appear in many studies comparing aggregate or average incomes
across occupational groups. However the range of incomes within
similarly qualified groups is often greater than the differentials between
neighbouring strata. Nor can these differences be explained by differences in either productivity or in personal job tastes.

One is therefore forced by the evidence to conclude that market
imperfections exist on a scale too large to be considered 'frictional' or
short-term. While ignorance of market opportunities may explain some
apparent inefficiencies in the allocation of labour, the statistical pattern
of employment suggests systematic discrimination against certain types
of people, for example women, coloureds, immigrants, the very young,
and older active members of the work population. At very least the large
and persisting differential in earnings and in job opportunities displayed
between these groups and that of prime white males is a challenge to
orthodox economics. By assuming the existence of exogenously determined tastes or preferences among employers the orthodox economist
offers little by way of explanation of the basis for these discriminative
practices and for the sub-optimal workings of the economy that results
from them.

Theories of discrimination–atomistic or structural?

More recent works in labour economics have used one of three approaches in their analysis of the market. The most widely used in
theoretical analysis is one which assumes the existence of a continuum of
workers and firms in perfect competition on either side of the market. In
empirical work segmental models tend to be more useful. Studies that
place firms and workers in discrete occupational, geographical and
industrial categories are mapping segmentation in the market. The
advantage of such models over continuous queue models is that one can
better define who is in the line for a job. Moreover, *within the boundaries*
of the market so defined one can make assumptions about the nature of
competition between employees and between firms which are more
credible (that is, the model seeks to define partial equilibrium conditions
within a sub-system).

The discovery of a large body of apparently disadvantaged workers has led to the formulation of a third approach which has come to be known as the 'dual labour market model'.

A dual labour market may be defined as one in which:

1. there is a more or less pronounced division into higher and lower paying sectors;
2. mobility across the boundary of these sectors is restricted;
3. higher paying jobs are tied to promotional ladders, while lower paying jobs offer few opportunities for vertical movement;
4. higher paying jobs are relatively stable, while lower paid jobs are unstable.

According to this theory the labour market may be divided into two sectors, one characterised by 'good' jobs, called the primary sector, and the other characterised by 'bad' jobs, called the secondary sector. A worker who is unemployed in the primary sector has been made so in the involuntary, Keynesian sense. He may accept less attractive work temporarily, but essentially he is waiting to regain a similar position to the one from which he has been replaced. Secondary jobs tend to be self-terminating or to be so unattractive as to provide little incentive to stay. Hence aggregate unemployment in the secondary sector is made up of short-stayers who move in and out of work frequently—a condition described as 'frictional', or self-adjusting, in orthodox theory.

This dichotomization must be viewed as an abstraction from a complex multi-sector market. In reality jobs and careers may be judged against those conditions considered appropriate within a given occupation, region, or industry. In this sense the dual market concept may be viewed as a continuum in which certain tasks or jobs are rewarded in a manner which denotes lack of competition between primary and secondary workers for the same job.

On what basis does this dichotomy occur? Dual market theory offers no clear answer in itself. There are perhaps four main theoretical perspectives:

1. individual stigmatization;
2. internal labour market mechanism used unconsciously;
3. internal labour market mechanism used consciously; and
4. industrial reserve army.

1. Stigmatization is a social process by which a dominant group attributes impurity to features of a subordinate or foreign or 'outside' group. It involves training the young and new entrants to the 'in-group' in appropriate responses and behaviour towards the outcasts or 'untouchables'. It is normally a defence of an economically privileged position which cannot be 'rationally' justified. It is usually psychologically internalized and often unconscious. Although resulting from a group ideology it is therefore exercised unknowingly in everyday individual actions.

2. The internal labour market (ILM) is a description of the structured processes by which companies, and other employing bodies, allocate labour and distribute rewards. These processes follow the internal administrative rationale of the organization; they are more or less insulated from the competitive pressures of the external market according to the position of the job within the firm. Kerr (1954) was the first scholar to conceptualize an ILM model. He described the structure of rules by which 'portals of entry and exit' to the ILM were defined, and the 'seniority ladders' and 'job clusters' which provide routes for movement within it. Doeringer and Piore (1971) provide a social and economic rationale for the development of the ILM. Enterprise specific skills are developed within such an organization. These offer higher immediate returns to employers than more general training. They also enable on-the-job training to take place, which is less costly and more task directed. Once trained in this manner the 'permanent' worker is seen as part of a work team rather than as an individual, if he leaves the productivity of the group declines overall. To these economic forces for stability and permanence Doeringer and Piore add the social constraints of 'custom and practice'. Custom seems to form most strongly around internal wage relationships and job allocation procedures.

In the external labour market the establishment of an ILM (sometimes referred to as a 'manorial' market) encourages other employers to attempt to achieve a similar monopsony over a specific supply of scarce labour. Trade unions encourage ILM's in two ways. Within companies they institutionalize the protective customs of their members and, through collective bargaining, reinforce existing regulations. Outside the firm they create their own ILM, as do professional associations, whenever they can control entry, training and/or qualification. These are sometimes described as craft or guild markets.

For Doeringer and Piore the crucial importance of the ILM is seen in its part in creating the wider dual market segmentation. Previously Kerr had spoken of the 'balkanization of labour markets'. Both authors are referring to the manner in which the employing establishment discriminates between workers in its hiring and training practices, and therefore provides differing career chances in wider society. Theoretically the importance of the ILM concept is in shifting the focus of labour economics away from a somewhat abstruse concern for the boundaries of occupational, industrial and regional markets to the point at which wages and jobs are created (i.e. in which MC = MRP). As such it poses an obvious threat to economic orthodoxy.

3, 4. The ILM may operate as a result of the purely localized concerns of employers, recruitment officers, work-groups and shop stewards. However there is considerable evidence that employers have consciously manipulated their environments to create a 'manorial' situation. Neo-Marxian economists (known in the United States as 'Radicals') analyse labour market segmentation as arising from the deliberate pursuit of welfare capitalism. Employers are alleged to have consciously fostered occupational and ethnic divisions in the external market and to have established insulated segments with different criteria for access in the internal market.

More orthodox Marxists see this subjective and individualized behaviour as reflecting nothing more than the 'objective' structural conditions of mature capitalism. Discrimination against minority groups may take the form of stigmatization. Individual employers and economists may act in their own best interests within the existing social-political arrangements. Objectively the result is the same: the concentration of production within a few multi-national corporations produces a monopoly(in the product market)–monopsony(single employer) situation. The need to produce increasingly higher surplus value with expanding capital/labour ratios creates the 'industrial reserve army' that is required to keep the system in being. Both theoretically and empirically this is a tenuous argument, but one that is rarely debated except from the equally unrealistic assumptions of neo-classical competitive models.

Empirical evidence of segmentation

Does the dual labour market exist? If so where is it most manifest–at occupational, regional, industrial or at company level? Can we find evidence to support the ILM as a prime factor in its causation if we adopt a 'null-hypothesis' approach to the problem? Several propositions stem from the dualist literature. The crudest proposition is:

1. that stigmatized groups are identifiable because people with their characteristics are 'crowded' into low-paying jobs with no upward career prospects, with low security of employment and with bad working conditions.

More refined hypotheses include the following:

2. that stigmatized groups with defined characteristics *but who otherwise possess similar educational qualifications* to those of non-stigmatized groups are crowded into jobs possessing the above defined features, to a greater extent than are the latter groups (pre-entry discrimination).
3. that stigmatized groups possessing *qualifications similar* to those of the non-stigmatized and *occupying similar jobs* are paid significantly less than the latter and are also subject to worse job and career conditions (post-entry discrimination).

A number of more contextual propositions may also be included which help in explaining and locating the cause of the problem, namely:

4. that smaller companies and companies with low capital/labour ratios;
5. that a number of defined industries;
6. that defined sectors of employment within and across industries may all become stigmatized employment opportunities in themselves.

These are also identifiable by the concurrence of high labour turnover (low stability or seniority ratios would be a more appropriate index), a high frequency of lay-offs together with an absence of 'structure' in the ILM as defined by Doeringer and Piore.

These contextual propositions are an important part of the 'radical' (neo-Marxist) account of the market process described by them as 'negative feedback'. In the historical institutionalization of markets, the attachment of stigma becomes a *job* characteristic. Certain occupations have become 'labelled' in this way through time immemorial. When combined with the inherent characteristics of the group that most frequently holds down such stigmatized posts, a reinforcive matching of man/job characteristics may occur. This is given a continuity and permanency through the formalized procedures of recruitment and selection for such occupations.

It is of course the permanency of segmentation and stratification that is at the heart of the 'radical' critique of neo-classical economics. The broad social basis of the occupational disadvantage has been described by a British right-wing radical, Sir Keith Joseph, who suggested that 'much deprivation and maladjustment persist from generation to generation through what I have called 'a cycle of deprivation'... People who were themselves deprived in one or more ways in childhood become in turn the parents of another generation of deprived children' (Joseph 1972).

In an overview of the studies of disadvantaged groups Rutter and Madge found that 'continuities over time regarding high rates of various forms of disadvantage can be seen in terms of schools, inner city areas, social classes, ethnic groups and other social and cultural situations... The reason for the intergenerational continuity may not be familial at all but rather may reflect the influence of a common social environment or factors which lie outside the family' (Rutter and Madge 1976). Even with respect to familial continuities, common social environment or the effect of a similar communal structure on successive generations was found a major determinant factor by these authors.

Policy implications of segmentation

Dualists discount two recent conceptual developments in neoclassical analysis. One is the development of 'human capital' theory in so far as it rests on the matching of a lifetime expectation of career earnings to a universally accepted hierarchy of educational achievement. The second is the concept of 'job search' with its concomitant costs of the imperfection of information. Neo-classicists explain the mismatch of skills and jobs that occurs in orthodox models of local and occupational job markets in this manner. From these two modifications to the neo-classical perspectives one may deduce the following policy implications:

1. If employers are discriminating in their patterns of recruitment on the basis of characteristics other than prior formal training or educational programmes then *manpower training or retraining* external to the employing company is of limited value: it will be acceptable only to small employers without the resources to invest in their own specific forms of human capital. Secondary workers have all the human capital they need – what they lack is access to good jobs. 'They fail to find jobs which pay a living wage because of racism, sexism, economic depression, and uneven economic development of industries and regions... Given the opportunity to escape to the high-wage sector, many low-wage workers would perform admirably'. (Bluestone 1970: 121-123). Magnum agrees: 'The basic manpower obstacle is still the supply of (good) jobs. Even during 1966-68 when labour markets in general were tight, there were never enough jobs in rural depressed areas or central city ghettoes within the occupational ranges attainable by the disadvantaged' (Magnum 1971: 109-110).

2. State-run employment exchanges will do little to improve the matching of skills to jobs because increased knowledge would not help to increase the job chances of workers in the secondary market. Such 'bourses' will carry only a list of secondary jobs; companies operating in the primary sector will tend to develop their own networks within 'manorial' job markets.

At a macro-economic level these departures from neo-classical theory have their implications for the orthodox interpretation of the causes of structural unemployment and of the 'deepening' of long-term unemployment. Non-discriminatory monetary or fiscal policies designed to stimulate overall demand, and even the more discriminatory attempts at selective 'pump-priming', seem condemned by a dualist interpretation of public policy. According to them, there may be more than enough jobs in the secondary market, but they are 'bad' jobs, characterized by poor wages and conditions. The cause of the deep unemployment is to be seen in high turnover resulting from a lack of incentive for workers or employers to maintain stable employment relationships.

To illustrate this point consider the effect of expanding the demand for labour uniformly throughout the economy. According to classical theory, adding workers to the primary sector would require employers to reduce hiring standards, to recruit from among previously rejected or excluded sources of labour, and to enlarge their training and upgrading activities—in short, the secondary sector would provide the major supply of new recruits in the primary sector.

The logic of this form of 'queueing' would indicate that a policy of full employment, if pursued long enough and far enough, would either eliminate the secondary sector or, through competition for scarce labour, cause secondary sector jobs to conform more closely to those of the primary sector. Unfortunately, however, full employment policy is too crude an instrument to insure that a tightening of the labour market would expand the primary sector. Employers often seem to favour temporary solutions to tight job markets, solutions that do not provide the newly hired with the full career benefits of primary employment. Thus one finds companies in the primary sector relying on *subcontracting* and the use of *temporary workers* to avoid the costs and risks associated with giving primary market status to workers from the secondary sector (Doeringer and Piore 1971).

Much of the preference for temporary solutions is traced to the employers' historical experience with 'stop-go' growth. Recessions reduce labour demand in the primary sector, but they do not provide corresponding relief in the costs of the employers' commitment to career employment. 'These costs, combined with aversion to uncertainty, and with race and sex issues that inevitably accompany the expansion of the primary sector, often lead to the avoidance of structural adjustments to the ILM that might be irreversible' (Wachter 1974). Increased overtime working enables primary sector workers to improve their earnings during upturns in the product market whilst keeping down the marginal costs of production. Expansions in aggregate demand may therefore serve only to exacerbate differences between employment sectors.

The same pessimistic view is taken of short-term help to the under-employed and destitute. If, as appears to be the case, a large proportion of unemployment is 'voluntary' in that jobs may be available but are undesirable, then payments provided to support job-search activities are clearly being wasted. This view of un-employment has gained a variety of adherents, particularly among those advocating free market and fiscal solutions. For them it provides a challenge to the interventionist thinking that has shaped employment and training policy in Europe in the post-War period. 'From such data, it is but a short step to argue that responsibility for unemployment should be shifted from the public sphere [where it rested in the 1960s] to individuals' (Doeringer and Piore 1971).

Needless to say dualist and radical economists do not accept this 'solution' to structural unemployment if for no other reason than the lack of recognition given to the underlying problem of the dual structure of the market. On the other hand neither do they accept piecemeal attempts at manpower planning. As Doeringer puts it:

If low pay is to be remedied, it must involve either the transfer of workers from the secondary to the primary sector, or the conversion of secondary employment so that it provides the upward mobility paths that characterise employment in the primary sector. In short, a combination of external and internal market policies must be followed (Doeringer 1974).

However, Bosanquet and Doeringer have also argued that:

Programmes to facilitate the transition from secondary to primary employment provide only a partial solution to the problems of low pay. Presumably primary employment opportunities are limited, so that at some point after shortages have been met, moving additional workers into primary employment will imply displacing others into secondary employment. Moreover, work habits exist or may be developed in the secondary sector that are incompatible with primary employment. Thus, some thought should also be given to a new area of policy endeavour—the restructuring of internal labour markets in the secondary sector. Little is known about factors affecting the design of work and the selection of production techniques in the secondary market. At a minimum, however, some attempt should be made to interrupt the cycle of work force instability, minimum investments in enterprise-specific training, and lack of promotion opportunity. One possibility might be the subsidisation of on-the-job training to reduce the costs of turnover to employers and to encourage internal training and promotion in enterprises such as hotels, where skill hierarchies are already present but are only occasionally used. A second strategy might be to improve the quality of managerial resources in the secondary sector in order to encourage new and more efficient forms of work force development and organisation (Bosanquet and Doeringer 1973).

Both approaches to the problem of job-creation for workers 'trapped' in the secondary sector are based on the notion of breaking into the cycle of economic disadvantage that exists on both sides of the secondary market. In this dualist and 'radical' solutions depart from the neo-classical assumptions which lead to a policy of only limited public intervention designed to 'set the signals' to which the forces of free competition can respond.

Neo-classical explanations and policy recommendations

Neo-classical concepts of the job and wage markets can be made to account for monopolistic 'barriers' and 'screens' in their explanations of market segmentation with little difficulty. These institutional boundaries can be reduced by the same economic forces which caused their erection: all that is needed is a 'lagged' function in the explanation provided. If such barriers to free competition are not fulfilling a function which helps 'the system' to work efficiently then market forces will, in time, erode them or modify the direction in which they operate (the purposes towards which the system is operating being exogenously determined). Time and balance are of the essence in neo-classical analysis. Market systems almost always have a tendency towards equilibrium. However they may never reach it within the finite career span of an individual worker nor may all the sub-systems in which he plays an economic role all move towards a determinate solution simultaneously. Therefore in real life a range of 'second-best' aids to survival are devised by employers and employees, all of which are amenable to orthodox economic analysis.

To the neo-classicist discrimination can be treated as an external economy: for example, employers, uncertain as to the skill of job applicants, hire prime-age white males for the 'good' jobs because the demographic group has, on average, the highest average educational achievement and, at least, may be believed to have the best job records (Wachter 1974).

The same author defines the boundaries of the ILM in terms of an imperfect 'screening system' which constitutes the most effective, least-cost, solution to the problem of dealing with an imperfect environment.

Collective discrimination may, then, be regarded as an 'external economy': nationality, religion, sex, or other *statistically* ascertainable data can be filtered and classified according to an assessed employment risk. In periods of 'loose' markets, applications which are attributed with a high-risk loading appear too far down in the queue even to be processed. Skin colour and other visible characteristics may require more costly processing (i.e. it may not be ascertainable without an interview). For the employer there may well be an economic advantage to be gained in discriminating against groups whom he believes, on whatever basis, to have low skills or against an individual whose job history suggests a chronic personal instability and lack of perseverance.

It is difficult, however, to judge whether blacks are seriously disadvantaged in labour markets currently, given the endowments they bring to the market. Their endowments may be inaccurately measured because of the inability to measure the quality of schooling and to capture feed-back from such variables as the socio-economic status of the parents (Wachter 1974).

Thus, say the neo-classicists, if as the 'radicals' suggest, the sources of disadvantage lie *outside* the labour market, it is unlikely that significant changes in their situation can or will be brought about through changes within the ILM. Blanket *counter*-discriminatory measures on the part of the state or courts are seen as potentially disastrous. There are two main reasons for this belief:

1. The economic inefficiencies that supposedly result from preventing the would-be employer from pursuing a profit-maximizing recruitment strategy in his best available manner (i.e. a 'second-best' screening system);
2. Counter-discriminatory measures would insulate the poor systems of education and primary socialization from free market forces which should eventually bring them up to the standards of those of the primary sector.

For the neo-classicists, feedback models do not support the conclusion that better jobs, rather than better training, are the answer to the low-wage problem. They do suggest that manpower training of adult workers is likely to be a costly process, which must remedy not only deficiencies in past education, but also the discouragingly negative signals that the worker has received from society. Orthodox theorists suggest that the allocation of educational resources should be focussed on the early years of schooling in the hope of a long-term solution. Neo-classicists come to terms with institutional barriers by moving their frame of analysis from one market segment to another so that each one becomes a discrete system whilst under their analysis. Thus it is possible to assume that free competition exists within the boundaries of the market so described: the economic processes within it can therefore be analysed according to the 'laws' governing such competitive forces. By moving the sources of disadvantage out of the labour market the neo-classicist consigns such matters to the separate and autonomous markets for education, for housing, and for social services. Within each of these areas efficiency is brought about through the existence of some measure of free competition. Remedial measures which may be perceived as necessary when viewed in terms of their outcomes in the labour market, are subjected to a separate analysis in order to determine the consequences of their provision for efficiency in the appropriate sector. Therefore what might be considered as necessary reform on a first (segmental) analysis, becomes eliminated when the same rationale is imposed on related areas of the economy.

Apparent alliances between neo-classicists and 'radicals' in the application of their analysis to policy directives are therefore more apparent than real. Whereas the 'radical' sees the removal or substitution of institutional barriers as a first priority and will work to that end through a system of institutional reform combined with cross-subsidization (and even 'shadow pricing'), the neo-classicist will attempt to restore and maintain price-competition *within* each market segment in the belief that, ultimately barriers *between* markets will be eroded by these same competitive forces.

Does the dual market exist in Europe?

Most of the available statistical evidence of discrimination originates from the United States. This accords with the size of the problem to which these data are addressed in that country. Few other economies outside South Africa contain such an indigenous population of secondary workers equal to that of the American blacks. No others have experienced an influx and settlement of foreign workers on the scale of American immigration. In order to re-establish the industrial basis of their economies a number of EEC countries actively promoted the immigration of foreign workers from less-developed Mediterranean countries after World War II. The UK became the less and less willing recipient of Commonwealth immigrants over this period.

It was no accident that the dualist hypothesis arose in America. Equally it is no accident that the bulk of the evidence on discrimination refers to blacks and to women. Both groups have become important pressure groups and have exponents of their cause among academics. In the European context foreign workers are the subject of widespread and pervasive prejudice leading to discriminatory practices. The relative dearth of appropriate data on immigrant workers and other minority groups in Europe is perhaps equally significant as the wealth of recent American studies.

It is possible to demonstrate the existence of a pool of itinerant labour in most industrial economies. A large amount of unemployment in Europe, as in the United States, is short term and contains a significant number of chronic job-changers. Yet differences between countries are significant, especially insofar as they relate itinerancy with the market behaviour of particular minority groups. Black workers in Britain have more long-term unemployment and less chronic job-changing than in the US; women too show greater stability in employment. Apprenticeship programmes are used more frequently by European boys than by American to bridge the gap between school and ultimate career, and to structure the choice of that career; rates of job-changing among girls are quite similar in all countries.

The 'crowding' of minority groups into bad occupations, bad industries and bad regions can be shown to occur in Europe; but the cultural/institutional structuring of this 'crowding' appears to be different across countries. The pattern of behaviour within market segments may therefore also differ between countries. But when we refine our hypothesis to take in 'pre-entry' or 'post-entry' discrimination our evidence is largely confined to Britain, Germany, France, Belgium and the Netherlands. In these countries both forms of discrimination can be shown to exist and it is a reasonable assumption that this would be so of other EEC countries were the analysis to be done, and were the data available upon which to carry out the exercise. Age, aptitude, physical handicap, migrant origin, sex and education can all be shown to affect market changes in Europe's labour markets. But the manner and direction of these influences, at any rate into the foreseeable future, will be culturally induced and may therefore vary between countries. As pointed out by Jain and Sloane (1977):

The essence of segmentalist theories is the all pervasive nature of barriers to mobility. 'Labour supply schedules may differ among otherwise similar groups because of differences in education and training, geographical location, or work history, whilst labour demand schedules may differ because of differing industrial structures, discrimination by race and sex or trade union barriers to entry' (cf. Wachtel and Betsey 1972). As a result there are a whole series of possible wage and employment equilibria for particular groups of employees.

One of the problems in using the dual labour market concept is the implied adoption of many assumed characteristics of a traditional market place, i.e. that the single market boundaries for the services of labour face a single aggregate demand function. One may be led to assume that therefore the services on offer can themselves be 'added up' to make a single supply function. Clearly this is not so of the women, blacks, immigrants and others who offer their services in a variety of occupational and industrial fields. Even within any one stigmatized group, such as women there are, as we pointed out earlier, large differences between the 'temporary' work of a qualified nurse and that of an assembly worker on an evening shift.

An alternative to the dualist approach might be that of an occupational hierarchy of markets in which a 'residual' position was taken by stigmatized workers at each level. The 'internal'/'external' market dichotomy remains since we have to assume that some discriminatory mechanism is at work to create the residual element. The barrier between the primary and secondary market provided by the ILM becomes movable and malleable according to the circumstances surrounding the sources of discrimination within each labour market.

On the other hand as Kerr (1954) has pointed out the occupational market for many 'blue-collar' secondary workers barely exists: 'In a depression, a 'waitress' may consider herself also available for work in a laundry.' The tripartite market model put forward by Lutz and Sengenberger (1974) contains (1) the residual sub-market *'Jedermannsteilarbeitsmarkt'*; (2) the craft sub-market; (3) the firm specific sub-market. Like neo-classicists these authors and their colleagues at the Munich Institute for Social Research see the variable return on human capital investment as the principal reason for market regulation. The employer response to the need for investment in training is associated with the *later* part he attempts to play in job-regulation and the imposition of bureaucratic control.

Piore (1975) has suggested that the primary market is better divided into upper and lower tiers relating to upper working class and middle-class occupations, while the secondary market is made up of the lower working class. As in the dual market model, Piore's social classes are related to core and peripheral jobs in the ILM. Mok (1975) develops this relationship further by dividing both the internal and external market into a primary and secondary sector, giving four sub-markets. In this model the primary/secondary axis represents the differentiated security of jobs and rewards. The internal/external segmentation distinguishes between the nature of the tasks and their place in relation to the firm-specific ILM.

The lack of the superior career chances combined with an obvious superiority in human and physical capital possessed by professional and administrative workers as compared with those of manual and clerical workers is clearly a debility in the dualists' global description of a ''primary' market; the more so when it is so often represented in their more specific description of the ILM. In both Europe and America the level of job security, the range and opportunity for promotion etc., may often vary more among those defined as primary sector employees than between hourly paid manual workers and those defined as peripheral or marginal. A move towards a multi-segmental model can only serve to reflect the complexity of social class and ethnic differences between marginal workers. This, in turn may enable the development of more precise analysis and prescription than has been possible hitherto with the cruder dual market concept.

On the other hand the existence of such a theoretical model serves to highlight the practical weaknesses in any state-sponsored job-creation programme which focusses on the manufacture of peripheral work. The effect of socialization in such jobs may well bring into being a new segment of itinerant workers.

The internal labour market in Europe

In general the structure of organizations in Europe appears to be less formal than in America. Internal labour markets therefore have boundaries and career paths that are more permeable. Studies in the Netherlands have, however, demonstrated the degree to which custom and practice shape the use of technology. They have also demonstrated the existence of primary and secondary markets *within* the employing company. Other work, Brown's in particular (1975), has traced the effect of internal social structures on earnings levels on the shop floor. On the other hand British and French studies of work organizations have demonstrated the effect that product market environment and trading conditions have on the choice between technological and social determinants in the creation of jobs (Roberts et al. 1971; Loveridge 1973; Erbes 1977) within the ILM. The precise nature of the mediating processes by which the internal pressures generated in the ILM mesh with environmental forces is bound to be idiosyncratic and unique to each firm. Yet for the concept to develop from its present heuristic role it must be possible to devise more specific predictions on the general direction and form that these processes take.

Many of the characteristics offered as typical of an ILM in America are to be found in European firms. In their original thesis, Doeringer and Piore (1971) suggested that large firms that are union organized are more likely to create ILM's, and that small non-union entrepreneurial ones are more 'open'. So far the relationship between size and formalization has not been tested by economists. Sociologists have discovered a significant link between the size of a company or establishment and its structure (Pugh et al. 1968). Yet if the ILM is not so much a function of the *size* of the firm per se but rather of the bureaucratic control system that is associated with it then large size may not be a necessary characteristic of an ILM. Small firms in stable environments may develop such structures, as they may also when operating in a bureacratic business environment. This appears to have been the effect of state intervention in Swedish business activity for example.

The trend of legislation in Europe has been towards reinforcing the security of employment for workers in the primary sector—the length of probationary service before coming eligible for statutorily enforceable job rights appears crucial in determining who benefits from state inter- vention. It is an often expressed intention of such legislation that the employer should be forced to plan his manpower requirements in a more long term manner if he is to take on the overhead costs of a body of permanent workers. Temporary workers may therefore become un- necessary or may be elevated to permanent workers. The de facto status of the permanent workers becomes 'de jure' and therefore restrictive work practices are seen to give way to greater internal flexibility of movement and the development of 'generic' skills. To believe that this is the necessary outcome of the legislation is to make assumptions about the rational behaviour of employers and work groups and to ignore the structure of the existing ILM and its effects in shaping the responses of workers and managers to such statutory intervention.

Policy considerations in Europe

While there are considerable differences in approach between member states it may be said that the European approach to social security, training, job creation and discrimination has been generally more stable in direction than that of America. In this study we attempt to deal with each problem of unemployment and under-employment in Europe sepa- rately. Jain (1977) has characterized the European approaches as being divided between:
1. the fair employment concept designed to eliminate discrimination at work, and at school in particular;

2. the income distribution focus which we describe as that of the national minimum wage or solidarity approach;
3. the segmented labour market approach particularly in relation to job-creation programmes;
4. the selective social underpinning of less competitive groups such as foreign workers;
5. the isolation of specific characteristics, such as physical disability, for special treatment.

These measures can be subjected to criticism of the kind advanced previously (see the section on policy implications). What may be said of them is that they have enabled us to learn more of the nature of the 'feedback' effects in segmental markets and of the workings of the ILM. Anti-discrimination laws have led to the revelation of common hiring and firing practices within companies. Training and retraining programmes have been particularly revealing of the existence of a dual labour market and the usefulness of the concept in policy terms. The British Training Act of 1964 for example was recently revised because of sustained opposition from secondary market employers led by Enoch Powell. The ferocity of this campaign (directed at reducing training levy grants paid by small employers) demonstrates a strong underlying economic motivation within ILM's for the existence of market segmentation. On the nature of the external market Wachter has commented:

The major policy of the dualists calls on government to create more good jobs, in either the private or the public sphere, but more in the latter. Although the dualists do not oppose manpower training, aggregate demand policies aimed at full employment, or transfer payments to the lower-income groups, they argue that these programmes have been largely ineffective. Hence the need for direct action. In concentrating on the issue of creating more good jobs, the dualists have ignored the implications of the feedback effects that are inherent in their own argument. In some ways, they have neglected the cycle of poverty and have assumed more equality among workers than they have evidence to justify. In a broader context, their recommendations can be reinterpreted as means for breaking the cycle at the point of labour market activity. Whether this is a least cost or even a viable solution is unclear. The social and psychological features of the literature on the cycle of poverty do not encourage optimism on this score (Wachter 1974).

Current public service programmes in Europe are still basically counter-cyclical. In spite of the recent moves by the secretariat of the European Community to support job creation programmes and the long-standing subsidization of regional development, secondary workers are rarely given priority in the distribution of funds by member states. The dualist policy of moving secondary workers directly into primary jobs is more likely to result from adjudicated cases of discrimination than from current legislative programmes. Once more we are directed to changing the discriminative practices of the ILM.

But in Europe the immediate problem of unemployment clearly arises out of the period of industrial rationalization and retrenchment in the early 1970s and particularly affects young people. In France, the Centre d'Études et des Recherches sur les Qualifications has suggested that the largest growth in jobs over the last decade has been in labouring or 'undifferentiated office work'. Nearly half of the present unemployed are under 25 years old and nearly half of these young people hold certificates or *brevets*. This situation of highly qualified unemployed and under-employed young people can be reproduced in descriptions of structural unemployment in all the member states.

Clearly the creation of a 'third sector' of employment in publicly supported jobs has to be considered. This involves a consideration of the goals of economic growth and of the allocation of resources within the economy as a whole. It is unlikely that purposive job creation on the scale envisaged by the dualists and what is required by the dimensions of the problem could be undertaken on a purely national basis. For individual states to embark on large-scale programmes could ultimately jeopardize the free movement of trade and employment within the Community.

This implies that the present use of subsidies to member states for the purposes of job creation along nationally determined lines should be reinforced by Community initiatives in investment location, etc. This is obviously a politically sensitive area. However one source of influence open to the secretariat is its nodal situation in an information network and its ability to monitor the ILM's created by the multi-national company with a degree of strategic neutrality not possessed by national govern-ments. It might also be possible to elicit market information in a form that could be fed back to member states as evidence of the existence of segmented markets within states and comparisons between states.

Market strategies among marginal workers

It is perhaps a contradiction in terms to speak of the 'strategy' of the 'marginal' worker. By definition many marginal workers can have little concept of futures–no 'projet de vie'–other than a continuation of the present uncertainty. Their strategies therefore consist of no more than a habitual resort to the short-term tactics that have ensured their survival to date. These people are the classical residual element described by the dualists. Essentially they differ from workers in the primary market in their ability to gain an institutionalized response from management. Employment opportunities and earnings levels may be set either on an individual or on a collective basis but either way it is the *institutionalization* of discrimination that creates labour market segmentation.

An evident response to the erection of institutionalized barriers is that of collective bargaining (in the broadest sense of the word) either as a means to gaining entry to an existing market, or as a means to securing and maintaining a new and old discrete market segment for those of one's own kind.

This bargaining may take place within the existing system of economic exchange or as a deviant activity such as street gangs organized for 'protection rackets'. An alternative response is an individualized one. In most European countries a proportion of the work force at all social levels is 'self-employed'. The entrepreneurial response is very common among permanent *immigrés*, and in urban ghettoes where ethnic specialization in particular economic activities is often to be found.

In our study we suggest that one possible categorization of the sub-segments of the secondary market might be achieved by treating groups within the market as having more or less of a strategic identity. We suggest four categories:

1. The individually disadvantaged: those whose source of economic disability is peculiar to their personal situation;
2. the collectively disadvantaged who conceive of their situation in personal terms and who are unaware of any means to rectifying this *personal* situation: these are the stigmatized groups of people upon whom the dualists concentrate their analysis;
3. the collectively disadvantaged who have become aware of their existence as an 'economic community' i.e. a group that is aware of the existence of a 'public good'—the concept of public good or common good being central to the study of welfare economics;
4. the collectively disadvantaged who have become aware of their existence as a 'political community' or pressure group, i.e. a group that has become aware of the legal-administrative means to acquiring a 'public good'.

In devising public policy we suggest that public administrators should be aware of the possible 'trade-offs' and 'side payments' to be made to groups in order to increase their cohesion, political awareness and active participation in the system of reward allocation. In other words we suggest that the labour market should be treated as an *arena* in which disadvantaged should be encouraged to act as a pressure group and taught how to be politically effective within the system. Only in this way do we see the required structural changes being maintained into the future. It is interesting for example to compare the current tactics of the 'economically' conscious group of unemployed school-leavers with those of women workers. While the problem of youthful unemployment is a new one and is therefore the subject of considerable public attention, the most serious problem of *under*-employment is perhaps the oldest in society, that of discrimination against women. So far there has been little pressure for a 'quota' system of good jobs for women only, or for job creation for women only. Unless the publicity given to adolescent unemployment can be used in support of an effective and permanent pressure group activity on behalf of the young, the institutionalized acceptance of a subordinate market position by some kinds of young people is a strong possibility.

Some areas for research

Much of the debate that has gone on between neoclassicists and 'radical' dualists over the last decade has been based on statistical analysis. The data may be criticized on three bases: first, its validity; second, its technicality; and third, its crudity. Technically the form of statistical analysis used by economists is largely that of regressing one set of aggregated data obtained from secondary sources against another set—ignoring the presumptions behind the act of drawing causal inferences from two sets of associated figures. Often the data bases that are used have been drawn from different sources and were originally for purposes entirely different from those for which they are currently being used. The data have therefore been taken out of the historical context from which they gained their original meaning, and are being used in a completely ahistorical manner to formulate general equations. Furthermore we cannot assume that this exercise is being conducted in a *neutral* manner. Instead of being used to test or invalidate a theory, evidence from fragmented and uncontrolled studies has been widely used by proponents of both persuasions to support and reinforce their preconceived policy prescriptions.

Given the remoteness of the aggregated data from the micro-processes that they purport to represent, some latitude in interpretation is to be expected. Debates take place at the level of technical interpretation as well as about the factual nature of the problem. For example neo-classicists accuse 'radical' dualists of statistically 'truncating' their samples through the omission of high earners or holders of stable jobs, or the highly qualified to ensure a correlation between the reverse of these and other unfavourable job characteristics.

The crudity of the data and the extenuation of findings beyond the limits of the data has led to a debate as to the nature of the facts, which could be settled relatively easily were those facts available. For example it has been suggested that the increase in work rates by women has led to an increase in less experienced and less able women employees and, ceterus paribus, the neo-classicist analyst therefore predicts a fall in the real earnings of people in 'female' occupations. But if the increase in work rates stems from reduced exit rates, the average experience of the stock of working women may have actually increased relative to that of men. Thus the 'radical' dualists may, by gaining supplementary evidence, use the same data to argue a precisely opposite point.

Particulars of the stocks and flows of labour within, and into and out of the employment system are critical, not only for planning the actual disposition of human resources, but also for the formulation of accurate explanations and theoretical foundations for prediction. The source of much of this data lies at the place of employment. Without accurate monitoring and recording of recruitment, earnings, career and exit data on all employees by employers and the local employment service (the latter especially in relation to job histories and out-of-work careers) then both theorizing and planning can be positively misleading in resource allocation at national or international level.

An alternative to rigorous and continuous data collection at plant level, which may be operationally and politically impossible to achieve, would be greater knowledge of how decisions are taken at that level in order to establish a micro profile by which macro data may be periodically adjusted. Very little attempt has been made to integrate the macro-level studies of economists and the micro-level analyses of institutionalists and industrial sociologists in a manner which would test the logic (and therefore the validity) of the framework used at either level. This is an almost universal weakness in social science findings: it is a link that has been attempted in the concept of the internal labour market. It is, as yet, too ill-formed conceptually to provide any generally useful statistical taxonomy in the manner suggested above.

We would therefore see the following areas of research as being of value.

1. An attempt to establish a more rigorous model of the ILM based on empirically grounded comparisons of the type that has been pioneered by organizational sociologists (these would be particularly useful in analysing the role of the small business and the multi-national corporation in creating labour market segmentation).
2. A study of the manner in which the public and private employment agencies operate and the degree to which state-supported services are geared to other institutional channels that structure markets (this may be more difficult than it seems, for example trade union representatives often sit on committees that authorize retraining schemes, but this does not prevent their members from refusing to accept retrained workers into their ILM).
3. Research to establish the nature of potential groups of disadvantaged workers and the kinds of measures required to get them operating as effective pressure groups.
4. More broadly, the need for new forms of data in the collection and collation of national statistics should be examined. Proposals for modification to existing methods should be based on a theoretical analysis of existing and future segmentation problems.

2. Labour market theories in historical perspective

Definitions

We define *labour market* as those mechanisms and institutions through which the purchase and sale of labour power are arranged.

Labour market segmentation is defined here as the historical processes whereby political-economic forces encourage the division of the labour market into separate submarkets, or segments, distinguished by different labour market characteristics and behavioural rules (Reich et al. 1973).

The process of *marginalization* is taken to indicate the movement by which jobs become related to particular segments of the work force who are available for full-time employment but who are unable to become fully integrated into a more permanent form of employment which utilizes their full work potential. Over a period of time particular segments of the work force become related to particular jobs, modes of work organization and employment practices to a degree which reduces their objective range of job choice, so that jobs as well as people can become marginal. In addition to *temporary work* we shall also consider *part-time* work and the extent to which both constitute a permanent mode of employment for this element of the work force.

The classical and neo-classical labour market

Labour markets have been defined in a number of ways. Traditional neo-classical analysis more or less treats the labour market as a unified entity in which allocation is regulated by the price mechanism. In neo-classical theory the labour market is treated as an exchange system, where buyers and sellers of labour meet each other individually as equals. In this it may be seen to differ fundamentally from classical theorists such as Smith, Ricardo and Marx. Neo-classical labour market theory is essentially only a theory of markets and market interdependencies without reference to its societal context. By contrast Marxian, and classical theory in general, links the mechanism of the labour market to the system of power and domination in society at large. In further contrast neo-classical theory is essentially a-historical, in that the experiences of actors in the labour market which mould the supply and demand schedules are seldom taken into account; instead the theory purports to lay down fundamental laws of market behaviour regardless of any changes in the underlying social relationships that may take place over time. Thirdly, in its purest form, neo-classical labour market theory is non-institutional, in that factors like trade union influence, collective bargaining and the state, do not appear as *necessary* conditions in the workings of their models of reality.

The competitive labour market model remains based on the following assumptions:

1. Employers and workers have fairly accurate knowledge about wages and job opportunities throughout the market.
2. Employers and workers are 'rational' in the economic sense–that is, employers act to maximize profits and workers act to maximize satisfaction from real wages.
3. Each employer and worker represents such a small part of the total demand or supply for labour that their individual decisions have no influence on wages.
4. There are no obstacles to mobility of labour and other factors of production.
5. Workers and employers act individually and not in concert with other workers (through unions) or employers (through associations) in making wage and employment decisions.
6. Labour within a particular market is homogeneous and interchangable (Levitan et al. 1972: 201).

Of course, this competitive model has never given a real picture of the working of the labour market, it has always been seen as an 'ideal type' in which each condition might be released under 'controlled conditions'. It has, however, been influencing the thinking of labour market theorists for more than a century. This competitive model may be seen as the product of what Marx described as the 'middle phase' of capitalism, which started with the industrialization of Europe and America. Britain, of course, was the first nation to be industrialized and to pass from the early stage of capitalism, which was characterized by the dominance of agrarian production and mercantile relations. In the middle phase the first precondition for the continued rise of capitalism was derived from the new possibilities of technology: the bringing together, under a single authority, of workers belonging to different trade and crafts into one 'manufacture' (Marx 1976: 455). This is the essential precondition for the division of labour which, in turn, gives rise to a specificity of skill and training needed to apply the necessary technology to the job. For, as Adam Smith observed as long ago as 1776, internal labour markets are mainly characterized by a specific technology and a specific skill structure.

Without the detailed division of labour exemplified in the modern factory Smith saw that the growth of capitalism could not have occurred. But it was only a necessary and not a sufficient precondition for this development. In order to progress to the 'middle stage' of industrialization the formation of competitive product markets was necessary. Following Malthus, Marx believed that to attract capital from other uses the entrepreneur had to offer a rate of profit big enough to divert capital away from direct consumption. That means the capitalist has to prevent too big a share of his profits going to labour. Marx therefore postulated that there must constantly be an unemployed reserve of labour to keep the supply of this commodity abundant and its price low. So, according to this reasoning, the most important condition for the development of capitalism in its middle stage is the existence of an industrial reserve army (I.R.A.), which exerts enough pressure from the 'external' market on the 'internal' market to keep down wages inside the factory or workplace.

But, of course, this is not enough in itself for economic development. What is needed are large enough markets for the commodities produced in the technologically advanced way. England's development was in many respects the early example of developments in all countries of Western Europe. As production increased, labour reserves were formed, first in the early agrarian way consisting of women and children as well as men. Later the laws everywhere, starting in 1833 in England, restricted the labour of children. National markets for commodities were developed by developing the infrastructure of the countries involved (railways, roads and canals) and this permitted the free movement of labour. But these were not enough for creating sustained growth: for sustained investment much larger markets were found to be necessary.

Entrepreneurs sought out markets in which invested capital could be sure of an element of monopoly in order to ensure high returns for their increasingly substantial investments. In terms of a single pre-industrial economy this would be an almost impossible condition. In a situation in which there were a number of co-existing economies, all at different stages of development, then the matter was easily resolved. The industrial goods of one country would simply exploit the markets of the others, whose relative backwardness would prevent effective retaliation (Rostow 1959). This is eventually how England's industrial revolution did develop: a labour reserve, a quickly expandable supply of raw cotton, and a technological lead just sufficient to sustain a super-profit incursion into the world market for craft-produced textiles. Indeed, from this point of view, the preconditions for pioneer industrialization were easy compared with what was required for some subsequent attempts (Foster 1977: 14).

Thus for the Marxian economist the historical trend in the evolution of capitalistic political economies is towards an increasingly narrow range of more or less monopolistic markets. In the short run it is more realistic to analyse the day-to-day workings of the economy in terms of a process of bargaining between competing but monopolistic producers, than it is in terms of a state of free competition—in which there are so many competitors that no one of them can do other than to maximise his short term goals and await the outcomes in the post hoc judgement of 'the market'. For the Marxian interpreter the fragmentation brought about by the division of labour is complemented by a reformation of class identities and new forms of collective strategies in the market. For the neo-classicist the same historical pattern represents not coagulation but a consistent erosion of interests and institutions by market forces. Often the argument is presented in terms of Social Darwinism: institutions either adapt to the inexorable pressures of competitive forces, or perish.

Labour market theory is very much the product of the history of economic development and of the interpretation of the relations of production made by the theorists. It would be misleading to suggest that there has been a clear and sequential unfolding of economic ideas which allows the part played by labour as the *primary* unit of value in early classical thought from its later regulation to its contribution to the sales price of the product. Adam Smith (1845) [1776] was intent upon discovering a measure of economic value, other than that of gold: a measure which related not only to 'scarcity' and to 'need' in the exchange of goods, but to productivity and to the value added by the process of manufacture. Hence, 'The wealth of a nation,' he says, 'will depend upon two conditions: first, the degree of productivity of the labour to which it is due: and secondly, the amount of useful labour, that is to say, labour productive of wealth, which is employed' (Roll 1957: 154). Profits and rents are quite separate constituents in the value of commodities but *productive* labour was that which earned sufficient 'surplus value' or profit to ensure its continued employment.

Labour remains, however, 'alone the ultimate and real standard by which the value of all commodities can at all times and places be estimated and compared' (Smith 1845 [1776] 32). The division of labour, its increased specialization and coordination, would result in increased productivity. But the value and amount of labour's output could also be increased by training.

The difference of natural talents in different men is, in reality, much less that we are aware of, and the very different genius which appears to distinguish men of different professions, when grown up to maturity, is not upon many occasions so much the cause as *the effect of the division of labour*. The difference between the most dissimilar character, between a philosopher and a common street porter, for example, seems to arise not so much from nature as from habit, custom and education (Smith: 1845 [1776] 28).

For the worker the choice of job was determined by the balance of net advantages and in the perfectly competitive market in which he was assumed to make his choice:

The whole of the advantages and disadvantages of the different employments of labour and stock must, in the same neighbourhood, be either perfectly equal or continually tending to equality. If in the same neighbourhood, there was any employment evidently either more or less advantageous than the rest, so many people would crowd into it in one case, and so many would desert it in the other, and its advantages would soon return to the level of other employment (Smith 1845 [1776] 99).

However, the very act of separating labour from its product through the division of labour created a distinction between the 'use-value' of the product, which might be measured in terms of productivity, from its 'exchange value', which was determined by the scarcities of supply and the current consumer needs reflected in the state of the market. In the 'unnatural' circumstances in which labour has been separated from its 'use value' and has become a source of wealth for entrepreneurs (through its 'exchange value'), Smith saw the long term wages of labour as being determined by the need to 'assure the survival not only of the man but of his species of producer' (1845 [1776] 67). In the short term he observed that bargaining between 'master and servant' was quite normal, viz:

What are the common wages of labour depends everywhere upon the contract usually made between these two parties, whose interests are by no means the same. The workmen desire to get as much, the masters to give as little as possible. The latter are disposed to combine to give as little as possible. The former are disposed to combine in order to raise, the latter in order to lower the wages of labour (1845 [1776]: 66).

Smith was under no illusions about where the balance of power lay in this process and he was free from the self-delusion, to become so popular later, about employment contracts between free and equal parties:

It is not difficult to foresee which of the two parties must, upon all ordinary occasions, have the advantage in the dispute, and force the other into a compliance with their terms. The master being fewer in number can combine much more easily... In all disputes the masters can hold out much longer... In the long run the workmen may be as necessary to his master is to him; but the necessity is not so immediate (1845 [1776]: 61). Neither should we suppose that because we know only of workmen's combinations, because they are so vociferously deplored by the masters, that the masters do not themselves combine: whoever thinks this 'is as ignorant of the world as of the subject. To combine to prevent the raising of wages is the usual, and one may say the natural state of things. Masters, too, sometimes enter into particular combinations to sink the wages of labour... These are always conducted with the utmost silence and secrecy, till the moment of execution, and when the workmen yield, as they sometimes do, without resistance, though severely felt by them, they are never heard of by other people.' (Smith 1845 [1776]: 66; quoted in Anthony 1977: 78).

The sheer comprehensiveness of Smith's work makes it the source of numerous, mutually contradictory hypotheses and by its very nature it therefore spawned conflicting schools of economic thought. (His desire for an absolute basis for value and for measurement might be seen to reflect the objective of all embryonic sciences: the movement to re-lativity may seem to be equally inevitable?) The neoclassical critique of Ricardian (i.e. Smith and Ricardo) economics began with Malthus' critique of his theory of accumulation in 1820 in which he developed the concept of *effective demand*, i.e. the level of demand required to call forth sufficient investment to employ the existing pool of labour. Criticism of classical theory was to recur in a variety of works having many different methodological starting points. But the focus of most of the criticism can be traced to the location of the ultimate sources of value. Ricardians hold to the distinction between 'use value' and 'exchange value', a dichotomy which, along with other aspects of Smith's thought, was to become an integral part of the Marxist thesis.

But before that integration was accomplished a shift in the theoretical dialogue could be observed when profits ceased to be explained simply as 'surplus value' or 'rent', and took on the property of a 'normal cost' of meeting consumer wants. This important difference in emphasis marks economists from Mill onwards as neo-classicists rather than classicists. It represents a shift in emphasis from production to consumption in the explanation of the generation of exchange value.

The demand for labour, as for all other factors of production (land and capital) is thereafter seen to be *derived* from the secondary demand for its product in the consumer market. The level of wages is also determined by the price, or revenue product, derived from the sale of labour's produce. Labour itself remains a source of value, but only insofar as it contributes to the costs of production. The level of these costs are determined by the price at which each worker is willing to sell his services, an offer price which reflects his subjective evaluation of the 'disutility' of the work involved. The employers 'estimate of the workers' revenue product has therefore to be set against the latters' desire to take the job in a transaction in which both are competing with others for the desired contract of employment.

The central assumptions of the competitive model of the neo-classicists are:

1. there is maximizing behaviour of all parties involved
2. there is perfect substitutability of labour and capital
3. there is a tendency of supply of labour and demand for labour to be balanced by wages.

The competitive model tends to present the demands for labour from the angle of the individual firm whilst seeing the supply as coming from one big pool consisting of the total economy. The labour reserve exists nationally (or even internationally).

The competitive model of the second half of the nineteenth century clearly reflects the need of theory to account for the consumer-led growth that was taking place. Everywhere in Europe neo-classical economists sought to account for the new phase of capitalism in their theories. Jevons, Wickstead and Marshall in England, Walras in France, Von Thünen in Germany, Barone in Italy and Von Böhm-Bawerk, Menger and Von Wieser in Austria (to name the most important ones) all attacked the classical theories of Ricardo and some (like Wieser and

Böhm-Bawerk) also attacked Marx as the potentially (politically) more dangerous theorist. Many of their works appeared around 1870: Marx' *Capital* in 1867, Jevons' *Theory of political economy* in 1871 and Menger's *Grundsätze* in 1874.

One of the problems encountered by neo-classicists, was that of translating a commodity theory of production designed to handle the inanimate elements of land and capital into hypotheses which encapsulated the inherent subjective propensities of labour. Whereas the owners of land and capital may take a decision on the balance of net advantages gained from investing their commodities in a number of different activities, none of which involve the investor in any personal sense, the owner of the skills embodied in labour may generally dispense his services to only one contractor at a time and must, over the period, engage or hold in suspense, all of his physical and mental faculties that are not so engaged. The services, and concomitantly, the rewards going to labour are therefore of a fundamentally different variety to those of other commodities. The problem was not one which preoccupied neo-classicists since labour only occupied a peripheral place in their consumer-oriented model. For Marx, on the other hand, it was the point from which to begin his analysis of the whole political economy. The separation of the economic value of labour postulated by Smith, for Marx represented the exploitations of one social class by another. It was accompanied by a separation of the labourer's self-identity from his purpose in the work environment: the exploitation was thus seen to take place at psychological level and in all areas of social activity. Just as capital ownership was seen to assume a monopolistic form so labour inevitably adopted a collective stance; at first through unions and later in the form of a revolutionary movement.

Had the neo-classical model remained constrained by the pre-suppositions of pure competition there is little doubt that its utility as a policy guide would have been very small. Jevons, like Walras, was concerned with establishing the ultimate laws of economics, analogous 'to the science of Statistical Mechanics' (Jevons 1924 [1871]). Like the Austrians he was concerned with establishing objective and universalistic propositions. On the other hand, Anglo-American marginalists were to become very much more pragmatic and concerned with the political implications of their work. Marshall's *Principles of economics* (1890) contain an eclecticism which owes more to political realism and a recognition of the existence of prevailing institutions than does that of his

Austrian and German contemporaries. Indeed the definition of labour markets with which we begin this chapter is almost identical to that used by Marshall (1890: 217). Sub-markets had already been identified by Cairnes (1874) who distinguished 'non-competing groups'. These groups divided the labour market into layers or strata—unskilled, skilled and professional workers. Marshall described the segmentation of markets by locality and by industry.

Modern social scientists such as Van Voorden (1975: 30) have criticized Cairnes' notion of non-competing groups as static and confined only to the supply side of a market for skills. However, in his development of segmental market theory Marshall postulated the concept of 'elasticity' in the measurement of market forces. In what was almost an aside, he thus contributed the basis for all modern analysis of 'imperfections' in the market and for dynamic (or at any rate, comparative-static) models.

He was able to do this because, unlike Continental economists, the British school developed theories which postulated *partial* rather than *general* equilibrium conditions. Simply by defining the characteristics of the parties involved in an economic transaction as being those which constituted a closed market system, discrete in its workings from those of wider society, it was possible for the analyst to treat each source of heterogeneity (monopoly) as a separate market; each in itself amenable to marginalist analysis. A second, and equally important aspect of post-Marshallian economics was the emphasis given to the difference between the short- and long-term time-horizons and to comparative-static analysis.

This was not, however, to save the assumptions of 'pure' competition. In a situation of monopoly the stability conditions so neatly established for any competitive system became indeterminate. 'This wreckage', as Hicks said, 'is that of the greater part of economic theory' (1934). The output-restricting and price-raising tendencies of modern economic institutions have long been observable for those who bothered to look. Eventually these empirical features of the economic world were successfully incorporated into a marginalist model by Chamberlain (1933) and by Robinson (1933). But the spontaneous tendencies to market equilibrium, so beloved by Pareto (1906) and the Austrian school, were shown as by no means inevitably leading to an optimal distribution of scarce resources. A series of economic crises, especially the depression of the 1930s, a world war, rising worker consciousness and the formation of collective defence mechanisms, like unions, led economists to pay attention to the influence of power relations on the allocation in the labour market (Van Voorden 1975: 30). The substitutability and homogeneity of labour was put to the test, competition proved to be less than perfect: 'Dans la réalité actuelle, le marché n'est ni unique, ni morcelé à l'infini et la concurrence n'est ni parfaite ni pure' (Ledrut 1966: 126).

One of the most evident effects of market imperfection was the long-term unemployment of the 1930s. Inspite of the development of a model of 'imperfect competition' neo-classical thinking itself remained (and remains) curiously segmented with a high level of insulation between its various component theories. Most neo-classicists believed (many still do) that the level of production would always be such as to generate full employment were it not for 'unfortunate' obstacles to the free movement of commodities and capital. The work of a number of European economists, most notably Wicksell (1906), demonstrated that the period of large-scale unemployment through which they were living was indeed conceptually possible within the neo-classical framework of economic analysis.

Keynes' *General theory of employment, interest and money* (1936) develops the Malthusian concept of 'effective demand' into the determinant of the level of employment within a closed economy (p.55). At macro level Keynesian analysis of the market is a clear step away from classical thinking in at least two important respects. It was a departure from both the traditional wage fund theory and a theory of investment in which money has to be tempted away from the current consumption. Therefore the preconditions for Marx's industrial reserve army were no longer present. For Keynes, capitalists, like all men, were masters of their own fate and not the puppets of history. If, by use of financial and fiscal measures, investment could be made profitable, then large-scale unemployment could be avoided. A subsidiary but important element in Keynes's criticism of Say's Law (supply determines demand) derived from the inflexibility of wage levels. In classical theory, the amount of money going to labour was fixed in proportion to the total revenue derived from the sale of its product. According to Say's Law, labour could never be unemployed; they would simply receive lower wages. Keynes pointed out that the wages often operated according to a 'ratchet' effect. Neither the individual expectation of the workers, nor the collective strategies of their unions enables wages to go down: they were, he said, 'sticky'. At a particular level of effective demand, job opportunities might therefore be sacrificed to retain existing wage levels.

Conversely he maintained that more jobs might be created at the *existing* money wage rate without pressure being encountered for higher rates of remuneration. As Lester has pointed out, this part of Keynesian theory is somewhat ambiguous: 'He fails to reconcile his continued adherence to the marginal productivity theory with his new theories of employment determination, based on effective demand' (Lester 1948: 63). This weakness in Keynesian analysis makes it particularly insufficient when applied to current problems of high structural unemployment conjoined with a high rate of inflation. Such conditions may be approached through classical thinking of two extreme forms; either the monetarism of Milton Friedman (1971) or the structuralism of the neo-Marxists, some of whose work is to be examined in this text (see the appendix to this chapter).

The period of economic recession through which Western economies were passing at that time did not encourage academic study of collective market strategies. However, during and after World War II a number of American scholars, described here as institutionalists, became prominent. Their work had been preceded by that of the Webbs, Commons, Perlman, Hoxie and Cole, among others. Each of these writers were concerned to explain the growing power of collective labour in conditions of rising demand. The Webbs were contemporaneous with the marginalists and were personally, as well as intellectually, acquainted with many of them. Their analysis of the varying strategems used by labour collectivities of 'restriction of numbers', 'collective bargaining', and legal intervention to impose a 'common rule' (Webb and Webb 1894) were later developed by modern labour economists in neo-classical terms (see for example Mc Cormick 1969).

The work of such American institutionalists as Clark Kerr (1950), Dunlop (1950) and Ross (1948) has led to a reconsideration of the firm as a unit of analysis. The neo-classical reduction of the firm to an abstraction solely made up of isolated and independent supply and demand functions has caused empirical observation of its working to be reduced to a minimum. Even today the small studies carried out by Hall and Hitch (1938) and by Lester (1946) are considered essential reading for students of economics because of the important criticisms of competitive theory they contain: in an essentially deductive discipline, the replication of investigatory research findings offers few career rewards. How-

ever, one of the results of the research done by institutionalists such as
Kerr et al. (1954) has been a rediscovery of the internal labour market of
the firm as a unit of analysis. Job mobility may be seen as the process of
socialization or induction into the work structure of the firm. For many
years British and American labour economists have been pointing to the
disparity of rates that exist in geographical, occupational and industrial
markets (Knowles and Robinson 1951; Robinson 1970). It remained for
two Americans, Doeringer and Piore (1971) to conceptualize the role of
the firm in bringing together these three sources of segmentation in the
market through the very act of creating each sub-market. In doing so,
these scholars have contributed to a new body of theory which attempts
to bring together existing knowledge on vertical segmentation (occupational stratification) and horizontal segmentation (local and industrial).

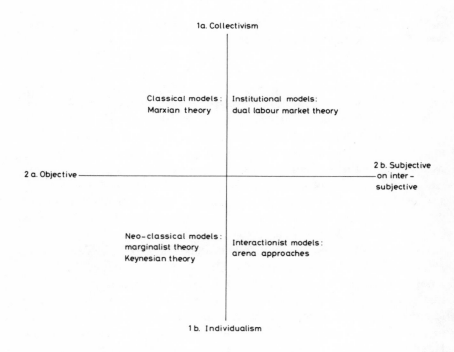

Figure 1. Labour market theories on two dimensions.

Recognizing the horizontal dimensions in the labour market next to the vertical one was the first step towards a new body of theory which had come to be known as the theory of the segmented labour market. This theory is by no means a unified body of theory, it is rather a collection of approaches which still lack unity. The advantages of segmentation theory is that it has undergone influences from many sides, although most of its origins can be traced back to Marxist and institutional theories. Segmentation theories got a lot of attention at the end of the 1960s and the beginning of the 1970s, at the height of the anti-poverty programmes and minority rights movements in the United States. The economic crisis since 1973 has stimulated interest in this body of theory in Europe too, although so far not much work has been done with the expressed purpose of testing the hypotheses contained in labour market segmentation theory.

The labour market theories mentioned here have been brought together by Mok and Bracke (1976: 615) on the two dimensions objective-subjective and collective-individual (Figure 1). In the figure the dimensions represent the following taxonomy (see Berting 1976):

1a. Theories of the labour market which regard phenomena as *sui generis*. Labour market systems and their constituent parts are regarded solely in their functioning for the society as a whole, for their socio-political consequences. These theories are regarded as collectivistic or *catascopic* approaches to the realities of the labour market.
1b. Theories which regard the totality of the system and the characteristics of its constituent parts as arising from the aggregation of individual choices, and are solely regarded as individualistic or *anascopic* approaches to the realities of the labour market.
2a. Theories of the labour market which depict that market as an objective reality which obeys fixed rules or laws, which arise outside of people's personal intentions.
2b. Theories of the labour market which depict that market as a subjective or inter-subjective reality. Behaviour in the market and the rules that guide it arise out of interaction between market parties and can only be explained in terms of the meaning systems which actors bring into that interaction.

The main differences that emerge between classical and neo-classical theory can be seen in the importance given to the demand function in the determination of price in the latter body of theory and to supply in the former. As such, neo-classicist theory is atomistic, dependent upon an aggregation of individual choices; while classical theory, particularly in its Marxist form, is structured by the intrinsic nature and artifacts of production. In this chapter the shift in theoretical emphasis has been related to the development of capitalism from its early reliance on land and labour to the growing role of the consumer and of rentier credit in economic expansion during the latter half of the nineteenth century.

However, as Roll (1957) has pointed out, there never has been a fixed and accepted corpus of economic knowledge but merely a collection of ideas which are revived again and again in response to the circumstances of the time. In recent years there has also been a return to a consideration of the wider problem of economic growth as a *self-sustaining process*, an approach which rests on a totally supply-dominated model of the economy (see for example Matthews and Hahn 1964). It may well be argued that this conceptual negation of the role of consumer preferences reflects our current economic world, dominated as it is by monopoly suppliers. Certainly the extension of economic modelling to the normative purposes of operations research and systems control reflects the ability to allocate resources centrally on a scale that could not have been attempted before the technological and social conditions of modern organization allowed. In these circumstances a new approach to segmental labour markets which incorporates the existence of such powerful institutional control mechanisms seems long overdue.

Appendix

Part of the problem in considering the evidence for any theory other than the neo-classical theories of market processes is the indeterminate nature of the outcomes, unless, that is, one can substitute ambiguous terms such as trade-union pushfulness for the rigour of Marshallian elasticities (Dow and Dicks–Mireaux 1959). But in a free market situation a direct link is made between the number of jobs on offer and the level of wages at which men will be taken on, the link-pin being the revenue product derived from the last man employed. Once one abandons this strict mechanistic relationship it is extremely difficult to make any exact statement on employment levels.

Unless one can be assured that there is some tendency in the system towards employing people at the level of their marginal productivity, then the relationship between jobs and wage levels breaks down. To use Clapham's famous (or infamous) remark neo-classical economics becomes little else than a 'series of empty boxes' (1922). It may be argued that even in a freely rather than a perfectly, competitive world market, entrepreneurs will neglect productivity at their peril. This is, of course, the nub of current criticism of post-Keynesian economics. It can equally well be argued that the degree of institutional structuring of the market is such as to give little meaning to the concept of marginal productivity, and to any related series of production functions, or more accurately that these functions are politically determined.

Such production functions are derived from a complex series of socio-political interactions within organizations. A modification to the neo-classical theory suggested by Clay (1929) is that unions (and presumably other collectivities such as professional associations) will attempt to maximize the earnings of their members within the constraints provided by job opportunities. In this way Clay provided a role for marginal theory within the arena of collective bargaining; for the employer may be seen as having the minimization of labour costs as his goal, within constraints provided by the individual employee's willingness to work rather than take leisure, or to take an alternative job/occupation, *and* the employee groups' willingness to undertake the cost of collective action.

3. Segmented labour markets

The movement in the nineteenth century thought towards consumerism was marked by a growing recognition of the heterogeneity of consumer tastes. Hence the concept of segmented markets developed most rapidly in the marketing of products. As defined by W.R. Smith:

Segmentation is based upon developments on the demand side of the market and represents a rational and more precise adjustment of product and marketing effort to consumer or user requirements. In the language of the economist, segmentation is disaggregative in its effects and tends to bring about recognition of several demand schedules where only one was recognised before (1956: 5).

The existence of separate demand schedules indicates that the consumer preferences differ and that their response to price changes may vary; in other words the supplier no longer faces an unlimited and perfectly competitive market. Moreover the existence of identifiable and discrete submarkets indicates that consumer preferences do not vary randomly, but in numbers large enough to be recognized as separate entities or groups, and long enough to be regarded as stable and predictable sources of trade.

Given these limitation to market boundaries it becomes feasible for a single, or few, suppliers to control the input of goods to the market and to vary the supply of its products *in response to changes in price*. Hence the concept of elasticity as a measure of the consumer's or supplier's response to a given change in price (or other inducement) became an important indication of monopoly power (Hicks 1936). Similarly the degree to which the consumer finds himself able to substitute one product for another indicated the height of barriers between markets (Shackle 1956).

These, and other uses of elasticity as a measure of interdependency, were freely transferable to the employment contract (Hicks 1936; Shackle 1956). At the same time the theory of bargaining, and still later, of economic gaming were developments which allowed alternative methods of analysing a price mechanism worked through confrontations or alliances between monopolistic buyers and sellers (Von Neumann 1948). However these latter concepts represent a major departure from the competitive model and may indeed be looked upon as being in direct conflict with its interpretation of the workings of the political economy. Inspite of attempts to synthesize these approaches (Scitosky 1963) it cannot be said that the movement from a competitive model to a gaming or bargaining model is an easy one to accomplish: it remains with the analyst to choose the more apposite of the available alternative explanations of reality when confronted by an empirical or administrative problem.

In neo-classical economic theory the market for labour is a commodity market in which the ultimate value of the employees' services is determined by the sales value of the product of these services. The cost of supply reflects both the disutility of work for the recruit, and his equalization of net advantages between jobs. For modern labour economists, the assumption that entrepreneurs require identical inputs of labour and that new recruits will therefore possess similar skills (the conditions of free competition) is an unrealistic one. Hence segmental labour market theory has grown out of need to explain differences between *shared* needs and commonalities *within* each group of consumers (employers) on the one hand and suppliers (employees) on the other. In this way it has been possible to carry on assuming the existence of perfect competition on both sides of the market *within* the boundaries of labour markets thus defined. Unfortunately, as Adam Smith recognized, the existence of shared needs bespeaks a commonality of *interest* which may lead to the repression of competition between individuals in favour of a collective bargaining strategy vis à vis other groups who have a share in the distribution of rewards or allocation of resources. The analyst is therefore forced to shift his model from one of limited competition in which there is still a determinate outcome, to the much less predictable outcomes of gaming theory (Pen 1971).

The structure of sub-market boundaries described by Marshall and others consisted of three segments:

1. Occupational (OLM),
2. Local–regional (LLM),
3. Industrial (IM).

In spite of the recognition thus given to market distinctions, the boundaries of each segment are seen to be explicable in terms of the workings of economic forces. They are therefore subject to long-term change through movements in the market such as might be brought about by a change in demand for the product, or a change in production technology which affects the number or type of jobs on offer. The costs of entry to each segment may be considered low or high by those who wish to enter, that is the market may be 'open' or 'closed', (sometimes described as 'unstructured' or 'structured') or increasing or reducing in cost ('opening' or 'closing'). The nature of these structural costs include training, redeployment, geographical location, etc. They indicate that a significant amount of time is taken in overcoming or reducing the barriers against entrance to the market. Perhaps as many as several generations may be required before residents in a depressed area 'learn' that they have to move to find employment, for example.

Because of the nature of comparative static analysis, 'time' becomes the most important measure of the costs of imperfection. Ultimately constraints to the perfect mobility of labour between jobs are seen by neo-classicists as essentially of an only temporary nature: even trade unions and employer associations can only exist and seek to mould their environments within the 'laws' of the marketplace. But other, demographic factors, such as age, sex, racial or ethnic origin, cannot be regarded as malleable over time. They are, in fact, often translated into dummy variables representing *qualitative* differences in the labour services on offer: for example women are often distinguished as being better qualified for manipulative work than men. Categorization of this kind renders employer perceptions of the labour force more amenable to analysis in terms of an economically rational choice (see for example Wachter 1974), but by the same token is in danger of being tautological.

Structural obstacles to the movement of labour between jobs, between forms, between regions and between occupations have been seen to be located in a number of physical and social institutional factors. The distinction made between 'frictional' and 'structural' unemployment has led to the formulation of public policies, and to a complementary compilation of official statistics, which recognizes the longevity of differences in employment prospects within the work force. One of the problems of this format is the degree to which it contains the tautology referred to above. The inability of neo-classical economists to explain the existence of institutions which express the long-term tastes of workers and employers, prevents any explanation of the means by which market segmentation came into being in the first place or can be eliminated in the long run, assuming market forces fail to do so.

One important attempt at an explanation of institutional blockages is to be found in the recent development of 'human capital' theory. In many ways labour possesses the immediately expendable aspect of other commodities but it also possesses the characteristics of capital equipment. It is, moreover, an unusual form of capital in that its stock of future services may actually appreciate or accumulate rather than depreciate or diminish over time. Through the effects of learning, labour may actually become more efficient and therefore more productive, rather than less. A number of neo-classical economists have developed this analogy into the concept of 'human capital'. The stock of skills possessed by a worker are, somewhat tautologically, judged in terms of his or her experience, or by their level of formal qualification (see Becker 1964; and Schultz 1964). However, unlike non-human capital, its services are irrevocably bound up with the tastes and preferences of the owner of a given set of skills. Moreover a whole set of social constraints exists to make labour unlike any other 'commodity' utilized in the production process. Hence the computation of net advantages arrived at in any employment contract represents a socio-political as well as an economic transaction to an extent that cannot be true of others. For this reason employees may do well to protect their investment in skills, just as employers will seek to maximize their returns from any investment undertaken in the skills of their employees. For both sides of the employment contract the existence of the human capital represented in that contract may be the subject for conflict or co-operation; it is certainly a source of power. This will be reflected in the influence that one party has upon the actions of the other, but it also relates to the control that each exercises on the rest of society.

The contribution of the 'radical' and 'dualist' scholars to economic theory is in their attempt to integrate the existing analyses of sociologists and industrial relations scholars in explaining the nature of the 'structure' which creates labour market segmentation. The former tend to see this in class-related terms: differences in career expectation related to the ownership of wealth (variously defined). More particularly they have emphasized that the effects of time may be to allow 'positive feedback' to take place. That is to say that the occupation of an advantageous or disadvantageous position in the market gives the occupant access to varying levels of resources with which to secure that position against the possibility of future market changes and eventually even to dictate movements in the market to his own favour. Lack of such resources or of the ability to control one's future may, on the other hand, cause the actor to become inured to his situation and to take a short-term or fatalistic view of his prospects. Either way the 'feedback' received from the market in response to the worker's efforts to find employment and to secure his position would lead to habitual responses over time and to a rigidifying rather than to a relaxation of market boundaries. A control role is seen to be played by the family unit in stabilizing the ownership of financial and physical wealth. More particularly it is seen to provide differing amounts of 'human capital' in the form of early socialization and training new entrants to the labour market with all of the concomitant aspirations and expectations, goals and objectives that they bring with them (this theme has more recently been explored by neo-classicists also: see Schultz 1971).

The work of dualists, more particularly Doeringer and Piore, has been associated with the development of the concept of the 'dual labour market'. The dual approach to labour markets revolves around four inter-related hypotheses. First, that it is useful to dichotomize the economy into a primary and a secondary sector of employment opportunities. Second, that the wage and employment mechanism in the secondary sector are distinct from those in the primary sector. Third, that job mobility between these two sectors is sharply limited, and hence workers in the secondary sector are essentially trapped there. Finally, that the secondary sector is marked by pervasive under-employment because workers who could be trained for skilled jobs at no more than the usual costs are confined to unskilled jobs. In this sense emphasis should be placed on 'good' versus 'bad' jobs rather than 'skilled' versus 'unskilled' workers.

Another, perhaps more important contribution, made by these two authors is that of integrating the work of the institutionalists and neo-classicists in the concept of the 'internal labour market' (ILM). In this concept they have succeeded in eliminating, whilst not entirely destroying, the neo-classical theory of the firm. The model presented by traditional theorists presents the firm as a series of demand and supply schedules, behind each of which are still further schedules matching the preferences of consumers to entrepreneurs on one side of the internal (company) market and those of employers to investors and to the technical needs of production on the other. The internal matching of these schedules has been a 'black-box' exercise for most economists and a series of descriptively anthropological studies for most other social scientists. Yet quite clearly the division of labour that gives rise to the occupational markets and to the industrial markets takes place within this 'black-box'. It also provides much of the character and wealth of the community described as a local labour market.

In the rest of this chapter we propose to give a brief review of some of the literature on each form of labour market segmentation.

Occupational labour markets

Occupational labour markets spring from a similarity in the needs of companies for skills or services, hence giving rise to a *general* level of expertise or experience which is useful in a number of *specific* work contexts. According to Reder:

Economic theory has a ready-to-hand technique for analysing the wage differentials associated with skill... i.e. to treat workers of different grades of skill as representing different factors of production, and analyse the behaviour of their relative wage rates by means of the theory of related (factor) markets (1955: 833).

Such treatment is much better afforded to occupations representing narrowly defined skills in which specific entrance qualifications are generally recognized across or within industries (where the cross-elasticity of substitution between factors is very low, to use Reder's terminology). When labour is freely interchangeable between a *broad* range of tasks, or even between jobs within a plant, an occupational identity is difficult to identify within that establishment let alone between establishments and across industries.

Yet occupational labour markets appear to have a long term stability in form and in membership which denotes their wider socio-economic significance in the hierarchy of status and authority within society. Their basis is an institutional framework which extends beyond the work environment (Wootton 1958; Fogarty 1961; Routh 1965). The definition of this hierarchy has been the concern of both economists and sociologists: the definitions of the former being phased in 'objective' aspects of occupation (wealth and income) the latter with 'subjective' (status and prestige). In general the economists's definitions have been provided by the needs of policy makers in government and in industry. Although these are now becoming more detailed and more explicit in form, official occupational definitions remain somewhat amorphous. Most attempts at analysing occupational wage differentials concern themselves with distinguishing between broad categories of skills used in similar occupational work contexts; this concern is demonstrated by Knowles and Robertson (1950). Their usefulness as tests of the operation of market forces may therefore be called into some question. Since these categories represent neither similar rates of marginal productivity on the demand side of the market nor the balance of net advantages on the supply side, any similarity in these recorded rates of earnings within 'occupations' might be considered to be largely fortuitous.

Recent developments in neo-classical thinking in the direction of human capital theory has caused economists to seek out more precisely defined occupational forms in order to measure earnings over the long term, not in relation to that of other occupations, but rather as returns to the training and qualification required for entrance to the occupation (see for example Blishen 1958). However, the separate research carried out by the authors suggest that the process of job creation at plant level is a highly idiosyncratic exercise in which the short-term exigencies facing the employer rank fairly highly. In this process technological changes, which at macro level appear to be the long-term source of occupational change, is mediated by local circumstances, including the strength of vested interest represented by local work-groups. For this reason the attempt by economists to define and to categorize 'tasks' by standardized 'categories' (i.e. to group skills in a manner which reflect a modal value of training/productivity) appears doomed to insurmountable difficulty.

In a seminal contribution to the theory of occupational rewards Reder (1955) related movements in occupational rewards to the trade cycle. He suggested that in periods of high demand in the product market occupational skills become 'diluted' by the transference of tasks formerly considered to be those of skilled employees to unskilled workers, hence a reduction in earnings differentials which historically were rarely properly restored (his theory also encompasses the employers' use of an external 'reserve army of unemployment'). Loveridge (1971) has suggested that a similar process may in fact take place at the introduction of any major change in work process i.e. that an internal market imperative dictates the employers' pressure towards the use of an existing division of labour rather than seeking a fresh one. Doeringer and Piore (1971) stress the importance of custom and practice and the degree to which the internal labour market is already structured by existing job clusters.

As against this internal explanation of the formation of skill differentials most institutionalists emphasize the importance of unions as an *external* force. While these theories were pioneered in the work of Dunlop, Kerr, Ross, Freedman, Ullman, Lewis, etc., the most specific investigations were undertaken by Turner (1957). Basically these theories put forward the view that 'wage contours' within and across industries *can* be identified. These arise, not out of any working of the free market system, but out of the use of comparative wage rates as bargaining references by union negotiators. Their choice of reference points is seen to be dictated by socio-political factors as much as by economic considerations.

Neo-classical economists have reported that such processes serve, not to destroy the market, but rather to make market forces work more effectively. Information flows more freely in the bargaining context so that comparisons can be made by employers as well as employees on a more informed basis. Such is the uniformity of rates that results across occupations that it may even be possible to establish a national job evaluation scheme. Similarly the institutions of collective bargaining simply reflect the pressures of competition for labour, therefore such systems have a tendency to equilibrium at the most efficient level of wages and location of labour. However the bulk of the empirical evidence to be examined in this study argues against both the similarity of rates of earnings within occupations over any long period and the existence of a single economic rationale in the bargaining strategies pursued by unions and by work-groups (Brown and Sissons 1975).

That is not to say that a well-established hierarchy of occupational rewards does not exist, or that it is not perpetuated by the conscious use of institutionalized power. Studies across countries and industries demonstrate that roughly similar places are awarded to identifiable occupational groups in the distribution of financial and honorific rewards—e.g. in Lipset and Bendix (1954). Moreover these crude differences in remuneration obviously reflect clear points of delineation in public attitude towards what might be described as 'working-class' occupations and 'middle-class' occupations, with other segments much less clearly defined in the public mind (Psacharopoulos 1977). However within the extremes of this hierarchy steps in income tend to be overlapping rather than at discrete intervals representing uniform differentials.

The largest groups to move *between* occupations are young people (below 25) and others whose physical, social or ethnic characteristics make them the subject of employer or union discriminatory practices (Hunter and Reid 1968). Mobility up the occupational hierarchy is usually of a short range variety.

Thus social scientists have noted both the stable nature of the actual distribution of wealth, income and career chances, and the potential range of increasingly differentiated job opportunities. Like economists they divide into those who stress the structural nature of the job market and the helplessness of the individual in overcoming institutional barriers to promotion or self-advancement, and those who stress the 'open-ness' of job-competition and individual achievement within an institutional framework (See Mok 1975). An original contribution to the debate at a somewhat more pragmatic level than is usual was that of Broom and Smith, who suggested the existence of an 'occupational system':

> The idea of an occupational system is designed to identify the potentiality for mobility or immobility inherent in particular forms of employment. It expresses the view that men develop social attributes through their work experience; and that these attributes may govern further job-choice and mobility. Within an occupation system a certain range of job experience is combined with a certain set of attributes to give distinctive opportunities for or restrictions on labour mobility (Broom and Smith 1963).

These authors identify six types of occupation system: (1) bridging, (2) closing, (3) preparatory, (4) career hierarchies, (5) incremental hierarchies, (6) residual. These systems do not correspond with the conventional divisions of the labour force into industrial or 'activity' categories. In any given industry they can occur in combination: but it is the occupation system and not the industry in which it is found which assists or blocks the potentially mobile worker.

Bridging occupations, for example are those providing through work experience the conditions and opportunities for movement across occupational frontiers (Dibble 1963). Attributes developed in the bridging occupation include resocialization (exposure to new influences), interdependency (severing of ties to kin or community), a relatively high standard of health or bearing, access (to influential or useful people), financial competence (skill in managing or acquiring resources). The mark of a bridging occupation, as in the examples of domestic servants, the military, schoolteachers and others, is that it develops attributes that are marketable in another type of employment.

Closing occupations, by contrast, tie workers to narrow lines of employment, since the skills associated with them are linked to one particular activity and even to one particular place, as in the case of miners, farm-workers or fishermen.

Preparatory occupations are those providing well-established routes into the labour market, usually for juveniles e.g. apprenticeships and traineeships.

In the advanced technological society, the predominant occupational systems are the hierarchical forms. In the first of these, *the career–step*, jobs are ranked in steps of increasing responsibility, reward and status. Such a system is characterized by frequent mobility and in all directions–upwards, sideways and sometimes downwards. Since this form is commonly found where employment is with large-scale organizations, mobility may in fact take place without a change of employer; indeed, it may be necessary for the employer to move the employee in order to retain him. We regard such job changes within the same employment as an important form of labour mobility in an advanced industrial society, since they have consequences for the demand for labour, and generate mobility elsewhere. The *incremental hierarchy* type consists of jobs graded not by power and prospects of further power, but by seniority. Rewards increase by predictable but small degrees, and the system has its own barriers which those who are satisfied with its modest but secure benefits must eventually acknowledge.

The *residual* category consists of those jobs outside even the most highly articulated labour market. Examples include most forms of unskilled manual labour and temporary or casual employment. These jobs are mainly irregular and short-term–workers may be hired by the day or even the hour–and do not build into the job holders skills or attributes that equip them for a different kind of work. In this they resemble the closing occupation: but not in their lack of skill and insecurity of tenure. As such they have probably the highest frequency of mobility, but at the same time the lowest degree of effective job choice (Roberts and Smith 1966).

We can see that this system provides us with some portals of entry to an institutionally 'closed' occupational market through *preparatory occupations* and also bridges for movement between occupations in mid-career. In general, however, it assumes that the active work population in mid-career may be categorized as being in career-step, closing or residual occupations. As such it provides a useful structure within which to categorize job opportunities. It tells us little about the propensities which steer the choices of the work force as between the different types of occupation, or the forces that are acting upon them whilst they are making the choice. A great deal has been written on the subject of job choice, more on that of new entrants to the work force than on the mid-career changer (Brown and Smith 1963).

Hunter and Reid (1968) have summarized most of the available data on occupational mobility. About half of all job changes in French, British and American studies are accompanied by a change in occupation, but a large part of this movement takes place in low-status 'residual' occupations. The highest rates of stability are to be found among professional and craft workers who in Blau's (1965) terminology are net consumers of new entrants. There is more upward mobility than downwards, but, as we have already suggested, this is only of a short-range kind and, horizontally, it is likely to be an 'adjacent' industrial or skill group. There does, however, tend to be little upward mobility from *manual to non-manual* occupations in spite of the heavy outward flow of male clerical workers into manual employment.

One of the reasons for professional, supervisory and craft groups being net consumers rather than producers of 'human capital' for investment in other occupations, was the apparent attachment of these groups to their original career choice. Technician grades were, in both French, British and American experience, net consumers of recruits from other occupations. Yet these, like the latter occupations, tend to be closing (or terminal) occupations. For a majority of technicians and craftsmen their present occupation provided the upward limits to their career mobility. This was so of virtually all but an infinitesimally small proportion of manual workers: professionals also remain outside the career streams of those large organizations that provide 'long-range' careers.

Local labour markets

Economic orthodoxy has long cherished the model of a local labour market. According to this model, competition between employers determined the level of pay for each category of labour within a given area. It is assumed that, in the long term at least, the firm that pays below the market rate will lose its labour; the firm that pays above will lose its profits.

Geographically, the labour market has strong, though not fixed, local boundaries. Within these notional boundaries the effective limits of the market are likely to be set by a system of communications which links buyers and sellers. For manual workers this system is unlikely to extend beyond the immediate neighbourhood, such as the area covered by local news media, employment agencies, and the geographical range within which friends and acquaintances work. Copious, but largely American evidence, attests that blue-collar workers acquire their jobs largely by informal means, gaining information from and being referred by friends working for alternative employers (Rees 1966). Little is known of these information networks in Europe, but their boundaries are unlikely to be fixed in a spatial sense. It seems more likely that the boundaries of spatial labour markets, e.g. for manual workers, are marked by zones of transaction between the different spheres of influence of adjacent employment centres, and that 'the market is defined by resistance points on a scale of mobility' (Kerr 1950), rather than by fixed frontiers. Carter suggests that the special dimension of the labour market concept might be visualised by imagining a map of the country with rings of concentric circles extending outwards from each locality, becoming fainter as one moves further away from the present locality. Within the inner bands a worker is more likely to be responsive to job opportunities, since he does not have to change residence and is more likely to have access to better information, etc. (Carter 1967).

Phelps Brown considers the market to be defined by 'potentialities of individual access' and '... more often than not the effective labour market is restricted to one locality, whose bounds lie within a radius of less than a day's journey from where the workers are living' (Phelps-Brown 1962). Given modern means of transport 'less than a day's journey' is extremely flexible. But Kerr suggests the boundaries are largely determined by the ideas in people's minds, and considers a local labour market to be 'merely an area of indistinct geographical and occupational limit within which certain workers customarily seek to offer their services and certain employers to hire them' (Kerr 1950). Thus we have a picture in which the market for the supply of labour may be defined in terms of information networks with subjective boundaries drawn by individuals in terms of their personal 'resistance points on a scale of mobility'. Defined in this manner some markets will be more diffuse than others.

Geographically the term the 'labour shed' describes a line enclosing the area which supplies labour (at some percentage) to a nodal point, such as an individual plant, a group of factories, or the complex of economic activities embraced by a conurbation. 'Employment field' is that area in which residents of the enclosed area actually work. The more closely the two boundaries coincide the more easily identifiable and the more selfcontained is the local labour market area. Such lines are much more easily established in Europe than is the extent of intra-market spatial mobility. The distance of journeys to work in metropolitan areas vary enormously even among manual workers (Vance 1960). Even so occupational patterns may be distinguished. Generally white-collar workers seek employment over a wider area than manual workers, and younger people travel farther than older. The effect of aging—or rather marriage—is much more evident among women. Young girls and single women are more likely to travel to city centres than are young men: married women prefer to work close to home (Duncan 1956; Loveridge 1967). At the extremes the market for senior executives and some professional occupations may be a world market, but again, extremely reliant on occupational information networks.

Generally the important distinguishing feature between these groups (white/blue collar, young/old, employee/executive) is *not* the distance of journey to work (though this *is* an important distinction in metropolitan areas) but *the attachment to place of residence.* The degree of 'perfection' of the defined local labour market can then be established by expressing the local day population as a proportion of the night population. Using the Registrar General's definitions of conurbations and the data for 1961 these figures were 97.8 and 93.6 per cent for the West Midlands; for Merseyside 93.6 and 93.0 per cent; and for the S.E. Lancashire conurbation 97.2 and 94.8 per cent (Goodman 1970). The psychological importance of a feeling of 'belonging' to a community neighbourhood is certainly an explanatory factor in determining the boundaries of local markets (see for example Young and Willmot 1956). Almost certainly the importance of the finance capital represented by an existing residence is of supreme importance to the maintenance of their living standards among low income groups and older employees. So important is the attachment to place of residence that a large proportion of the work-force will change their occupation rather than move. There are clear *national* differences in this attachment to the place of residence but in general lower income groups are most likely to change their job rather than their house (Loveridge 1969).

Whilst one may demarcate occupational markets within a spacially defined market, degrees of occupational attachment will vary, principally with the investment in specific skills. For unskilled workers occupational attachment has been shown to be low. For example, Robertson has observed: 'The need to change occupation when changing a job is not of special importance for the unskilled or semi-skilled, since such training as they receive is usually given in the form of internal training at each new place of employment' (Robertson 1961). Faced with the choice of giving up his investment in specific task skills or his investment in (1) localized and personal information networks; (2) transfer of a tenancy or of house ownership, it is not surprising that most low income employees are geographically immobile and see their attachment to their employer in this specifically local context. However it is notable that a significant proportion of manual workers *do* commute long distances, thus denoting a strong attachment to both place of residence and to their job. These are most likely to be skilled workers.

The evidence of wide earnings dispersion in local areas is increasing. The implicit questions surrounding these analyses centre on what order of dispersion is consistent with the 'effective' operation of market forces in neo-classical terms. However:

in view of the costs of search and since competitive theory does not predict equality of pay, but rather of net advantages, it is questionable whether evidence of wide dispersions at one point in time is an appropriate test. What seems more crucial to traditional market theory is the examination of changes in inter-plant differentials for 'homogeneous' occupational groups, i.e. whether inter-plant differentials are stable over a sequence of time periods and how movement can be explained. That buyers and sellers have imperfect knowledge is one explanation of wide dispersions. If this were the critical factor, it might be explained that, ceteris paribus, inter-plant differentials would narrow with the passage of time. If, assuming no change in non-earnings elements of net advantages, no narrowing tendency was found, this could be interpreted as the equilibrium position. Otherwise the explanations would seem to lie in other than simple market factors... unchanging intra-plant differentials in a situation of occupationally differentiated changes in labour availability or demand in the external market would suggest that institutional factors were stronger than market factors (Goodman 1970).

To examine the influence of market pressures, changes in intra-plant occupational differentials in plants in the local labour market would need to be assessed in the light of the state of the external market. Goodman suggests that:

the validation or rejection of traditional market theory applied to labour is notoriously difficult, if not impossible. Despite its use as proxy, the theory does not postulate wage and pay equality, but merely a tendency towards equality of net advantages. This compendious balancing item can be used (or misused) to explain away very wide dispersions of earnings for apparently similar types of labour service (Goodman 1970).

Examining a local labour market from an employer's point of view, Robinson defines it as:

> that geographical area containing those members of the labour force, or potential members of the labour force that a firm can induce to enter its employ under certain conditions, and those members of the labour force, or potential members of the labour force that a firm can induce to enter its employ under certain conditions, and those other employers with whom the firm is in competition for labour (Robinson 1968).

This usefully distinguishes workers he might be able to attract and the sources of external pressure on the firm's ability to retain labour. It also indicates the locationally specific institutions from which it draws its market information and which it shares with other local employers such as local news media, local union officers, and employment agencies (Rees 1966).

Management action following periodic ad hoc earnings surveys may also promote stability of inter-plant differentials even if it does not reduce dispersions. These surveys frequently reveal considerable intra-occupational dispersions between geographically adjacent plants, with little tendency for 'league table' positions to change over time (Knowles and Robinson 1969; Doeringer and Piore 1971). Employers appear to divide their competitors into broad categories, e.g. high, average, and low payers, and they seek to retain membership of one of these groups, rather than constantly responding to marginal changes within each sector or aiming at the average or at the top. Low-paying firms seem able to recruit labour without changing their relative positions, if at some cost in terms of labour turnover and labour force 'quality'.

The market imperfections arising from the shortcomings of the information held by buyers and sellers are well known. So, too, is the presence of trade unions and employer's associations and supply inelasticities introduced by training and other conventions. That the local market is imperfect is, prima facie, a statement of the obvious, but more recently doubt has been thrown on the entire significance of its part in the allocation of labour.

In summary, on the demand side an important factor for recruiting policy is the size and boundary of the area from which personnel is recruited. On the supply side a local labour market can be described as a geographical area in which there is a concentration of labour demand, and in which workers can change jobs without changing their residence (Lulofs 1960: 25). The essential points about a local labour market are that the bulk of the area's population habitually seeks employment there and that local employers recruit most of their labour from that area. Both employers and workers in any community will have a fairly precise notion of the relevant market area for them in normal employment conditions, though for certain types of specialised labour the extent of the market will be much wider in scope, while for certain key jobs a firm will wish to spread its net wider than the normal market area (Hunter and Reid 1968: 42).

The relative attraction to the worker of job alternatives in the local labour market is an important fact to discover (Mann 1973: 43). The distinction between voluntary and involuntary movement between jobs (or to unemployment) has been proved to be important in several Danish, Dutch and British studies, which we shall deal with later. The way in which job search is effected has important consequences for the subsequent integration in the employment situation, or the persistence of a situation of under-employment (Doeringer and Piore 1975: 70). Work done in this area suggests that (un)employment is the outcome of a process of job search where workers have limited information about the labour market, and are certain to have faulty expectations about it. People begin looking for a job on basic information about the labour market and their chances in it. If the jobs they encounter first do not come up to their expectation, they either make a more realistic evaluation of the available jobs and adjust their expectations accordingly, or leave their job aspirations unaltered, which gradually leads to discouragement and withdrawal from the market.

But a labour market can only work effectively if there are adequate channels of communication between supply and demand. Much depends on the methods used during job search, as we shall see. By using informal channels of information (friends, relatives) a worker can have far more realistic knowledge about the labour market than by using formal channels. Indeed, one researcher (Granovetter 1974: 14) even found that among graduates in industry the better jobs (often newly created, growth jobs) went through informal channels and that by recruiting friends of workers there was more chance of an early integration in the work situation and less mobility among newcomers. Quite a few authors suggest that job search is often casual and unsystematic and that many employers rely on informal methods of recruitment (Mackay et al. 1971: 347), like casual calling at the gate and applicants with relatives or friends in the firm. Formal channels, such as employment agencies and advertisements, are also used, but in many investigations employers report a preference for informal channels. Much depends on whether firms restrict their recruiting to their local market, or are prepared to go beyond this. If they go outside the local labour market, they will be less inclined to rely on informal channels. This, of course, leaves the *local* public employment exchange, as a *formal* channel, rather in the cold, as is proved by results of investigations in Britain, Belgium, Holland and Germany.

Yet in view of the important role of public employment offices in national manpower policies we think that labour market segmentation due to communication barriers should not be underrated. Limited knowledge of job opportunities seriously hampers the worker's possibilities of voluntary movement in the labour market. After involuntarily leaving his job the worker's re-entry is much dependent on his perception of alternative jobs open to him as well as the availability of such jobs. Locational preferences may tie a worker to his geographical area but so may ignorance of opportunities existing elsewhere.

As Palmer has noted: 'Basically mobility is a subjective concept concerning a persons' willingness or unwillingness to make such [job] changes' (Palmer 1954: 81). It concerns (1) their capacity for mobility (e.g. the openness of entry to the job market); (2) their willingness for mobility (e.g. a worker's motivation for future potential movement); (3) their actual movements (a job history which conditions but does not determine future movements e.g. the frustrated actor or musician who has cleaned windows for all his career). Cousins (1976) quotes a study of under-employed workers who were laid off, waiting for recall by being 'tipped the wink' by an employed work-mate. Without some prior knowledge of the way these men perceived their career as being attached to a particular plant it might seem that these men were deliberately remaining unemployed. By the same token it may be concluded that when the worker's strongest attachment is to his neighbourhood community he may be less strongly attached to a particular occupation or industry.

Most studies of strong community linkages have, however, associated such attachments to a single industry, plant or occupational identity (for example studies of coal, steel, textile, and shipbuilding communities etc). The existence of such monopsonistic local markets are also familiar in the new, large 'batch' or 'process-control' industries of the United States. In these situations the effective of membership of all such community attachments may be mutually reinforcive. The reinforcing mechanisms of these neighbourhood communities are such that Kerr (1954) coined the term 'manorial markets' to describe their feudal characteristics. Long-serving and plant-centred careers of a 'liege' or 'yeoman' variety are common among employees of these plants as is the employment of several generations of the same family at the same location.

Internal and external markets

In their work on internal labour markets and manpower analysis Doeringer and Piore (1971) define the labour market as an administrative unit within which the pricing and allocation of labour is governed by a set of administrative rules and procedures. The internal labour market is to be distinguished from the external labour market where pricing, allocating and training decisions are controlled directly by economic variables. The two markets are inter-connected, and movement in and out of the internal labour market occurs through ports of entry and exit, to use Kerr's term (1954: 101).

Internal labour markets are present throughout the economy. Doeringer and Piore (1971: 39-46) call the formation of internal labour markets a logical development in a competitive market in which three factors (usually neglected in conventional economic theory) may be present:

1. enterprise-specific skills,
2. on-the-job training, and
3. custom.

Doeringer and Piore summarize these factors and the consequences of their presence as follows:

Enterprise-specific skills are those which can only be utilised in a single enterprise in contrast to general skills which can be transferred among many enterprises. The effect of skill specificity is twofold: it encourages employers, rather than workers, to invest in training; once the investment has occurred it leads employers to stabilise employment and reduce turnover so that they can capture the benefits of the training.

On-the-job training is characterised by its informality. In many ways it appears to occur almost automatically by 'osmosis' as the worker observes others or repeatedly performs his job. Because on-the-job training is informal, is a joint output of the production process, and is limited to the skills required by work actually being performed, it appears to be an economical training process. Skill specificity tends to promote on-the-job training by reducing the number of persons learning a particular skill, thereby deterring more formal training programmes with their concomitant fixed costs. Moreover, because skill specificity is often the result of elements of work which are difficult to codify in a formal training curriculum, on-the-job training may be the only way to transmit skills from one worker to another. The informality and adaptability of on-the-job training, in turn, permits skill specificity to increase inasmuch as the need to codify or standardise the training process is not a constraint upon the evolution of job content.

Custom, or customary law, is the natural outgrowth of the psychological behaviour of stable groups. Where stability of employment is encouraged, a work group will begin to develop customs based upon precedent and repeated practice. As work rules become customary through repitition at the workplace they come to acquire an ethical, or quasi-ethical, status within the work group (and violations of these customs tend to be punished by the group). Even where work rules may have initially reflected economic forces, custom imparts a rigidity to the rules and makes it difficult to change them in response to dynamic economic forces. Custom seems to form most strongly around wage relationships and internal allocation procedures. This accounts for much of the long-term stability in the wage and allocative structure of internal labour markets and is an important influence in the maintenance of internal labour markets over time.

When one internal labour market emerges in a previously competitive labour market, some workers and some jobs are withdrawn from general market competition, thereby encouraging other workers and managers to institute internal labour markets within their enterprises. Managers will do so in order to retain their 'competitive' position in both product and labour markets. Incumbent workers will do so in order to protect or enhance their employment security and promotion opportunity. Once these markets are prevalent, workers and managers will seek to stabilise the work relationship and to reinforce further the internal labour market. Much of the interest of trade unions in seniority, internal promotion, job control, and equitable treatment at the workplace can thus be interpreted in the light of these effects. Similarly, management's interest in stabilising its workforce and in maintaining flexible work assignment procedures reflects its desire to retain an effective work force while protecting its prerogatives from the encroachment of customs which will interfere with the profits of the enterprise (Doeringer and Piore 1971).

Stability of employment is the most salient feature of the internal labour market. With stability comes rigidity and irreversibility in the administrative rules governing such markets. Not only are they irreversible, but, as argued above, they tend to spread and to grow stronger over time among all enterprises. Internal labour markets are favoured by employers because they reduce the costs of turnover among workers who have been provided with enterprise-specific skills. Because skills are not transferable among enterprises, because employers seek to induce stability through economic incentives, and because mobility is frustrated by actions taken in other internal labour markets, workers become increasingly protective of such markets and the privileges which they confer.

Finally, the gradual removal of the industrial work force from its agricultural antecedents, the decline in economic fluctuations, the increased specialization of machinery, and the rise in non-wage compensation and social welfare payments have all worked to increase gradually the stability, and the incentives for stability, within the internal labour market (Levitan et al. 1972: 215-216). In that way enterprise specificity of institutional arrangements is a crucial condition of the internal labour market, and so institutionalization of the labour market is almost synonymous with organization.

Organization means the structuring of the division of labour into specific job territories, which are themselves sub-markets where institutional rules exist to establish and maintain specific occupational boundaries. Van Voorden (1975: 223) defines institutionalization as 'the conscious attempt to preserve or the unconscious process of the preservation (stabilization) of norms, values or goals, which in their most far-reaching forms are precipitated in a structure.' According to Van Voorden two kinds of (conscious) institutionalization processes may be discerned, one in which market behaviour is controlled by the parties involved in the exchange between supply and demand, the other whereby some outside agency, like the government, structures that relationship with an eye to some external objective, e.g. welfare. (We shall come back to Van Voorden's interesting analysis of the role of the Dutch government in labour market policy when criticizing his approach precisely on the grounds that successive Dutch governments have neglected the formulation of an active labour market policy oriented towards the internal labour market.)

In sum, institutionalization of the labour market is a result of all sorts of agreements between parties involved, employers, unions as well as governments. Institutional rules are established by formal agreements (including the law) as well as by informal understandings within and between firms, unions and governments. The structuring of the internal labour market by more or less rigid rules and procedures was described by Kerr (1954: 91) as the 'Balkanization of labour markets'. In Kerr's terms, institutionalization of labour markets causes some of those markets to be structured and some to be structureless.

A structureless market has the following characteristics:

1. an absence of union influence;
2. a fleeting, impersonal relationship between employer and employee;
3. a low skill level of the workers;

4. payment by unit of product; and
5. little use of capital or machinery.

This Kerr contrasts with structured markets, in which all sorts of institutions and rules exist. This, of course, comes close to Doeringer and Piore's distinction between internal and external market, but there is an important distinction to which we shall return later. The structure brought to the employment situation by institutional rules most usually relates to specific occupational skills, attachments to the work group or the firm, and attachment to a specific locality. In all cases these structural elements tend to isolate the institutional market from the workings of external forces.

Kerr distinguishes between two main types of structured labour market, the craft and the industrial. In the former, knowledge and tasks are regarded as common to the group, in the latter skills are 'private property'.

In labour markets like building and printing, the workers have control over all jobs because they control the occupation's recruitment and training policies. Unions as occupational associations will then be able to restrict entry to their particular submarket and to control the conditions under which the work is done. If the employer wants to hire a worker, he has to address himself to the union, because he is bound by contract or custom to observe the rule. Attachment to the enterprise is thus achieved through attachment to the occupation. Because wages and other material conditions tend to be equalized, workers can quite easily move from firm to firm.

In Doeringer and Piore's terms this is an 'occupation specific', not 'firm specific' internal market. In the former the social status of the individual is determined by the collectivity to which he belongs. Individual mobility is geographical or horizontal in nature. If a worker wants to be vertically mobile, he must leave this form of structured market in which he is tied to the collective fate of his occupation.

In the industrial type of structured labour market, such as may exist in textiles or electrical appliance industries, the internal market is the firm. The workers have preference for clear job ladders and give heavy weight to seniority to determine which workers will fill what job. Here the workers' fate is determined individually (by seniority and/or productivity), and movement is mainly within a family of jobs. Unions in this case are not organized along occupational lines, but on an industry or enterprise basis.

Vacancies are filled when they occur at the bottom after the promotion of senior workers, so ports of entry for workers in the external market are restricted to the lowliest jobs in the job families. Competition between the workers in the internal market and in the external market is restricted:

Competition among workers is reduced, the internal and external labour markets are joined only at restricted points, and within the internal market, craft jobs are likely to be fairly standardised and industrial jobs filled in accordance with seniority, so that workers are not actively contesting with each other for preference. Beyond this, the distribution of work opportunities by the craft union and the rehiring rights of the industrial contract tend to hold unemployed workers in a pool attached to the craft or plant and thus keep them from competing for jobs so actively elsewhere (Kerr 1954: 96).

This works two ways. It tends to restrict mobility of workers within markets more than between markets, and it also guarantees the enduring presence of an industrial reserve army big enough to challenge the power of unions not to exercise pay restraints:

Reduced mobility is one of the main ways in which institutional rules isolate workers in the internal labour markets from external competition. The potential mobility of workers is the main sanction that makes wages rates interrelated. Once a worker builds up a certain amount of seniority in a plant, his mobility is undoubtedly restricted, and the penalty for his withdrawal from the internal labour market becomes greater and greater. It might, therefore, be very difficult for a worker to find another job with comparable pay and status if he withdraws from a particular labour market (Levitan et al. 1972: 217).

This analysis of labour market segmentation was first developed in the United States, as an explanation of urban poverty and under-employment (Gordon 1972: 43). Dual labour market theory arose out of the studies of local labour markets in the negro ghettos of Chicago, Boston, Detroit and New York. From these studies it emerged that characteristics which economists had conventionally associated with high productivity, such as years of schooling and training (i.e. human capital), had almost no influence on the employment prospects of large numbers of urban employees. In many instances they were rejected for jobs which, objectively speaking, they were as fully qualified or even better than those who were actually hired. The work preferences of ghetto workers were unfulfilled compared to those of non-ghetto workers, and the characteristics of the jobs ghetto workers did hold were less varied. With some exceptions, those jobs were typically menial, lowly paid, with low status and requiring little mental effort. Job instability (i.e. a high turnover) seemed to be accepted by employers and in many cases even to be expected or encouraged. Most important: all of these jobs were dead-end jobs, with no connection to any promotion ladders.

The dual labour market

It is from these studies that the dual labour market (DLM) approach was developed by American economists, especially by Doeringer and Piore of Boston University and the Massachusetts Institute of Technology. In this exposition of the dual labour market approach we shall rely heavily on their work and on the account of it given by Gordon (1972: 46-48).

The labour market is seen as divided into primary and secondary sectors. The primary sector contains the better-paying, steady, and preferred jobs in the society. Those employed in this sector possess job security and opportunities for advancement, high wages, good working conditions, employment stability, equity and due process in the administration of work rules. Work in the primary sector is associated with an established position in the economy. Workers here tend to identify with institutions: the company for which they work, their union, their occupation. One who has lost a primary-sector job is unemployed in the involuntary, Keynesian sense. He has not chosen to go and look for another job, but has been laid off because of contradictions in the economy or in his industry. He may accept less attractive work temporarily, but essentially is waiting to regain the clearly identified position from which he has been displaced.

As Barron and Norris (1976: 52) argue, individual firms will try to minimize the impact of economic fluctuations, like a fall in the demand for the firm's product, upon its key workers:

In a situation of periodic fluctuations in product demand, a firm cannot control its output either by trying to stabilise the demand for its own products and thereby forcing the instability in the product market on to other firms, or by organising its production system and job structure in such a way that fluctuations in its overall level of product demand can be accommodated by adjustments in the numbers of people employed on those jobs where employee instability is less costly to the firm. Firms which want to retain their key workers by raising their earnings levels, may have a limited capacity to raise wages and will therefore try to keep them low in other areas of their job structures. Levels of job security and earnings in the two sectors are therefore crucially interdependent and the growth or decline of one sector is bound to affect conditions in the other sector. If it is in the interest of employers to maintain and expand the primary sector, it may also be in their interest to ensure that instability and low earnings are retained in the secondary sector. Of course, this strategy is necessarily related to the availability of a supply of workers willing to accept the poor pay, insecurity, low status and poor working conditions of secondary jobs.

The existence of a secondary sector is of crucial importance for the maintenance of the marginal jobs. Secondary sector jobs tend to be self-terminating, or are basically unattractive, and provide little incentive for workers to stick with them. We must be careful, though, not to conclude that jobs are secondary because of marginality of the workers: it is very easy to confuse the propensities of jobs with the characteristics of job holders. Individuals who are confined to a particular sector of the labour market will acquire histories and attitudes which reflect their jobs and which mark them off from workers who do not share the same experiences (Barron and Norris 1976: 50). It is here that the problem of job search and of the acquired level of aspirations, of expectations, and of orientations to work, gains importance. If certain groups in the population are to be found predominantly in the secondary sector of the labour market this raises important questions for policy. If young people, women, foreign workers or ethnic groups are over-represented in secondary jobs, we must ask whether this is so because of some inherent characteristics of those workers and their concomitant aspirations. In the course of his discussion of women as employees in industry, Brown (1976: 30-34) sees this problem as arising out of the interplay of socialization, life-cycle experiences and opportunities available, and concludes: 'the majority of women are employed on jobs whose demands on them and rewards for them are not such as to increase their involvement in the world of work at the expense of their central life interests in the home and the family'.

Much, of course, depends on the availability of jobs in the local labour market, to which women are often consigned. This raises the question of whether whole firms, and even industries, can be assigned to the secondary sector or whether primariness and secondariness cuts through firms and industries. From Mann's study of industrial relations in the West Midlands area it can be concluded that there is a strong technological influence on whether jobs are 'good' or 'bad'. A continuous process plant is so capital intensive that the machinery will be operated stably and not intermittently. The employer will then recruit those which have proved to be stable employees, to value promotion ladders and to be willing to move their home if their job is relocated–all characteristics not usually attributed to women (Mann 1973: 216-217). This easily starts the circular argument on cause and effect with which labour market litera- ture is so richly endowed. It shows how difficult it is to decide whether the processes involved originate on the supply or on the demand side of the market.

What should concern us most are the actual causes of primarization/ secondarization, when seen as the result of an historical process. Piore (quoted by Gordon 1972: 46-48) has the following description to offer. First, he suggests, 'the most important characteristic distinguishing jobs in the primary sector from those in the secondary sector appears to be the behavioural requirements which they impose on the work force, particularly that of employment stability'. Secondary workers are gener- ally barred from primary jobs because they tend to work unreliably and intermittently.

Second, 'certain workers who possess the behavioural traits required to operate efficiently in primary jobs are trapped in secondary markets because their superficial characteristics resemble those of secondary workers'. Two kinds of discrimination seem important. There is dis- crimination 'pure and simple' where employers simply dislike employing workers with certain characteristics. There is also 'statistical discrimina- tion'. In this case, employers tend not to employ members of certain groups because their superficial characteristics seem to be statistically associated with undesirable behaviour traits like unreliability. As Doeringer and Piore (1971) are careful to note, of course, many workers in the secondary market will work stably despite the extent to which their jobs encourage instability.

Third, the distinction between sectors is not so much technologically as historically determined. Many kinds of work can be technologically performed in either sector. 'Work normally performed in the primary sector is sometimes shifted to the secondary sector through subcon- tracting, temporary help services, recycling of new employees through probationary periods' and so on. Different jobs within the same plant can share the characteristics of either or both sectors. But once jobs come to be rooted in one sector or another, through a process of historical or institutional evolution, 'shifts in the distribution [of jobs between sectors] generally involve changes in the techniques of production and manage- ment and in the institutional structure and procedures of the enterprise on which the work is performed'. Since these changes are difficult and expensive they are infrequently made.

Fourth, 'the behaviour traits associated with the secondary sectors are reinforced by the process of working in secondary jobs and living among those whose life style is accommodated to that style of employment'. Those who are channelled into the secondary sector as a result of discrimination 'tend, over time, to develop the traits predominant among secondary workers'. This grows both from work patterns on the job and from life style in the ghetto or in the family.

Finally, a wide variety of historical forces have interacted to increase the likelihood of sharp separations between the two markets. The following hypotheses draw largely from Piore (1968) and Doeringer and Piore (1971). The increasing importance of skills acquired through on-the-job training has raised the incentive of employers to retain some (stable) employees, and has tended to create a division between these jobs and other jobs which do not require such employee retention. Trade-union organization and social welfare legislation may have 'operated in the postwar period to sharpen the distinction between stable and unstable jobs'. The rise of national (federal) social legislation, and particularly of minimum wages, 'the income ceiling upon the tax base of social insurance programs, the ceiling on the tax rate in the experience rating for unemployment insurance taxation, and the limited coverage of the legislation' (Piore 1968: 26), has tended to encourage employment stability in those industries affected because the 'employer has an incentive to minimise the number of people on his annual payroll and avoid absenteeism, turnover, and fluctuations in demand which disperse the wage bill over a large number of workers' (Piore 1968: 25).

Other institutional factors such as the differential rise in union strength across different American industries, and the differential industrial coverage under the National Labor Relations Act also tend to separate industries into those with stable and those with unstable work arrangements. Most important, the interactions between the process of economic growth and the changing behavioural characteristics of disadvantaged workers have accentuated these trends. Disadvantaged workers, especially those recently off the farm, have always had trouble responding to the discipline required of them in industrial organizations. That transition was traditionally abetted by the 'stick' of the sharp penalties attached to unemployment and the 'carrot' of the example of successful transition by previously assimilated groups. As Piore writes:

Earlier migrants made their transition at a time when the penalties for unstable work habits were more severe. Public welfare programs have since reduced the cost of life without work and rising wage levels the threat which unemployment, especially temporary unemployment, poses to subsistence... The completion, by a greater and greater proportion of the total labour force of the transition to industrial work, combined with the effects of union organization and social welfare legislation, has tended to create a discontinuity along the spectrum. If workers (and jobs) of intermediate stability have not been completely eliminated, their numbers relative to those with unstable work habits may have become greatly reduced. This implies, in turn, a decline in the alternative behavioural models to which the very unstable are exposed and in the number of social groups that can serve as waystations in their transition to stable life styles (Piore 1968: 28-30).

Conclusions

The emphasis in neo-classical theory has tended to make labour market segmentation a product of the *interdependently* working forces of supply and demand (Marshall's allusion to the 'blades of a scissor'). Dual-market and radical theorists have set out to demonstrate the interdependency of the supply and demand curves for labour. In doing so they have shifted the emphasis from that made by neo-classical economists in segmented market theory in which the heterogeneous nature of the supply of labour (encapsulated in human capital) is seen to be the most important boundary condition. Instead the varied employment practices of the modern corporation are believed to cause the dichotomy between the primary and secondary markets. These practices are seen by dualists and radicals to reinforce and extrapolate present distinctions between differing forms of available labour by shaping the objective and subjective nature of the commodity environment from which the organization draws its labour. In this way those parts of the labour market that are currently deficient in human capital, remain in an inferior and possibly worsening situation over time and over a succession of technological changes in which work tasks, jobs and even occupations undergo considerable change.

In the introduction to his seminal work *The Balkanization of labour markets* (1954: 92), Kerr discusses the extent to which the supply and demand curves for labour reflect an adding up of individual preferences to obtain an identifiable and homogeneous market. Kerr's description of the waitress who finds herself working as a launderess (or vice versa) may be considered typical of that large proportion of the work force in residual, closing, occupations (Brown and Smith 1963). It is doubtful whether the conscribing boundaries of an occupational identity have any great meaning in the case of this waitress, the boundaries of the market for her services, necessarily, coincide with that of a local neighbourhood community. Instead of moving freely to alternative openings for waitresses, if she wishes to remain both in the same occupation *and* in the same neighbourhood, it becomes necessary for her to erect certain protective barriers or 'shelters'. In this case the employer and employee have to either explicitly or unconciously accept the existence of such 'shelters' as marking certain boundaries to their conduct in employment practices and day-to-day job management. Their dimensions are set not by the whims of workers and employers but by rules, both formal and informal. These rules state which workers are preferred in the market or even which ones may operate in it at all and which employers may or must buy in this market if they are to buy at all (Kerr 1954: 93).

The view that is being put forward by dualist theorists is that the marginality of work arises, not, as the neo-classicist would have us believe, out of the essential characteristics of either the job or its occupants as evaluated in a free and rational choice, but rather from the result of a constrained situation in which preferences are shaped by the very nature of the choice open to the worker within that situation. Furthermore, it is being postulated that since the market is segmented by institutional rules, the rules themselves will maintain the situation in being until they are changed. This leads to the question of whose rules they are. *Cui bono?*

4. Forms of discrimination and their measurement

One can see in segmentation theory a new 'queue' theory: just like neo-classical economists perceived of workers as standing in a queue according to their marginal productivity, so now workers are lined up according to their aptitude for certain market segments.

Suppliers of labour all have personal characteristics which can be seized upon to be labelled as superior or inferior qualities in a given context of the labour process. People are never superior or inferior as such, but only potentially so, until recognised in the response of the employer and of other market institutions; that is in the employment contract or in the unemployment context. Superiority or inferiority becomes manifest when confronted with employment situations which differ fundamentally from the ones originally happened upon at an earlier point in their career. The French author Ledrut (1966) gives the following traits according to which supply is judged on a 'superior–inferior' scale:

Age: Being young or old gives a greater chance that one will be offered an inferior job, especially when viewed in combination with other characteristics. Being young equates with a lack of experience in the labour market and a lack of specific skills. Here much depends on the way entry into the labour market is organized. Where a system of vocational training is well developed, like in Germany, there are fewer entry problems for the young than where no such system exists, as is the case in Belgium. Even where vocational training is well developed it may not be used to the full extent: young girls in the Netherlands and in Britain make little use of the system of vocational training and education. As a result there are marked differences in under-employment figures between boys and girls in these countries. Being old means a greater likelihood of having many physical and social characteristics which can be regarded as inferior (Koopmans et al. 1976: 78). Here again structural differences can be very great, for instance 'pensioning off' at an early age lowers the chance of a label of inferiority for the older workers in the labour force.

Aptitude: Being physically or mentally handicapped brings about an inferior position vis à vis 'normal' persons. This is not to say that handicapped persons always have relatively inferior chances in the labour market. The report cited above (Koopmans et al. 1976), which contains the result of an investigation into the characteristics of un-employed persons in the Netherlands (commissioned by the Dutch government), has some interesting observations on this. It appeared that some unemployed with 'low aptitude' had no difficulty re-entering the market, while some employed with high aptitude did have considerable difficulties. Much depends not only on the extent of the demand for labour, but also on aspirations and expectations of workers. Those who are content with being confined to a certain segment of the market, apparently, had no difficulty with re-entry, in spite of their handicaps.

Migrant origin: From research done for instance in Belgium (Martens 1973 ; Haex et al. 1976), it appears that being a 'guest worker' in Western Europe is indeed an inferiority trait. Haex et al. (1976: 214) conclude that foreign workers form a kind of buffer segment to screen the 'good' segments of the market from the 'bad' ones. This makes one think of what Piore, and Barron and Norris (1976: 52) have to say about (for instance) women: firms try to screen their hard-core workers from the instability caused by a fall in product demand and so have a need for a peripheral work force. In this way there is no competition within the total work force, but only within the particular segment to which the worker 'belongs'.

Sex: We have already said that being a woman confines one to certain segments and bars the way to others. In Europe, women in many ways take the place of negroes in American studies. But it is more complicated than that. As Barron and Norris (1976: 47) say, one cannot understand the position of women in the labour market if one does not refer to women's place in the family and sexual division of labour. Of the breeder-feeder-producer triad (Boulding 1976: 95) the first two are exclusively assigned to women. It is interesting to note that quite a few authors have remarked that in the enterprise that predated the industrial revolution, women were involved in the productive process in partnership roles with men (Boulding 1976: 106). It is quite possible, say Elise Boulding and others, that the small-scale craft-guild enterprise provided the setting of a more egalitarian, less exploitative work and parenting relationship than any other kind of work setting.

As soon as the separation of work and the family was realized, and women (and children) came to work in capitalist-owned enterprises under the exclusive authority of male supervisors and managers, this egalitarian relationship disappeared. Women became important members of the new 'industrial reserve army'. Unemployment among women is almost as high as, and in some countries (like Belgium) considerably higher than, that of men.

Education: Lowly educated people, without specific skills and experience, have inferior positions in a labour market that tends to stress the advantages of an education or of specific experience in progressing their career.

Industry: There are some industries which as a whole tend to have an "occupational" unemployment coefficient and can be dubbed inferior: they tend to be labour-intensive and old-established. The Belgian report on migrant workers (Haex et al. 1976: 215) gives as examples of 'inferior' industries: clothing, textiles, cleaning, hotels and restaurants, and some pharmaceutical firms. Others are as a whole 'superior': gas, electricity, oil refineries—all without any 'guest workers'. Of course industry is an objective characteristic of the employment situation rather than of the worker himself. Over a period of time the worker who is confined to a certain industrial segment by virtue of his market position tends to become 'labelled' in a way which identifies him with the best or least attractive characteristics of the job.

Region: Some regions are backward and 'inferior', giving people living there fewer chances in the labour market. Regional differences may account for certain inferiorities, for instance from lack of specific experience (agrarian workers in an urban labour market) or from other traits, like a strong accent, which will foster people's chances of being confined to specific segments. In part this is the same factor as the first one (geographic origin).

Of course, these 'superiorities-inferiorities' do not each in themselves confine people to certain segments ('good' or 'bad' or 'in-between') but in a cumulative way may have precisely that effect. Being a young migrant woman with little education or experience in industry from a backward region may severely handicap a person's chances of getting work in the 'good' or even 'in-between' segments of the market if she *wishes* to move from either the job or the region. But in itself this need not be true. There are two other factors involved: the structure of demand and the level of aspirations and expectations, and the attitudes people bring to their work.

The statistical evidence

Any attempt to explore the existence of *particular* kinds of market segmentation is faced with three major difficulties. The first is technical, the second methodological, the third conceptual.

Regarding the latter, conceptual, problem we discover that market boundaries are largely set by the analyst in terms of the perceptions of the would be employee and/or the employer; the 'potentialities of individual access', to quote Phelps Brown again, may consist of a series of objective physical and institutional barriers but each have to be observed through the frame of reference used by the actors. Hence when an American judge was called upon to enforce anti-discriminative legislation within a *local* labour market he was unable to find a theoretical economist who could help him in setting the physical boundaries of such a market and was forced to do so on an arbitrary (common sense) basis (Jain and Sloane 1977).

Writing of the dual labour market analysis, Cain (1975) employs the same criticisms and more. He suggests that Piore does no more than to list several good characteristics of jobs in the primary sector and several bad characteristics of jobs in the secondary sector:

Of course, all this provides a taxonomy, not a hypothesis. Indeed, as a taxonomy there are some vital missing parts. No rule is provided to designate which jobs go into one or the other sector. No specific hypotheses are stated that use this particular taxonomy; therefore, we are left to interpret the meaning and purpose of the 'duality' on our own... Clearly, both tests of the dual hypothesis require some criteria for determining in advance what assigns a worker to a primary or secondary sector and what degree of bimodality or immobility would be considered sufficient to justify the dual label. Surprisingly, almost no discussion of these criteria has been forthcoming (Cain 1975: 41).

Although it is possible for Ledrut (1966) and for others to construct a schedule of 'least desirable' factors on the basis of the historical (objective) measurement of discriminative behaviour it is extremely difficult to predict their effect on any given employment situation. A measure of dynamic ambiguity surrounds all labour market boundaries. For example, a worker classified as a skilled man in one place of work may not be so categorized in another; nor a plumber be able to substitute for a mechanic, yet this ambiguity in definition does not inhibit economists from pronouncing the future needs for 'skilled tradesmen'. Yet it may be said that the objective basis of job discrimination in this case, however contentious between employee and employer or craft union it may be, is more objectively discernable and therefore more likely to remain stable as a market parameter than are those surrounding new occupations such as that of computer technician.

But the essence of the dualist case is that the various forms of stigmatism listed above *do* tend to act in a cumulative fashion and, according to the radicals, to be self-perpetuating and mutually reinforcing. The neo-classicist, on the other hand, will tend to treat each form of stigmatism as a discrete source of market imperfection. To repeat Jain and Sloane's contention: 'As a result there may be a whole series of possible wage and employment equilibria stemming from the multi various demand and supply schedules that represent discrimination of one sort or another' (1977).

It may indeed be the case that the nub of the argument between modern neo-classicists and the new segmentation theorists rests in their different interpretation of the nature of stigmatization. The former, neo-classical theorists, see it as arising out of the exercise of narrow prejudices which may or may not serve a 'rational' economic purpose, but however justifiable in economic terms, may be treated as localized phenomena on an ad hoc basis. The dualist, and certainly the radical, sees the problem as existing within a wider societal framework in which the social, political and economic needs of each group of actors serves to sustain and to reinforce an identifiable dichotomy in the market conditions facing two distinctive groups of workers. The very difference in the frames of analysis used by the two schools makes the data they use to support their competing claims difficult to compare.

A related difficulty is the difference in methodology used in pursuit of these claims. Neo-classical economists have by tradition generally regarded 'empirical research' as being confined to a form of multi-variable regression analysis which uses secondary source data of an aggregated nature, collected that is, at a national, industrial, or occupational level. Their view of the market as being freely competitive within each of these defined limits allows them to generalize about the overall effect of other variables such as sex, age and colour as if all undefined and (at that level) undefinable factors are being held constant for the purposes of their experiment. (Usually their conclusions included a provision of 'ceteris paribus' in the small print!) Most of the empirical evidence brought to bear on the problems of employment segmentation by both sides has been couched in the form of such multiple regressions on aggregated statistical data. Dualist economists trained in the use of neo-classical tools continue to deploy such methods in attacking their alma maters.

This results in two major weaknesses in the presentation of their case. Firstly that the available statistical data from official sources has not been collected or categorized in a manner which enables it to be easily amenable to the dualist taxonomy. For this reason crude impositions of new groupings have to be made on existing data. For example Osterman (1975) employs a test of duality in which he first classifies occupations according to his personal judgement about the autonomy and stability of occupations. Andresani (1973) simply selects the three-digit occupations and industries where median earnings are below the thirty-third percentile of the labor force to define secondary workers. Cain, quite rightly, points to the tautological nature of the 'proof' thus obtained and to the related distortion of the statistical results produced in the regression analysis (Cain 1975).

The second, and perhaps more important distortion that appears in the dualists' presentation of their case is in their attempt to demonstrate the existence of an essentially micro-level phenomenon, the internal labour market, with data collected at a macro level. For, inspite of Cain's claim that segmentation theory lacks a hypothetical basis, if a single source of causality is to be found in dualist theory one must look to the ILM to produce that explanatory force. For the neo-classical economist the firm represents a 'black-box': certain laws, largely those based on the concept of marginality and declining returns to scale govern their approach to the processes of production and the allocation of labour. Much of the work done to 'demonstrate' the workings of the firm on an empirical basis are no more than the measurement of aggregated indices of what are assumed to be the internal activities of firms and attitudes of entrepreneurs and workers. Thus to test the existence of the ILM one might resort to measuring the level of employee concentration within defined local labour markets–on the assumption that big plants create manorial markets where they are in a monopsonistic position (Bunting 1962). However it is clear from micro studies by Addison (1976), Brown (1976) and Mann (1973) that size alone does not provide either the sole source of employment stability or company prominence as a local reference group in wage bargaining. Descriptions of the ILM that appear in Doeringer and Piore's definitive text (1971) and in other parts of the dualist literature contain considerable obscurities and, for the industrial sociologist, a certain amount of naivity. The multitude of regulative processes that exist in the work place and the nature of their relationship with different product market conditions, with technology and the forms of organizational structure deployed by management and the unions across different situations–as well as to ascertainable differences in attitudes among particular forms of labour and types of employer–are nowhere well explored.

Here we have to differentiate between much of the American literature and that of European theorists (with the British having a foot in both camps!). The Anglo-Saxon literature is dominated by positivistic theorists using regression analysis of an aggregative nature and often attempting econometric models. This is the literature reviewed by Cain (1975) and Wachter (1974) after which the latter concluded that 'A rigorous empirical test of the dual under-employment hypothesis, however has not been attempted, and given the available data, may not be feasible.'

In the next chapter we supplement these studies with a review of similar data collected in Europe. We observe a different perspective presented in the work of European theorists, most particularly by the Munich School of sociologists. This body of theory is based on a much more disaggregative approach, concentrating on the analysis of internal or 'manorial' markets and extrapolating their findings upwards to macro level, rather than downwards, as is the case with American empiricists. The assumptions about the nature of market relationships made by these European analysts are also markedly different from those of the American theorists, reflecting both their different academic tradition (often Marxian rather than neo-classical) and the differences in national cultures which give rise to variations in the way social 'problems' are perceived and their solutions defined. These differences are explored in Chapter 6 on the internal labour market.

The third difficulty we encounter in our consideration of the evidence is one that we have already mentioned, the technical problem of matching data collected for one purpose to the requirements of proving another hypothesis altogether. Labour force statistics do not generally provide a precise means for determining the boundaries of the primary/ secondary market. Workers with 'disadvantaged' characteristics are not necessarily used as categories for the collection and collation of macro-statistics. One is forced to resort to small and unsystematically produced micro studies and to composite aggregations or to generalizations made from these often unrelated data bases.

Some of these problems are mainly ones of technique or lack of uniformity in technique. For example methods used in the collection and collation of unemployment statistics vary considerably across the European states. It is generally agreed that for the purposes of policy analysis the American method of separating the production of data on unemployment from the process of registering for benefits is a more effective one. The method used in Britain and other countries has been shown seriously to understate the level of unemployment among some groups of marginal workers, particularly women, adolescents, and itinerant occupations like construction workers (National Institute for Economic Research 1971; Standing 1972).

Similarly studies of relative earnings often employ different definitions of earnings. Some use 'basic weekly pay' others 'basic pay' when all possible bonuses and fringe benefits have been added. The differences between these figures may be considerable. Clearly when making such comparisons a 'consolidated hourly rate' would be the best unit across industries and occupations. These are rarely obtainable (Addison 1976) and even if they were, in comparisons between individuals and family units they leave out the not unimportant opportunities for 'moonlighting', 'foreigners' and other extra mural activities. It is clear than many 'marginal' workers occupy this latter status in more than one organization at a time!

The recently introduced list of Key Occupations for Statistical Purposes (kos) which in turn was derived from the new Classification of Occupations and Directory of Occupational Titles (codot) had greatly improved production of New Earnings Surveys and Social Trends Statistics produced in the UK. Similar detailed occupational breakdowns have also become available in other E.E.C. countries. Yet it is important to recognize that far from helping the identification of *sources* of discrimination these attempts to standardize occupational codes are often motivated by the normative purposes of comparing jobs across industries as means to state or managerial control over incomes and employment practices. Localized 'custom and practice' is ignored and discounted, and is certainly disparaged by agencies engaged in manpower planning or incomes control at macro level. An example of how the process of occupational definition actually works at local level is produced in a description of the compilation of training statistics for 'technicians' employed in 14 plant studies by Roberts et al. (1971). Employers sometimes translated ambiguous task clusters into 'occupations' with a view to maximizing their own returns from training levies rather than meeting the criteria required by national planners! More often however employers resisted the creation of new occupational identities that lay outside of their own existing local job grading structure.

In other words it may be possible to say that any form of occupational categorization may be a point of contention and as such represents the political institutionalization of a given market relationship. Once more one has to ask of any given form of categorization—*cui bono*? Statistics on labour market discrimination based on employee stigmatization may be extremely difficult to collect but so for that matter are accurate occupational statistics. The fact that they exist only in a fragmented and unsystematic way may be taken as an indication of the low order of priorities set on this form of social control by state authorities until comparatively recently (Berckmans et al. 1975). This brings us back to the differences that exist between the two schools of analysts in their occupational bases which reflects in their methodological approach. Thus Wachter (1974) rightly suggests that many people *prefer* low-paying and dead-end jobs because they value these or other characteristics of such employment. Indeed if one accepts the radical's account of the low aptitude and negligible amounts of 'human capital' possessed by peripheral workers as being related to their work and social environment, then we have one explanation of why this might be so. But whereas neo-classicists see no reason to explore the reasons for the expression of individual preference in the market-place, the latter would see it as necessary to expose the structural position which they believe to have helped create the propensities being expressed by the labour force.

5. The empirical evidence of segmentation

Does the dual labour market exist? The evidence is fragmentary. Cain (1975: 41) suggests 'One of the first questions in evaluating the D-R position is the factual content–the 'realism', if you will–of the 'duality' or 'segmentation' of the labour force.' In Piore's words:

The basic hypothesis of the dual labor market was that the labor market is divided into two essentially distinct sectors, termed the *primary* and *secondary* sectors (1972: 2).

Piore goes on to list several good characteristics of jobs in the primary sector and several bad characteristics of jobs in the secondary sector. But in order to examine the evidence more rigorously we may attempt to form some null hypotheses. These were set in the first chapter. The broadest proposition is:

1. that stigmatized groups are identifiable because people with their characteristics are 'crowded' into:

   A. low-paying jobs, or
   B. jobs with no upward career prospects, or
   C. jobs with low security of employment, or
   D. jobs with bad working conditions.

   The existence of these conditions will be taken as support for what we shall refer to as the Crude Dual Market Hypothesis.

2. A more refined hypothesis might be that stigmatized groups with defined characteristics *but who otherwise possess similar educational qualifications* to those of non-stigmatized groups are crowded into jobs possessing the above defined features A, B, C and D to a greater extent than are the latter groups. This may be described as the *Anti-Human Capital* or the *Job Discrimination Hypothesis*. If proven

it demonstrates differential returns to similar levels of education and training which cannot be explained in the neo-classical framework of 'human capital' theory adopted by Becker (1964), Mincer (1958) and Schultz (1963).

3. A third version of the theory states that stigmatized groups possessing similar qualifications to those of the non-stigmatized and *occupying similar jobs* are paid significantly less than the latter and are also subject to conditions B, C and D. This is the clinching, necessary and sufficient, condition needed to demonstrate the existence of discrimination between individuals or groups in exactly the same market situation. It is sometimes referred to as the *Wage Discrimination Hypothesis*.

The Job Discrimination Hypothesis may also be described as *Pre-entry Discrimination*, that is to say stigmatized groups are seen to be kept out of certain occupations or industries, whilst being 'crowded' into others. For example, in neo-classical terminology it asserts

that women are contracted within a narrow industrial/occupational range as a result of, say, the pressure applied by male trade unions.

This overcrowding results in an excess supply of females to such sectors, which, if the market is to be cleared, acts to depress female marginal productivity to a relatively low level and hence to reduce female relative earnings (Addison 1975).

The arguments for the existence of Wage Discrimination (Condition 3 above) are also called upon to support the existence of *Post-entry Discrimination*. Those economists who do so appear to believe that it is the institutionalized practices operating *within* the ILM that bring about earnings differentials within the same occupation. For example a woman is paid less than a man who is doing a similar job in the same work context. Paradoxically this provides them with a basis for suggesting that no major structural changes in the *external* job market should be necessary for comparability in earnings to be achieved. Statutory measures to curb discrimination should be focussed on equalizing wage and salary levels leaving the matching of skills to jobs to the free workings of the market (Chiplin and Sloane 1976). (For a fuller understanding of this dialogue the reader is referred to the discussion of 'marginality' in Chapter Two, in which we describe the distinction drawn between the 'job market' and the 'wage market' in the neo-classical explanation of segmentation. This contrasts with feed-back models in which emphasis is placed on the *type* of job and the regularity of income.)

The dualists would claim that *both* forms of discrimination are in operation but might be expected to place more emphasis on Pre-entry Discrimination than neo-classicists. Their explanations would differ significantly from those of the latter economists particularly in the emphasis given to contextual features of a labour market namely:

4. smaller companies and companies with low capital/labour ratios;
5. a number of defined industrial features (and associated geographical areas);
6. defined sectors of employment within and across industries which have become stigmatized employment opportunities in themselves. These are also identifiable by the concurrence of high labour turn-over, a high frequency of lay-offs, together with the absence of 'structure' in the ILM as described by Doeringer and Piore (1971).

We should also examine the contextual data for evidence of so-called 'feed-back' effects i.e. all those influences which reinforce or undermine institutionalized barriers to mobility into, out of, and between labour market segments.

The crude 'crowding' hypothesis

In Britain as in Belgium, industries such as laundries, distribution, catering, and some parts of government employment all have low earnings. In addition, according to the few surveys available, low-paid work is marked by undesirable working conditions and few promotion opportunities (Marquand 1967; Haex et al. 1976). That discrimination exists, in the crude 'crowding' sense, is demonstrated by the fact that women and immigrants are disproportionately represented in such low-wage employment in all European countries. Both Rose et al. (1969) and Hepple (1970) showed that black male immigrants in Britain were over-represented, compared with the indigenous population, in some parts of manufacturing, transport and communication industries but under-represented within distributive trades and service industries. Bosanquet and Doeringer found coloured workers to be highly concentrated in foundries, textiles, clothing, bakeries and bus transport (1973).

Women, especially from the West Indies, were particularly likely to
work in hospital or medical services and were also over-represented in
low-status positions in professional and scientific services. The virtual
exclusion of West Indian men and immigrant women from clerical work
and sales work was especially striking. London differed somewhat from
the rest of Britain both in the wider range of jobs held by immigrants and
in the greater differences between immigrant groups (Richmond 1973 ;
Rutter et al. 1975). This may, of course, be taken as evidence of the
efficacy of local labour market forces in eroding the barriers of social
stigmatism, but the evidence is fragmentary and often conflicting.

Both Rose et al. (1969) and Jones and Smith (1970) suggested that
patterns of job tenure were generally similar for immigrant and indigenous groups, although immigrants were more likely to suffer during times
of rising unemployment. However 1971 census data showed that, even in
areas of high employment, the unemployment rate among young West
Indian males was twice that of the general population of the same age
(Community Relations Commission 1974). The opcs Survey (1973 and
1974) confirmed that West Indian school leavers took longer to obtain a
job and were more often unemployed during the next two years than a
matched group of white school leavers. An interview survey of unemployed young people, black and white, showed that nearly half had
not registered at an employment exchange, implying that official figures
underestimate the extent of unemployment (Community Relations
Commission 1974).

One of the few attempts to relate discriminative practices to market
forces in a dynamic and rigorous analysis was carried out by Kudat and
Sertel (1974) in respect to *Gastarbeiter*. In an analysis of employment in
Germany over the period 1966-1969 they calculated an elasticity of
'firing', and one for 'hiring' for Gastarbeiter (or *Ausländer*), and similar
indices for natives (*Deutsche*). From this they calculated a 'discrimination factor' (r) for the sequence of economic recession, recovery, and
consolidation into which they divided the time period of their study.
Their findings indicate that the relatively large decline in the employment
of foreign workers in Germany in comparison with that of indigenous
workers during the recession was not symmetrically compensated for by
the corresponding rates of growth of employment in the recovery phase.
This inspite of the apparent growth in aggregate employment among the
immigrant workers during this period of economic recovery.

This differential treatment of the two working groups during the phases in question can perhaps be better seen from the following findings. Within the first period – average 1966 to January 1968 – total employment declined by 918,000. During the following recovery period the increase in employment was 974,000. When we examine the relative contribution of the Gastarbeiter and the indigenous employees to these figures, we observe that 31% of the total unemployed were Gastarbeiter, another 5% other foreigners, and 64% were Germans. During the recovery period, however, *Gastarbeiter* contributed only 17% to the total increase in employment, while the corresponding figure is 80% for the Germans. In simpler terms, the ratio of respective contributions of the two groups to the increase in employment during the recession is 0.49 and to the increase in employment in the recovery period 0.12 (Kudat and Sertel 1974: 12).

Differences in patterns of under-employment

The conditions of immigrant workers in European states has been the subject of a recent adverse report published by a newly formed action group (Minority Rights Group 1977). Yet it is clear that differences exist between industrialized countries in the manner in which discriminating practices produce unemployment and/or under-employment. Evidence from studies of the work experience of black men in the United States suggests that the greater burden of unemployment borne by them is not simply the result of their being at the end of an hypothetical hiring queue. Black unemployment rates are consistently twice that of whites because of the higher turnover associated with the peripheral jobs they hold in disproportionate numbers (Freedman 1976). Yet there is significantly more long-term unemployment (as a proportion of all unemployment) and less chronic job changing among the labour force in Britain than in America. Women in Britain appear to have unemployment rates slightly below the average, rather than slightly above it as in the United States. Women in Belgium have a much higher unemployment rate than the men: in 1977, 16.8 per cent of the active female working population was unemployed, as opposed to only 5.8 per cent of the male work force (total unemployed figure: 9.4 per cent). In Holland the similar figures were 7.1 per cent, 4.8 per cent and 5.3 per cent (but, of course, the participation rate of women in the Dutch working population is much lower than that in either Britain or Belgium: 21 per cent against 37 per cent in Britain and 34 per cent in Belgium). Over the period 1961-1964, Wright suggests that turnover in Britain, unlike that in the United States, was lower among coloured workers than among white workers in similar jobs (Wright 1968). In general, the dispersion of unemployment rates

among socio-economic groups is less in Britain than in the United States
(Bosanquet and Doeringer 1973).

In all industrialized countries most job changing takes place in
adolescence and in the early twenties. Apprenticeship programmes are
used more frequently to bridge the gap between school and work in
Holland, Britain and in Germany than in the United States and Belgium,
and coloured youths appear to be less prone to employment instability in
the former countries. However, the method of recording unemployment
in these countries is not the same as that used in America: it may disguise
much of the short-term unemployment especially where, as among
women, the system of social security penalizes registration for unemployment benefit.

It remains true that it is extremely easy to demonstrate the existence of
a pool of itinerant labour in most industrial economies including those
European states. In spite of differences between countries a large
amount of unemployment in Europe, as in the United States, is short
term and contains a significant number of chronic job changers. Most of
the available evidence on this phenomenon stems from Britain. The
Government Social Survey on Labour Mobility in Great Britain between
1953 and 1963 shows that although over half the work force remained
stably employed over periods as long as ten years, 15.4 per cent of the
men and 6.7 per cent of the women continuously attached to the labour
force held more than three jobs; 29.1 per cent and 12.1 per cent of the
men and women respectively held six or more jobs (Bosanquet and
Doeringer 1973).

Sources of stigmatism

In every European country it is possible to demonstrate crude earnings
discrimination against women. The crude average earnings figures
reproduced in Table 1 (Coventry Engineering Employers Federation
1971) may be complemented by the more sophisticated analyses
attempted by Addison (1977) discussed in a later section. It should be
noted that not only were continental countries ahead of Britain in
achieving equal earnings but the rate of increase in female earnings was
in excess of that in the latter country.

Table 1. Female earnings as percentage of male earnings, October 1970.

N.I.C.E.	Industry	Germany	France	Italy	Belgium	Luxem-bourg
34	Metal manufacture and primary conversion	71	78	74	67	57
35	Manufacture of metal metal goods	70	81	83	73	—
36	Manufacture of non-electrical machinery	72	83	86	73	82
37	Manufacture of electrical machinery, goods and equipment	74	84	86	76	73
38	Manufacture and repair of vehicles (including shipbuilding and repairing)	78	82	88	77	72
39	Miscellaneous manufacturing industries	74	76	77	85	—

Source: Coventry Engineering Employers Federation (1971).

In Britain progress to equal rates of pay looks particularly slow now that the transitional stage of the Equal Pay Act is over. Women's earnings as a proportion of men's earnings went up from 54.8 per cent in 1970 to 64.3 per cent in 1976. But as the Equal Pay Commission points out, this is the lowest proportion of any country in Western Europe, Italy included (Equal Opportunities Commission 1977). The excuse of economic recession is not a sufficient explanation. The Commission draws the conclusion that the difference is due to greater 'political will' and commitment from employers in other countries: 'People in authority in British industry appear to be spending more of their time trying to circumvent the sex legislation than in implementing it'.

Table 2. United Kingdom female earnings as percentage of male earnings, October 1970.

Iron and steel	51
Aluminium and aluminium alloys	57
Agricultural machinery (except tractors)	58
Metal-working machine tools	57
Industrial plant and steelwork	52
Electrical machinery	61
Electric appliances for domestic use	64
Shipbuilding and ship repairing	57
Wheeled tractor manufacturing	–
Motor vehicle manufacture	61
Aerospace equipment, manufacture and repair	58
Locomotive and railway track equipment	56
Manufacturing industry	58

Source: Coventry Engineers Employers Federation (1971).

Table 3. The structure of unemployment rates in tight and loose labour markets in the United States.

Group	Unemployment rate		Change in unemployment rate
	Tight Labour Market (1968)	Loose Labour Market (1961)	1961-1968
All	3.6	6.7	− 3.1
Men 20+	2.2		
White	2.0	5.1	− 3.1
Non-white	3.9	11.7	− 7.8
Women, 20+	3.8	6.2	− 2.4
White-collar	2.0	3.8	− 1.8
Craftsmen	2.4	6.3	− 3.9
Operatives	4.5	9.6	− 5.1
Labourers	7.2	14.5	− 7.3
Teenagers, 16-19			
Male	11.6	27.0	− 16.4
Female	14.0	16.7	− 2.7
Fifteen weeks or more of unemployment	0.5	2.1	− 1.6
Construction	6.9	14.1	− 7.2
Manufacturing	3.4	7.7	− 4.3
Services and finance	3.3	4.7	− 1.4

Source: Freeman *Labor economics* (1972: 30).

In the United States age is found by Freeman (1972) to be the most important variable affecting access to better jobs (see table 3):

Young workers, defined as those under 25, are found disproportionately in the lowest wage labour market segments. For white males this is generally a temporary status; they are able to secure better jobs as they mature.
Black males, however, fare less well than whites in moving out of the youth labour market. During this critical period of work establishment they experience higher unemployment rates, lower earnings and more involuntary mobility than their white counterparts.

The same applies to other countries, of course. In Holland, for instance, the highest unemployment figures are found among the under-19 year olds. While the unemployment figure for the working population as a whole stood at 5.3 per cent in 1977, that for young men stood at 11.9 per cent, and for young women at 11.6 per cent (Ministry of Social Affairs 1978).

Neo-classicists have no great difficulty in explaining this concentration of stigmatized groups in jobs characterized by low skills and high employment. Interpreting the American data (Table 3) Freedman explains:

Nearly 20 per cent of non-white males are labourers compared to about 5 per cent of white males. Non-whites also suffer from less education: in 1970 more than 57 per cent of the non-white work force lacked a high school degree compared to just 35 per cent of the white work force. Rough calculations suggest that from 40 to 50 percent of the difference between white and non-white unemployment rates is attributable to the unfavourable concentration of non-whites at the bottom of the skill ladder (Freeman 1972: 30-31).

Similar results emerge in Britain. If job tenure is considered, 19 per cent of the unskilled men have held their jobs for less than three months, while for professional and managerial workers of both sexes, the proportion was in the range of three to six per cent (Bosanquet and Doeringer 1973). Neo-classicists would therefore see in this hierarchical coupling of job security and income level with the level of education and training an expression of the market tendency to equilibriate at its most effective level. Traditionally the problem of low earnings has been treated as part of the general analysis of income determination. According to the neo-classical extension of this view, earnings can be expressed as a function of the 'human capital' endowments of the individual — formal schooling, on-the-job training, health, information and so forth. (Mincer 1958; Schultz 1963). More recently, attempts have been made in the United States to measure the effect of such exogenous variables as IQ, social class origins, race, and sex, upon earnings (Griliches and

Mason 1972; Hanoch 1967). Without dwelling at length upon these studies, it can be said that the results of their regression analysis are broadly consistent with the human capital hypothesis.

The dualists agree that some secondary jobs are filled with lower skilled workers–teenagers beginning their work careers with little education, or those only interested in part-time employment like some married women. These workers often have low aptitudes and hence low human capital and skills. The central claim of the dual approach, however, is that this successful matching of unskilled workers and secondary jobs is not correctly explained in the neo-classical model. Rather, the dualists support the contrary hypothesis: that *under*-employment is pervasive, in that good workers can be locked into bad jobs i.e. the Anti-Human Capital or Job Discrimination thesis.

The pre-entry (job) discriminatory hypothesis

The under-utilization of existing skills and training caused by the institutionalized 'closing' of certain occupations is the subject of considerable debate and controversy between methodologists rather than theorists. Multi-variate regression analysis has, for example, been used to *disprove* the human capital hypothesis in much the same way as it has been used to *prove* it. In order to understand how this can be so one has to examine the different data bases upon which the various comparisons are being made by the authors and to realize the extremely limited nature of the comparisons allowed by statistical techniques of this kind. We have therefore sought confirmatory evidence of the macro relationships attempted by such econometric analysis in smaller community studies made with less positivistic approaches and methods.

The argument for a prevailing under-utilization of existing skills and training is most easily proven in the case of immigrants and women.

Immigrants

Several studies have shown that black, particularly West Indian, immigrants tend to hold a lower status job after immigration to the UK than they did in their own country (Glass 1960; Daniel 1968; Richmond,

1973). Glass found that levels of unemployment were lower after coming to Britain than they had been in the West Indies: also, a few men moved up the social scale. Of those in unskilled manual jobs in the West Indies, a third obtained semi-skilled work in this country. However, although migration may well have brought other benefits, it seems that, on the whole, black people are likely to be in less skilled lower status work after arriving in England. Half of those who had been white-collar workers in the West Indies were in unskilled work in England and another two fifths were in semi-skilled manual jobs. Similarly, Richmond noted that 24 per cent of men from the West Indies were in non-manual occupations before immigration but only 6 per cent were in Britain.

A study conducted by Mehrlander (1969) indicates that the level of illiteracy among *Gastarbeiter* in Germany is very low (less than 3 per cent) and that a considerable number had obtained vocational training prior to their arrival in Europe. Few were working up to their level of technical qualification within their current job. Employers typically hire immigrant workers only for less skilled or temporary jobs or for those that have unfavourable non-monetary attributes.

Where tests of skills have been given to prospective employees, immigrants to Britain have tended to show a higher level of competence than expected (Radin 1966; Gaitskell 1969). There is evidence that careers officers tend to underestimate the intelligence of West Indian adolescents compared with white adolescents, even when the two groups have been matched in terms of qualifications (OPCS 1973). Several surveys both in the United States (Blau and Duncan 1967) and in Britain (Richmond 1973; Rutter et al. 1976) have shown that, for a given occupational level, black workers tend to have higher educational qualifications and/or longer schooling than white.

In general, the occupational composition of immigrant labour forces in EEC member states have shown little short-term change of a kind that suggests any substantial improvement in employment opportunity. Here one must distinguish between the temporary *Gastarbeiter* and the 'permanent' immigrant, although some *Gastarbeiter* are not 'guests' at all, but normal members of the work force. In Belgium in 1973 over 70 per cent of the immigrant workers were registered with normal civil registration offices, so they presumably meant to stay (Martens 1973). In the case of temporary workers it may be unlikely that career progression and full integration, either socially or economically, may be achieved in their short span of stay. In the case of immigrants, such as those from former colonies, who expect to establish a 'dynasty' in their adopted country, one might expect to find such integration taking place within the second generation. The fact that studies have demonstrated the longevity of discrimination against such permanent immigrés must cause us to reconsider the sociological 'melting pot' theories of the 1930s. Neither the 'temporary' foreign worker who stays on in the mainland European countries, nor the ex-colonial immigrant to Britain appears to become fully integrated into the community within one or two generations as this theory suggests.

The reasons are not hard to find: this theory was generated on the basis of experience in New York ghettos. The market conditions under which immigrants were absorbed into the American culture over the last half century are simply not present in Europe, nor, because of the later stage of economic development at which the influx of immigrants has taken place, are they ever likely to be. The physical and social infra-structure of Europe is far less malleable and permeable than that of nineteenth and early twentieth century America. Nationalism was often encouraged (in schools etc.) as a great integrating force in the U.S. (as paradoxically it has recently become in Canada–for all immigrants outside of Quebec) while in modern Europe nationalism has begun to be regarded as a somewhat reactionary force.

Job discrimination against women

The case of discrimination against women has also become the subject for debate between those who see discriminative practices as centring on job selection and those who see the relative level of earnings as the primary manifestation of anti-female prejudice. For both reasons, the social importance of this form of discrimination and the methodological implications of its investigations, we rehearse the arguments in some detail.

In a collection of studies covering Britain, U.S.A., Australia, New Zealand, Germany, Canada and Japan (Pettman 1975), the authors document the overall inferiority of the economic status of women. The empirical analysis relating to Britain (Chiplin and Sloane 1976), Germany (Addison 1975), and Belgium (Leroy 1975) are fairly similar. The authors address themselves to the question: What part of the wage differential between men and women is due to the fact that (1) women are paid less than men within a given occupation, or that (2) women are crowded into low-paying occupations and industries? Chiplin and Sloane attempt to answer this question by (1) assigning women the male earnings value prevailing in their particular occupation or industry and holding constant the occupation/industry female employment mix, and (2) altering the occupational/industrial mix such that females are represented in each sector in the same proportion as they are in the labour force as a whole, rather than, as currently, disproportionately represented in low-paying occupations and industries. On the basis of their efforts they conclude that:

Table 4. The effects of industrial redistribution on female average hourly earnings levels for selected countries, 1971.

Country/sector/effect	Computed average hourly earnings values (national currencies)
GERMANY	
Manufacturing industry	
W_1	5.15 (DM)
W_2	6.94
W_3	7.15
All industry	
W_1	5.14
W_2	6.95
W_3	7.26
ITALY	
Manufacturing industry	
W_1	596 (Lire)
W_2	703
W_3	751
All industry	
W_1	596
W_2	703
W_3	747
BELGIUM	
All industry and manufacturing industry	
W_1	55.41 (Fr)
W_2	75.10
W_3	80.12

Source: Addison, in: *British Journal of Industrial Relations* 13(2) 1975, 264.

the redistribution of females both occupationally and industrially makes little difference to the average earnings in comparison with granting females the male earnings levels in their existing occupations (industries)... this suggests that equal pay legislation is likely to be more significant than anti-discrimination legislation (1976: 14).

The results of Chiplin and Sloane's procedure as applied to a four-country sample by Addison (1975) are charted in Table 4. W^1 is the simple weighted average of female earnings in industry; W^2 is the weighted average of female earnings obtained after having granted females in each industry the appropriate male earnings value; and W^3 is the weighted average of female earnings after having industrially redistributed females according to their 'expected distribution and granting each element of the derived industrial distribution the appropriate male earnings value'.

The results clearly demonstrate that a redistribution of female workers across male-dominated jobs, whilst keeping earnings constant, appears in all four countries to make little difference to average hourly earnings in comparison to granting females the appropriate male earnings in their *existing* industries. The findings, although crude, are in conformity with those of Chiplin and Sloane and offer tentative support to their contention that equal pay legislation as opposed to anti-discrimination legislation may have more potential in closing the statistical earnings gap between males and females.

Table 5. Spearman's rank correlation coefficient between male earnings by industry and female employment (%) by industry, selected countries, 1971.

Country	Rank correlation coefficient	
Germany	− 0.52[a]	(22)[b]
Italy	− 0.18	(22)
Holland	− 0.86[a]	(9)
Belgium	− 0.36	(19)

[a] Significant in the five per cent level
[b] Figures in parenthesis indicates degrees of freedom

Sources: Statistiques Sociales, 1972 Annual, pp. 196-215; *Statistiques Sociales* 1, 1973, pp. 156-175. Reproduced by Addison in: *British Journal of Industrial Relations* 13(2), 1975, 263.

The relationship between the level of male earnings within each industry and the proportion of women employed within that industry is demonstrated in Table 5. In all cases the correlation coefficient is of the expected negative sign but only in two countries, Germany and Holland, was the rank correlation coefficient significant at the five per cent level. It therefore appeared to Chiplin and Sloane that although there is an unequal sex distribution by industry, in general, it would not appear that females are quite so unfavourably treated in terms of employment opportunities. In those sectors where women are employed in large numbers, wages received by men are also low.

Metcalfe (1976) considers this analysis to be simplistic 'because the occupational and industrial groups they have chosen to perform the exercise are insufficiently disaggregated.' According to Metcalfe, the reason women are paid less than men in each chosen occupation is mainly because *within* each group they tend to be crowded into the lower-paying segments; in teaching, for example, they are crowded into the relatively low-paying infant school segment and even in infant teaching they earn, on average, less than men. This is not because their earnings are lower, but because women are *under-represented* in the high-paying headship and deputy head segment of primary education. This example could be multiplied with evidence from other sectors. Metcalfe contends that:

The fallacy of the aggregate approach can be seen by consulting the NES [New Earnings Survey: a collection of statistics based on a one per cent sample of the work force taken every year in the United Kingdom since 1968] data. The occupational classification lists over 200 separate occupations yet in 1975 the NES provided comparative data on male and female earnings for only 13 such occupations: in other occupations there were insufficient women (or men) for valid comparisons to be made.

To conclude that in Britain equal pay legislation rather than equal opportunity legislation is the key to improving women's labour market situations is therefore wrong. While it may be true that in some sectors women are paid, ceteris paribus, less than men and therefore equal pay legislation is needed to reduce such discrimination, it is clear that the main cause of relatively low female pay is the unfavourable occupational and industrial composition of female employment. Thus measures to change the occupational structure are likely to be more fruitful than those aimed specifically at equal pay for equal work (Metcalfe 1976: 240).

Evidence of sex as a source of disadvantage, is also found in the data on differences in occupational mobility, in returns on investments in education, and in age-earnings profiles between men and women. Upward occupational mobility among women is somewhat less than among men, when broad occupational groupings are examined. With the exception of partly skilled manual workers, women are upgraded less frequently, are likely to be upgraded fewer steps on the occupational ladder and are more likely to be downgraded than are men. Similarly, women are slightly less likely than men to increase their earnings as a result of inter-employer mobility (Harris 1966).

When earnings data by age and sex are examined, a cross-sectional study of occupations (largely sales workers, managers, engineers and technical workers) showed that, after controlling for levels of education, women experience relatively less upgrading than men. A sample survey conducted for the Department of Education and Science as a follow-up to the 1961 Census of Population gave some very valuable information about the average earnings at various ages of male and female employees who had experienced different types of higher education. These are summarized in Figure 2, which shows that highly educated males earned more than their female counterparts even at the lower ages, and that this advantage becomes greater for the higher age groups. Only a minor part of this finding is likely to be due to different lifetime patterns of labour force participation between men and women (see also Ziderman 1973).

Metcalfe tried to make this analysis more general by combining the educational data for age-and-sex-and-occupation groups in the 1961 Census of Population with the earnings data for groups in the New Earnings Survey for 1970, which followed a broadly similar classification. The experiment was not sufficiently successful to justify a detailed presentation of the results: in a broad way, however, these were consistent with the results found from the Department of Education's survey noted above, i.e. at each educational level, males earn more on average than females at the start of their careers, and the gap is larger in the higher age groups.

In Belgium women's earnings in 1972 were also much lower than men's: female blue-collar workers earnings were 68.4 per cent of the men's: white-collar workers 59.5 per cent of the men's (*Arbeidsblad* 1977: 443).

It is often supposed that married women earn lower salaries in professional and administrative work because of the break in their service provided by child-bearing. In a national study of British teachers, Turnbull and Williams demonstrated that both men and women who come back to teaching after a break of two years or more suffer no loss in earnings when they return in relation to other people with a similar length of completed service: 'It seems that married women earn less than their

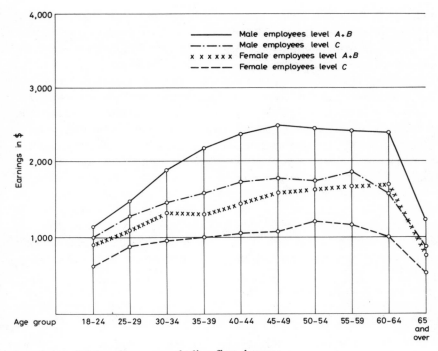

Level A = Higher degrees excluding first degrees
Level B = First degrees
Level C = Diplomas and certificates below first degrees

Source: Statistics of Education Special Series No. 3, p. 2, HMSO 1971.

Figure 2. Median earnings of employees by level of qualifications: England and Wales (1966-1967).

single colleagues and male teachers mainly because their supply price is lower' (Turnbull and Williams 1974: 255). The authors conclude that in spite of this: '*married* women are substantially worse off than their *unmarried* colleagues in both sectors. *There is furthermore no evidence that women teachers' position has improved since 1963; if anything it has worsened somewhat.*'

In promotional terms also the situation has become very much worse in recent years. In the past, women did not come into direct competition with men for promotion to head teacher and head of department: 'The result of comprehensive and co-educational re-organisation of secondary education has meant that this reserved labour market is much smaller and *women have not done well in direct competition with men'* (1974: 257). In medical nursing too, recent changes in the career structure that have brought women into competition with men have greatly reduced the number of senior appointments going to women (Salmon 1970).

Freedman (1976) suggests that 'occupational segregation is the basis of all other forms of invidiousness experienced by women workers.' Supporting Metcalfe's British data, Fuchs has suggested that 40 per cent of the earnings differential between men and women in hourly earnings in America would be completely accounted for if the occupational categories of the census permitted further disaggregation. In view of the limitations imposed by the statistical grouping of jobs, the degree of homogeneity discovered in female earnings and career chances in labour market statistics is all the more remarkable.

In fact, it is not the specific job title that describes the true extent of discriminatory practices but rather certain fundamental characteristics that serve to define the job content and the situation of its occupant:

In the case of typical 'female' jobs, what stands out is the specificity of tasks and the absence of promotional ladders. It is not that women fail to learn on the job or to benefit from experience, but rather that the jobs they fill are discretely fenced off from upgrading systems that might apply in other settings, even in the same firm (Freedman 1976).

According to Barron and Norris (1976: 53) this is so because women are needed as a secondary labour force: they are easily dispensible, easy to distinguish from other workers, they have allegedly low interest in training, set low value on monetary returns and are not easily drawn into unions. Valerie Oppenheimer has noted the extent to which typical female occupations require pre-employment training of a specific nature. In a survey of women between the ages of 30 and 40 she found that 90 per cent of her sample had received only *specific* training in clerical or service activities which meant permanent type casting in the labour market.

One result of this specialisation is an all-female work-force situated like an island in a sea of male workers, all but cut off from occupational mobility, either horizontal or vertical, like assemblers in electronics manufacturing who are hired because of their alleged dexterity and their willingness to perform repetitive tasks and who are isolated from the internal labour market operating for male workers in the same plant (quoted by Freedman 1976: 87-88).

Women are not only a source of cheaper labour for the skills they offer; they also provide employers with flexibility in the face of a proliferation of male workers seeking stability.

The ILM as a source of dynamic?

For the Marxist the trend must inevitably be towards the narrowing or dilution of job skills in such a way as to swell the secondary market (Braverman 1974). There is little statistical evidence of this process taking place in a *unilateral* manner within any of the available time series data (see for example Phelps Brown 1968 and 1977). New skills, particularly among service and administrative workers, have tended to take place of old craft or manual skills. Yet the growth of capital-intensive companies employing large concentrations of labour within single plant sites appears to have led to a growing dichotomy between 'permanent' and 'temporary' employees within such manorial markets (Dore 1973). But an alternative source of discrimination that Chiplin and Sloane raise in their defence of the pre-entry discrimination thesis is discrimination by *small* employers.

The Bolton Committee on Small Firms, for instance, estimated that the difference in earnings between employees of small and large firms was 20 per cent and that this difference was mainly due to lower wage rates for similar jobs with only a small part of the difference explained by the incidence of shift work, part-time work and overtime payments. The Report of the Committee also suggested that small firms employed more women than large firms. It is also interesting to note that a similar form of segregation is apparent in the United States. Mc Nulty, for example, found that differences in earnings between men and women performing similar tasks were much smaller within individual establishments than they were among groups of establishments. In line with these findings Buckley observed that the largest pay differences between the sexes occurred when the earnings of men in firms that employ only men in a job were compared with firms that employed only women. Thus, when earnings are compared for all establishments employing both men and women in a job, the earnings difference decreases substantially (Chiplin and Sloane 1976: 80).

The dualists have used similar arguments in explaining the cluster of low-paid workers in certain industries:

Low wage employment in Britain both is concentrated in industries with low skill requirements, highly competitive product markets and low capital:labour ratios. In manufacturing, low-wage employment is found in clothing and textiles; among the services, laundries, distribution, catering and some parts of government all have low earnings. Such low-paid work is marked by undesirable working conditions and few promotion opportunities (Bosanquet and Doeringer 1973).

Wachtel and Betsey (1972) and Bluestone et al. (1973), among others, have used regression equations to test for the existence of alternative wage processes in the American context. They find that 'demand variables' such as industry and occupations or workers, are the most important explanatory variables even after 'supply effects' such as education, job tenure, age, and the like are included.

Such evidence contrariwise tends to support the post-entry hypothesis but Wachtel declares that though providing fresh empirical evidence such studies hardly test the dualist model:

Their view of the neo-classical wage model is a straw man in that it consists merely of the relationship between wages and years of education. This type of equation has been employed by some who follow the human capital approach to estimate returns to education, but it is most often utilised when additional variables are not available. Indeed, multivariate supply-and-demand models of wages, of the type estimated by the dualists, have been a staple of neo-classical economists for the past twenty years (Wachtel 1974).

Other equally likely causal factors, he suggests, might be union closure or other oligopolist features of the market explored in other studies using the same methodology (Levinson 1976; Weiss 1966).

Disregarding the methodological difficulties we see the dualists as appealing to two distinctive and contradictory aspects of the structure of industrial demand for labour. One explanation appears to relate to a description of what the Marxist theorist might label as 'late monopoly capitalism' while the other describes a world of the owner-manager of 'primitive capitalism'. The concurrence of the two states and their relationship within the economy as a whole appears as another omission in the dualist thesis. This is a theme to be pursued in the next chapter.

Dean Morse has gone so far as to suggest the labour force dichotomization is part of a historical tendency in which the costs of flexibility (i.e. temporary employment) are shifted to the least advantaged worker groups—immigrants, racial minorities and women (Morse 1969). The 'peripheral' workers he studied were defined as those employed less than full-time or full-year, but whose availability was an obvious boon to enterprises that required their irregular staffing. Managements often expect or hope for turnover among the incumbents of such jobs, as in the case of an accounting department that prepared for the change over to EDP by staffing with women employees insofar as possible: 'It was hoped that the high attrition rate for women would alleviate the problem of reducing the staff when the change-over was finally completed' (Morse 1969).

There is something of a self-fulfilling prophecy in such plans. It is true that many young women retire from work, temporarily, because of pregnancy and child-rearing responsibilities. On the other hand, mature women, many of them returnees to the labour force, have tenure and turnover rates that compare favourably with those of men, even though their jobs are not of a type conducive to long tenure.

At the present time, women obviously fill a large part of this need. In 1970, 22 per cent of employed women in America worked part-time; of all part-time workers, women were 68 per cent. In Belgium in 1970 about 76 per cent of all part-timers were women. In the Netherlands this figure stood even higher (about 85 per cent). But they also offer advantages as full-time employees who, through their customary socialization, have traditionally demanded neither real nor nominal hierarchies for promotion, and who have been prepared to remain occupationally immobile. In the long run it may be that anti-discrimination legislation, as such, will not provide the central issue (Fogarty, 1961). Many of the occupational disadvantages are linked with sexual and ethnic discrimination in educational provision and in attitudes transmitted during schooling and in the community generally. There is thus a widespread acceptance of their fate on the part of economically disadvantaged workers which accords with their treatment in the work and market places.

The effects of cultural feedback

The proposition that workers are influenced by the instability of their jobs to become more unstable in their overall work attachments is only part of a larger system of feedback, in which workers are influenced by many socio-economic factors including their family background. We have already traced (albeit briefly) the impact of the woman's family situation as breeder-feeder-producer (Boulding 1976). In the dualist literature much more space is devoted to describing the materially impoverished environment of the ghetto dweller. In England, Rutter and Madge (following Sir Keith Joseph) have also emphasized the importance of good housing, hospitals, and schools in breaking out of the 'cycle of deprivation' (Rutter and Madge 1976).

Several British studies (e.g. Douglas 1964; Birch et al. 1970; Rutter et al. 1970; Davies et al. 1972) have shown that poor material circumstances such as poverty, overcrowding and lack of basic household facilities are associated with intellectual retardation and poor scholastic attainments. Lack of material resources make it more difficult for parents to provide the sort of environment needed by the children but it should be said that the effect of overcrowding and lack of facilities may be considerably less than is attributable to *social environment*. A number of studies have also looked at the effects of housing upon educational performance; it has usually been found that rehousing has little effect upon educational attainment.

On the other hand it is clear that the effects of early socialization on a child makes it more or less probable that he or she will experience upward social mobility through achievement in the job. The weight of evidence demonstrates the social gap that exists between the home environment provided in the families of low income or permanently unemployed workers and those of more stable, higher-income groups. According to Goodwin, welfare mothers communicate to their children a sense of inadequacy that may inhibit labour force behaviour. These childhood experiences may be the source of a good deal of the continuity experienced between generations of families whose *principal income earner* is a marginal or peripheral worker. Both early and contemporaneous family experiences have been found to be associated with poor adult employment records and consequent low social status (Marlowe et al. 1955; Hall and Tonge 1963; Gay and Tonge 1967; Stephenson 1975).

For many families, poverty is the normal state of existence over the period when children have to be maintained. Using the data collected by Smith and Townsend (1965) and Jackson (1972), Atkinson (1975) suggested that 'typically, the earnings of low paid workers reach a peak early in their lives and then decline'. This pattern is shown in Figure 3 where earnings are shown to be at their highest when the wage earner is in his thirties. Even then the needs of his family exceed his income by an amount shown by the dotted line (in the upper diagram) creating the deficit of family income against its needs shown in the lower diagram.

Furthermore, some poor children bear an additional handicap in that they are raised in relatively large families–a disproportionate number of American families with four or more children are in the poverty category. Evidence indicates that children growing up in large families tend to achieve less education and are otherwise less well endowed than those from smaller families (American Bureau of the Census 1973).

The 'feedback' from the workers' social environment may be seen to be irrecoverably bound up with his or her work role and therefore to the market segment in which he or she occupies a position. The level of variability or predictability in his or her income and career impacts on the

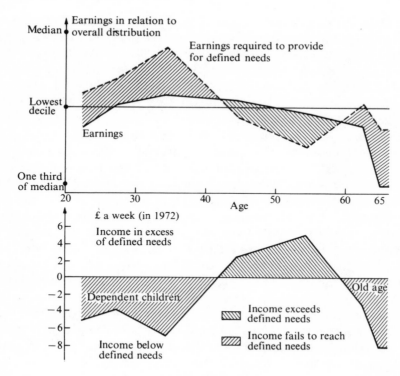

Source: Atkinson (1975: 201).

Figure 3. The life-cycle of earnings and need.

other social roles that he or she performs in society and in so doing helps to determine the level of expectations and aspirations that are passed from one generation to another. This inter-generational continuity is what Sir Keith Joseph meant by 'the cycle of deprivation' (Joseph 1971).

But the process by which the handicaps suffered by such groups is reinforced and multiplied is that of social 'labelling'. To obvious stigmatisms such as colour or sex is added a whole series of characteristics believed by the employer (or whomever it is that is casting judgement on the prospective employee) to be possessed by a black man, a woman, someone living in the Gorbals, or someone presently working as a kitchen porter (say). These are (since we *are* talking about stigmatisms) inevitably 'bad'. Thus blacks, women, school-leavers from certain residential districts, etc., are denied particular jobs and prevented from gaining house loans or rented housing (Daniel 1968). Other examples of 'labelling' include the way in which children of criminal adults may be more likely to be convicted of crimes because police surveillance of the family brings to official attention behaviour that would otherwise pass unnoticed (Woolton 1959; Cicourel 1968). More fundamentally a lack of verbal and social skills may cause the neglect of working-class children by their middle-class teachers (Tizard 1975; Bernstein 1965); similar accusations have been made of the biased format of intelligence ratings for working-class children (Ginsberg 1972; Mercer 1973).

For all of these reasons a 'culture of poverty' hypothesis has grown up which suggests that a distinct culture exists among certain of the poor. Poverty is defined not merely in economic terms but also by behavioural patterns in all aspects of community life (Moynihan 1968; Little and Brown 1960). The chief proponent of the culture of poverty has been Oscar Lewis, who made extensive studies of poor communities in countries such as Mexico and Puerto Rico (Lewis 1959, 1961, 1966). His thesis was that the culture of poverty develops to provide a structure and rationale for the lives of poor people who would otherwise have greater difficulty in coping with their problems. It is presumed to be an adaptation to their alienation from the wider society arising from their economic and social isolation. The subculture becomes self-perpetuating as it develops its own local solutions to its own problems and in so doing reduces its dependence upon outside institutions.

It is clear that regional differences in income, both social and private, may contribute to what may be described as the 'culture of poverty' in Europe. Himes (1964) has noted that the net effect of cultural deprivation is to generate a 'trained unreadiness for smooth transition from family, school and neighbourhood to the social world and technical roles of work'. The crucial elements in such deprivation remain ill-explored but probably include many of those listed by Borrow (1966) – limited life experiences, circumscribed and socially limited interpersonal relations, absence of successful achievement-oriented role models, lack of bi-parental child-rearing experiences due to parental separation, attitudes of distrust towards the law, negative or indifferent attitudes to school and to education, lack of encouragement from parents with respect to socially valued skills, also of recognition of the child's intellectual abilities, poor facilities and teachers in local schools, and a lack of opportunity for vicarious learning of the meanings and rewards associated with work. The social and geographical concentration of these labour force characteristics has been recorded in numerous regional studies.

The life-cycle hypothesis

If poverty is the normal expectation for many people at certain ages, it is clearly important to ask whether it is the *same* people throughout a single career and across generations. The data, fragmentary though it is, suggests that there is a large stable element in the population of the secondary market in some European countries. One source of discrimination that cannot be considered in this way is that of age, that showed towards the very young and the very old.

Research into labour mobility invariably reveals a tendency for persons to change jobs less frequently as they grow older. But the relationship between age and mobility is not simply inverse. The propensities of males to change jobs has been found by most investigators to increase up to the late twenties and then decline progressively until the years immediately preceding retirement when it again rises (De Wolff et al. 1965; Hunter and Reid 1968; Parnes 1954).

The young person's initial tenure of employment is brief, and frequent job changes occur during adolescence. Much of this movement is haphazard reflecting ill-defined objectives and the sceptical views of employers regarding his stability. As the young person matures his mobility is likely to increase. The breaking of parental ties leads to more job changing and especially to a rise in geographic mobility as job horizons widen. But mobility also becomes more purposive as the young person grows older. Job changing is increasingly directed towards a search for employment providing occupational training with good career prospects. When he marries and takes on the role of family breadwinner, his need for income increases. This leads to more intensive search for jobs in high wage industries with good promotion prospects.

Furthermore, the young worker, now in his twenties, finds employers more willing to hire him now that he is older. One labour market study reports that engineering employers hiring highly paid semi-skilled workers tended 'to discriminate against young and old applicants in favour of those aged 25-40 especially if they are married'. This attitude contributed to the rise of the mobility rates of young persons up to the late twenties.

For young people, the opportunity to improve income and career prospects through mobility rises until they reach the age of thirty. But beyond this age the benefits tend to decline and the costs start to rise. This can be expected for three reasons. First, the longer a person remains in a firm the more job security he enjoys. This is especially true in the United States, where the seniority system is 'more or less rigidly adhered to in sizeable sectors of the labour force'. It is less true in Britain where the principle of seniority is less firmly established. Nevertheless, long service still offers the employee some prestige within the firm and some protection against redundancy. Hence, it is an important factor to be taken into account before leaving a firm.

Second, persons over thirty are more likely to have acquired skills not easily transferred to other plants. Movement to another firm could well involve retraining and loss of income during the learning process. Conversely, the employer will be reluctant to lose labour trained to satisfy his specific requirements. He will try to retain persons who have acquired experience by offering them more attractive income and conditions of employment in order to avoid the costs of training replacements.

Clearly job-specific training is of some importance in reducing mobility in the primary sector of the labour market (Becker 1964; Mincer 1962) but as Mackay et al. (1971) have shown it is mainly skilled workers who are affected. The numerous personal and psychological costs associated with mobility increase with age and constitute a third and, possibly, decisive factor in determining mobility over life span. Family commitments and housing requirements reduce the geographic mobility of a man over thirty. Pension arrangements may tie him to a specific firm, although British evidence suggests the immobilizing effects of pension schemes are not very great.

It has been suggested by Sleeper (1975) that much of the mobility between industries (and, by implication between ILMs and, within companies, between job-clusters) can be explained by changes in personal propensities over the course of an individual career.

In Figure 4, four British industries appear in the upper panel. All exhibit a bulge in employment shares in the 20-40 age groups. In other words, these are all industries whose employment shares are the greatest for persons to prime working age. Notice that they also occupy four or five top positions in the earnings structure. The only industry missing is paper, printing and publishing. But net movements of persons under 30 from low-wage industries into this sector are known to be restricted by occupational barriers and union controls over entry.

Four industries are found in the lower panel. These exhibit a saucer-shaped pattern with movement across age groups: these industries are mostly at the bottom of the earnings structure. Their relatively low

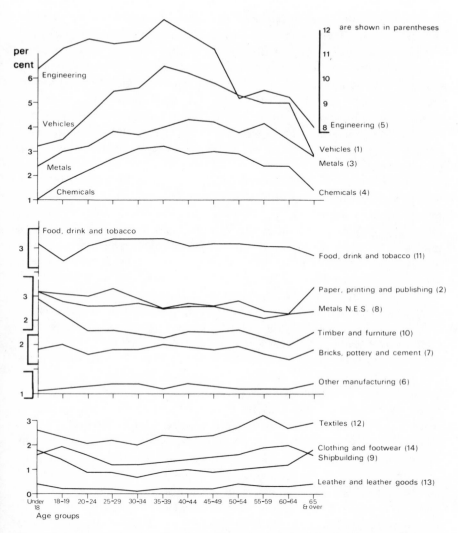

Figure 4. Average percentage of male employees in manufacturing industry by age group, 1961-1963 (Sleeper in: *British Journal of Industrial Relations,* Vol. XIII, No 2, 1975: 209).

employment shares in the prime working age groups reflects net losses to the higher-paying industries as the life-cycle hypothesis would predict. Rising employment shares in older age groups are unlikely, however, to result from reverse flows of older workers. These industries are all declining, and the large proportion of older workers they employ may reflect the unwillingness of older people to leave declining industries.

The industries in the middle of the wage structure have neither unusually large nor unusually small percentages of persons of prime working age. In the case of both men and women, agriculture, forestry and fishing, distribution, and miscellaneous services are net suppliers of manpower to the rest of the economy. Manufacturing appears in the middle achieving large net inflows from these sectors and simultaneously experiencing net outflows to the public sector, construction and the professions.

The behaviour of female net flow figures seems broadly consistent with at least the first half of the life-cycle hypothesis; the tendency is for people to enter the labour force through low-wage industries and move into higher-paying jobs as they grow older. Girls under eighteen have a tendency to enter distribution, as they grow older and marry, rising income expectation may lead to movement into manufacturing where average wages are higher. Similarly older women seeking lighter work tend to move back into the service sector. However, a large proportion of female mobility between manufacturing and non-manufacturing is comprised of administrative and clerical workers moving between jobs in which wages and conditions of employment vary very little. Hence, the second half of the life-cycle hypothesis is less likely to hold for women (Sleeper 1975). Rising psychological costs probably explain a good deal of the decline in mobility rates of persons over thirty. Mobility does not, however, decline continuously for the remainder of the working life; as people approach retirement their mobility tends to increase.

Sleeper suggests that these findings demonstrate that the weight people assign to the various net advantages they seek from employment vary over the life cycle. Frequent job changing amongst the young reflect an attempt to establish subjective estimates of these weights. Marriage and child-bearing force persons in their twenties to assign major priority to income and job security. As old age approaches easier and more flexible working conditions receive greater weight.

In a study using British and American data Sleeper (1975) finds a great deal of supportive evidence for this thesis. After examining the relationship of net flows into and out of industries Sleeper produces the chart illustrating the structure of age with earnings across industry (Table 6).

Once it is accepted that priorities do change over the life cycle the following mobility pattern may be deduced. Male employees tend to

Table 6. Net manpower movements between industries: men 1959-1966 (thousands)

Industry	Agricul-ture, forestry, fishery	Mining etc.	Distribu-tive trades	Miscel-laneous services	Trans-port communi-cations	Manu-factur-ing	Con-struction	Gas elec-tricity, water	Insur-ance, banking, finance	Public admin-istra-tion	Total net inflows	Total net outflows	Net flows (11-12)	Average (£) wages (manual workers only)
Agriculture, forestry, fishing											0·0	181·2	-181·2	18·08
Mining etc.	4·7										0·0	181·2	-181·2	18·08
Distribution	15·8	6·2									22·0	254·1	-232·1	20.08
Miscellaneous services	12·2	8·9	27·6								48·7	31·5	17·2	19·53
Transport and communications	12·9	5·8	17·0	6·1							41·8	69·9	-28·1	24·84
Manufacturing	48·2	71·1	126·1	6·3	26·4						278·1	112·5	165·6	24·97
Construction	45·2	28·6	23·8	7·4	7·5	31·7					144·2	43·1	101·1	24·59
Gas, electricity, water	4·5	3·5	7·9	2·1	3·7	11·2	3·4			2·0	38·3	2·7	35·6	21·89
Insurance, banking, finance	4·1	1·7	9·1	1·6	3·7	6·2	2·7	2·2			31·3	1·9	29·4	19·30
Public administration	23·9	12·1	23·3	6·8	18·1	38·8	26·3		1·9		151·2	6·7	144·5	20·54
Professional and scientific services	9·7	6·5	19·3	1·2	10·5	24·6	10·7	0·5	0·0	4·7	87·7	0·0	87·7	18·77
Totals	181·2	144·4	254·1	31·5	69·9	112·5	43·1	2·7	1·9	6·7	848·	848·0	0·0	23·56

Source: Sleeper, British Journal of Industrial Relations, Vol. XIII, No 2, 1975, p. 197.

enter the labour force through low-wage jobs, devote the prime of their working lives to employment in high-wage industries, and then return to low-wage jobs before retiring. This theory, the life-cycle hypothesis, may provide a partial explanation of inter-industry mobility. In particular, Sleeper says it can account for the consistently downward net movement of labour in Table 6.

First, the tendency for high wage firms to restrict recruitment of teenagers to those entering apprenticeships, combined with low income expectations, and haphazard job search would lead large numbers to enter agriculture, forestry and fishing and the two largest service industries. They are found at the top of the table because they act as a labour reserve for the rest of the economy.
Second, the net flow into manufacturing reflects a large gross flow of persons in their twenties whose income expectations rise as they marry and start families.
Third, the net flow into gas, electricity and water and the three service industries below it in the table reflect the movements of older persons from high wage manufacturing employment into less strenuous and lower paying service sector jobs. It is likely that the entire service sector experiences a net flow of older employees from manufacturing. However distribution and miscellaneous services appear at the top of the table because their losses of younger persons to manufacturing exceed their net intake of older persons, while gas, electricity and water and the remaining service industries are found at the bottom because they recruit small numbers of labour force entrants into manual jobs and hence fewer young persons to manufacturing. These industries rely most on recruitment of older persons seeking lighter work to fill vacancies in manual and low level clerical posts and their positions in the table are explained by job changing of this nature (Sleeper 1975: 200-201).

Are the hypotheses proven?

Whether one looks at macro or micro data the evidence suggests a more complex explanation than that put forward in the 'simple' dual market model of Doeringer and Piore. All three hypotheses formulated by econometricians to describe the nature (and by implication, the cause) of the DLM can be shown to be true in given circumstances. We are, however, left with the question of whether it may truly be described as a market in the sense accepted by neo-classicists.

From the empirical evidence there is little doubt that obvious differences exist between the characteristics regarded as debilitating in labour by employers. That is to say that separate demand schedules exist for male and female labour, for white and black labour, etc., which may or may not coincide in the case of a particular job requirement (e.g. a black female stenographer though not a black male stenographer). Similarly the circumstances giving rise to the sources of discrimination—the characteristics perceived as 'bad' by employers – vary enormously. To treat the multi-various demand and supply schedules which make up the primary or the secondary sector of the labour markets as if they were additive and therefore sensitive to similar socio-economic forces would be misleading in many circumstances. Change brought about in one part of the 'secondary market' for example may have little impact on another, and where it does the dual market theory, of itself, gives us little idea of the direction (or the process) in which the change may work.

In America the evidence for the 1948-1973 period–especially for the past decade–suggests that the incidence of unemployment has shifted to the disadvantage of demographic groups most likely to be represented in the secondary sector, particularly males aged 16-24 and females 16-44 relative to prime-age males. This opinion is based on results obtained by regressing the unemployment rate of each demographic group on the unemployment rate for prime-age males on a time trend (Gordon and Perry 1975). But the changing structure of employment has affected older workers through decreasing their participation rates rather than increasing their unemployment rates. These trends are especially striking in view of the relative increase in employment in non-manufacturing (a major source of jobs for older workers, according to Sleeper), and the narrowing of wage differentials between black and white workers, but *perhaps* only at the expense of others, that is, the active 'senior citizens'.

An important contention of the dualists is that the very concentration of poverty in certain segments of the population is proof that a non-neoclassical secondary sector exists. For example, Vietorisz and Harrison (1973) argue that

when bad jobs are found to be so widespread that perhaps 60 per cent of workers in the inner city fail to earn enough to support a family at even minimum levels of decency, conventional explanations based on individual differences in labour productivity become incredible.

Neo-classical economists would not disagree with these sentiments or with the evidence upon which they were based. They *would* suggest different methods of tackling the problem.

We are inclined to accept the evidence that both job (pre-entry) and wage (post-entry) discrimination exists in a permanent (institutionalized) form. This discrimination stems from prejudices which are directed at particular groups bearing obvious stigmata–femininity, skin colour, language, age, religion and ethnic origin being the obvious foci of group rejection. Whether the market conditions facing these multi-various groups are sufficiently *homogeneous* for them to be considered to be sharing the same market situation is to be doubted. Whilst women face the most diffuse and pervasive forms of discrimination, a young coloured or immigrant male member of the active work population is likely to be in a much worse short-term situation at any given time. The coincidence of racial discrimination with youth and inexperience may outweigh that of sexual 'superiority': the coincidence of any two or three stigmata tend to outweigh a single superior factor such as education in hiring and firing situations.

Quite clearly life-cycle effects are an important determinant of the supply of labour. Freedman's study suggests that the likelihood of multiple spells of unemployment bears a strong negative relation with age. But again both the incidence and the variability of these spells are related to colour and sex. It seems possible that while Sleeper's explanations of inter-industry flows of labour may explain the effects of age per se, that the coincidence of a number of 'accrued' stigmata may produce a large residual of marginal workers among the young and middle aged. It is upon this population that the present economic recession appears to have had the greater effect.

In general the evidence used by many of the authors we have reviewed had been 'stretched' to support, rather than to rigorously test, one theory or another. This is not so much a question of academic dishonesty as a tendency among writers to revert to 'the literature' for validation of their analytical construct when empirical evidence is methodologically impossible to obtain. The problem of validation becomes greater the more heroic are one's hypotheses. The concept of industrial reserve army, or of the 'permanent' 'temporary' work force, like all world-view frames of analysis, are beyond any rigorous statistical or other empirical verification. They take the form of an inductive and ex post facto rationalization of numerous data collected from numerous and various sources. Evidence must therefore be collected on a supportive rather than a null-hypothesis manner for, if one attempts the latter, there will always be 'an exceptional case' explicable in terms of 'exceptional' situational factors which nullifies any modifying effect it might have had on the general theory. Another means of verification available to us is therefore to examine the operation of policies which follow the rationale dictated by one line of reasoning or the other.

6. Labour market stratification and segmentation: some empirical models

Introduction

In the last chapter the evidence for the existence of a crude dual labour market was shown to be scanty and the concept itself was subjected to some criticism. Jain and Sloane (1977) were quoted earlier as subscribing to a belief in a whole series of more or less discrete wage and employment equilibria decided within more or less structured sub-markets. It was because of the obvious differences that remain between occupational and geographical markets that we suggested that the dualist concept might be considered as a heuristic model. Within each occupational market, at least within preparatory or career or hierarchical occupations (Broom and Smith 1963) there may be found institutional barriers to entrance which are not necessarily related to the potential productivity or to the productive skills of the marginal worker in the pure neo-classical sense.

On what basis does this dichotomy occur? We have suggested dual market theory offers no clear answer in itself. There are perhaps four main theoretical perspectives:

1. that of individual stigmatization;
2. that of the internal labour market mechanism used unconsciously;
3. that of the internal labour market mechanism used consciously; and
4. that of the industrial reserve army.

Clearly stigmatization is a source of unconscious bias in the everyday employment practices of most firms. But if we use the term social inequality we do not refer to inequalities which are due to personal characteristics of individuals, but to traits or characteristics which are shaped by particular societal relationships. Being a migrant worker or 'guest worker' in Belgium is not in itself an inferior position, but one that becomes so because being North African or Turkish determines the market position of a person of that nationality vis-à-vis the recruitment wants of the employer. It is that market relationship that makes the guest worker in Belgium a 'waste worker' (Martens 1973).

This, of course, is by no means confined to Belgium: 'In many contemporary European societies the lack of an indigenous ethnic minority leads to a 'transient under-class' [which turns out to be not so transient after all] being imported from the outside' (Giddens 1973: 220). And Castles and Kosack in their account of immigrant labour in Europe, write:

Virtually every advanced capitalist country has a lower stratum, distinguished by race, nationality, or other special characteristics, which carries out the worst jobs and has the least desirable social conditions (Castles and Kosack 1973: 2).

One of those other special characteristics, for instance, is being a woman. The connection between the social pattern of the labour market and the social grading of characteristics in society is quite obvious, as social status accorded in society at large is seized upon in the labour market. The labour market is the most important vehicle for social reproduction, that is the continuation of society as an ongoing process and of the continuation of the life experience of its members. Thus the 'untouchables' of one generation may occupy the same status in the eyes of the next generation, whether they are aware of it or not their 'objective' employment and career chances depend on the internalized biases of prospective employers.

The first step to rectifying this situation might appear to be that of modifying these attitudes. We are not unaware of the costs of doing so, the next question is therefore, at whose expense. There is a good deal of historical evidence to suggest that stigmatization may give way to a conscious strategy of 'closure' of certain occupations against 'outsiders' by employees as well as by employers. Kleindorfer and Sertel-Kudat (1974) report such attitudes displayed among German workers towards *Gastarbeiter*. We must therefore attempt to incorporate those forces which both give rise to and which maintain labour market segmentation. If we are to construct a model that has some use in explaining and predicting labour market behaviour it must bear some clear relationship to both the origins and forces that sustain market relationships.

Yet to take in the various and non-linear sources of segmentation contained within the diverse stigmata invented by human civilization is an impossible task. We must therefore look for theories which isolate

those forces which tend to *predominate* as significant causal features of
any given market situation and about which some measure of *generali-
zation* may be possible. Most European theorists have in fact followed
Morse in regarding stigmatism as important only insofar as it supplies a
source from which to draw a ready supply of cheap labour. The
European literature we review in this chapter is therefore centred upon
the demand characteristics of labour markets insofar as they are expressed in the concept of the internal labour market. But, as Marshall
suggested, to ask which is more important in any given situation, supply
or demand, may be an impossible question since they act 'as blades of a
pair of scissors' (1890). The restrictive (protective) practices erected by
labour are as often directed against their fellow workers as against the
employer, for example.

Of the three bi-modal segmentation models described in Chapter 2 it
can be said that the first one (internal-external) stresses segmentation of
the demand side, the third (primary-secondary) of the supply side and the
second one (local market-search and information theory) stresses the
relationship between the two sides. Authors who have used a twofold
segmentation model tend to see the barriers between the segments as
rather rigidly applied by employers. There are some authors who are
prepared to see labour market segmentation as a threefold affair. We
shall treat the two most important ones.

The 'Munich model'

In Germany, Lutz and Sengenberger (1974) have combined the segmentation approaches of Kerr (1954)–'Balkanization'–Doeringer and Piore
(1971)–internal-external labour markets–and Becker (1964)–human
capital–into the following postulated sub-market forms:

1. *Unspecific sub-markets*, which they call 'anybody's sub-market'
   (*Jedermannsteilarbeitsmarkt*), where qualifications are needed which
   are general and unspecified in nature, can be used anywhere and are
   easily substitutable;
2. *Craft sub-markets*, which will develop when there are workers with
   craft qualifications which can easily be transferred between firms, for
   instance typists, nurses and other medical personnel, and most
   building and other trades. People are only willing to invest in the

uman capital of craft qualifications when it is possible to get a return
ᴏn that investment, that is when there are enough firms in the locality
or region with a demand for their type of specific qualifications;
3. *Firm-specific sub-markets*, which will develop when there is a demand for qualifications which fill the needs of specific firms and
cannot be transferred to other firms. Substitution of these workers
inflicts considerable costs on the firm, which makes it worthwhile for
the worker to invest in this sort of human capital and a must for the
employer to employ the worker continuously.

These three markets are seen by Lutz and Sengenberger to arise out of a
conscious decision to invest or not to invest in specific forms of human
capital (qualifications) and thereafter to defend the returns derived from
the investment. In order to stabilize the return on human capital
investment labour markets have to be institutionalized, that is entry and
exit as well as rewards have to be regulated (see Gensior and Krais 1976).
The 'Munich School' postulates that qualifications are the main determinant of sub-markets. As in Becker's human capital theory it is taken
for granted that the costs of training are the main determinant of the price
of labour power. The conditions for investment in human capital are:

1. length of time over which a private (largely employee) return is
expected;
2. variability (or disturbance) in private returns over time;
3. continuity of the need for human capital by the investor;
4. relationship between costs and returns to the investor.

Conditions 1 and 2 are those that are most likely to cause changes in
supply; Conditions 3 and 4 are likely to cause discrepancies in demand
relative to any given level of supply. The stability of sub-markets is
derived from the importance of the return on investment in human capital
to the investors. In the Munich model, access to capital is almost
unlimited: qualifications, information, mobility, even social skills, are
available at a private cost to the investor/consumer be he employee or
employer.

It is hypothesized that workers in a privileged sub-market try to defend
themselves against encroachment from outsiders, because unequal life
chances are rooted in differential returns from investment. The official

labour market policy of the Federal Republic favours the traditional craft sub-markets, but the Munich researchers predict that the firm-specific sub-markets will gain in importance and pull away workers from the craft sub-markets, because firms offer better training facilities. On the other hand, firms try to let the government bear the brunt of the costs of training workers for the unspecific sub-markets, but that means that the workers themselves carry the risk and not the employers.

The threefold classification by Lutz, Sengenberger and collaborators is interesting, for it revives the old notion of the industrial reserve army, in the more sophisticated guise of the *Jedermannsteilarbeitsmarkt* and has attempted to relate this to the conflicting labour market strategies of different types of firm (we shall return to this in a later chapter). From other empirical research done in the Federal Republic of Germany it can be concluded that technological development may be leading to a strengthening of the demand for firm-specific qualifications, especially those demanding experience with specialized, high-technology machinery (Lahner 1975). It was apparent that a changing demand for a firm's product tended to induce that firm to manipulate its technology, and that this had important effects for the firm's skill structure. Similar research in America, Japan, France and Britain (see for example Scott 1964; Dore 1971; Erbes 1977) has suggested a similar development in other industrialized countries towards 'late monopoly capitalism' and the manorial market-place. One should however beware of making easy generalizations since significant differences in the nature of market places exist between these different cultural and economic contexts.

The neo-classical assumptions of Lutz, Sengenberger, and others, are, of course, quite similar to those of Becker and Schultz and have, by implication, been part of the neo-classical/institutionalist explanation of occupational strategies since Marshall and even before. The permanent income hypothesis by which Friedman explained differences in consumption patterns in the United States may be traced to the same notion of measuring income against the time span over which the worker attempts to plan his 'projet de vie' (1963). The Munich model has been attacked precisely on these grounds by Freiburghaus and Schmid (1975). They suggest that:

1. Few workers are oriented towards maximizing their monetary rewards either in the short or long term.
2. Job security is more important than wage differentials.

3. The labour market is opaque rather than transparent and this contributes to the lack of mobility between segments.
4. There is little inclination to move between regions or occupations.

In their investigations they have explicitly dropped the neo-classical assumptions that there is optimal mobility and homogeneity of labour in the labour market.

As we have pointed out before, the Munich researchers regard the labour market as an aggregate of sub-markets which are divided by institutional rules and procedures concerning entry and exit, allocation and rewards. Mobility within sub-markets is encouraged, but mobility between sub-markets is discouraged. Both parties in the labour market have an interest in the long term return on human capital investment. The greater the specificity and extent of this investment, the greater that interest. This depends, of course, on the conditions of employment, but labour market structure influences those conditions, especially if the share of human capital in total employer investment is very great. Their approach concurs with that postulated by the American M.W. Reder in his study of occupational differentials over time (1955).

The institutionalists have argued, contrariwise, that wage differentials have been greatly *affected*, though not wholly determined by trade union pressures (Turner 1957). Phelps Brown suggests that:

There is much evidence for the effect of trade unions on differentials. The impact of unionization, though marked, may be transitory, but sustained unionism has been associated with a raising of manual relatively to white collar pay, and among manual with a relative raising of the unskilled (1977: 99).

It is perhaps worth noting that inspite of the meticulous nature of Phelps Brown's compilation of evidence, he does not provide us with a definition of skill other than that contained within the officially produced statistics from which most of his data are obtained. This is quite normal in such economic studies conducted on the basis of secondary source material. In the experience of the authors, the employers' definition of 'skill' can change from one workplace to another and is itself the subject for constant union pressure. In the United States the practice of 'bumping' has become widely practised as a way of evading anti-discriminative legislation. That is to say that the jobs classified as 'skilled' are given to blacks or to women under the 'quota' provisions of legislation and the jobs done by whites are re-classified upwards. This kind of 'grade-drift' is similar to a well-known means of by-passing state-imposed income constraints practised by employers in Holland, Belgium and the U.K. So while the evident Achilles heel of the Munich model is the postulated correlation between qualification and reward and that a specific qualification carrier has a right to a specific position and reward, we may question the source of the empirical disparity that exists between the two.

A growing body of evidence gathered by British scholars puts a contrary hypothesis to that of the ILM; one which owes more to the earlier Dunlopian notion of 'wage-contours' (Dunlop, 1951). It suggests that while reference groups for the purposes of pay and job comparisons are located *within the firm*, for most groups the existence of unions tend to create bridges across which bargaining comparisons are drawn by union representatives. This is, of course, part of a formal political process of which the general membership may be unaware unless their active support is required by the negotiator in pursuing his bargaining strategy. Brown and Sissons (1976) have suggested, for example, that in Coventry and Fleet Street earning levels followed a pattern that was institutionalized *across* firms by collective bargaining arrangements. In other words in a strongly unionized situation the institutional arrangements for settling pay and conditions may take these matters out of the ILM and into a sub-market much more like that of the craft sub-market postulated by Lutz and Sengenberger. Evidence based on officially produced statistics of earnings and conditions in Germany might lead one to believe that this is a better description of the situation appertaining within bargaining arrangements that are highly centralized at *Länder* level.

We must however consider the equation between earnings levels and the extent of job control exercised by unions or professional associations (See Chapter 2). Our own observations of work-place bargaining as well as those of Sayles (1958), Kuhn (1961), Lerner et al. (1969), Behrend (1959), and of Brown himself (1971), support the view that this equation is one that can most easily be worked out at the point of production: that is within the ILM. The existence of institutional bridges, between work situations, such as unions and professional associations, does not ensure that the task that is actually performed by the worker within the ILM (or that his place in the localized, internal hierarchy of the firm) is exactly similar to that of his fellow unionists or professionals in other firms. Try as they might, external bodies can only impose a uniformity of conduct in the regulation of the workplace with the approval and compliance of the majority of members within that place, and, ultimately, that of the employer himself. The variability of technological and market contexts will serve to modify the influence of national or regional formal rules of conduct across different work situations.

The Piore model

This problem is also tackled in Piore's work on the relationship between labour mobility and social stratification (Piore 1975: 125-150). But the main focus of the author is upon the macro working of the economy and its relationship to behaviour within individual ILM's. Piore develops a threefold model of labour market segmentation. He distinguishes the three following segments: a primary segment divided into an upper and a lower tier, and a 'catch-all' secondary sector. The characteristics of work in the three divisions are closely related to the lower-, working-, and middle-class subcultures, which Piore seems to regard in the same way as sociologists view the class structure, for he calls them 'sociological' distinctions (Piore 1975: 128). These subcultures are differentiated by two main features. One is the type of 'mobility chain' or sequence of jobs an individual might expect to move through during the course of his career. The other is the subjective learning process that complements this chain and the degree to which learning is formally specific or general or whether it is an automatic acquisition of the traits needed to perform the job: this learning is seen to be fairly directly related to the technology in use.

The so-called 'core technology' of an enterprise dictates what jobs lend themselves to be incorporated in the mobility chains of the primary segment and what jobs can be detached and formed into a secondary segment. There is also a complementary or peripheral technology, which gives rise to the jobs in the secondary segment as well as in the higher tier of the primary segment. These technologies are reflected in the structure of the economy as a whole through the existence of certain key manufacturing and service sectors alongside a variety of tertiary and less central service functions.

Two main sources of new labour are seen to exist within 'any given economy'; these are young people and migrant workers. Young people are seen too come into the labour market whether they be from lower- or upper-class homes and schools. As these groups age, the middle-class flows tend to move into the upper tier, and the working class into the lower tier, leaving the lower class in the secondary market. The factors effecting the direction of this flow are largely structured by class position and background:

That derivation is a complex function of several variables. But one of these variables is the availability of stable employment to youths at the point of transition to adulthood. Lower-class workers at this stage of their lives are particularly adjustable to one or the other kinds of job structures, depending upon what kind of work is available (Piore 1975).

The career choices open to social classes may be shown to differ as may the context in which the choice is made (Rees and Schultz 1970).

The second major determinant of the supply of labour is the history of mass migration to be found within any given labour market. The lower-class subculture is seen to be particularly affected by migration. As a given incoming stream of migrants settles down and acquires a community structure the dominant racial or ethnic group norms emerge or are restored. Given a stable infrastructure—particularly an educational system—the available supply of primary sector workers grows:

If there is an excess demand for secondary workers, new migration should be encouraged or the stabilization of older migrant communities retarded, or both. If there is an excess supply of secondary workers, then, conversely, the stabilization of older migrant communities should be hastened and new migration retarded (Piore 1975).

Labour supply to the primary market, and particularly to the upper tier of the primary market (professional, administrative and technical workers) is seen to involve more complex processes. A major role is obviously played by institutes of higher education. Recent flows between upper and lower tier jobs, and even into secondary jobs, are seen to be the result of mismatches in the supply and demand for educational personnel:

The supply of upper-tier workers depends heavily upon the output of the school system, and this appears to introduce a certain asymmetry of responses. It is difficult to expand supply beyond the upper bound which that output imposes, but an excess supply will simply fall into the lower tier through specific employments which that sector has to offer (Piore 1975: 148).

Bottlenecks in the supply of educated personnel may, on the other hand, lead to an increase in standardization and mechanization within the core economy and thus force jobs onto lower mobility chains (that is jobs having a shorter range of promotion prospects):

Thus in sum, adjustment can take place on either the demand or the supply side of the market. On the demand side, it will have to occur through changes in the distribution of output between the periphery and the core, or through changes in the composition of final demand. It can also occur by detaching jobs at the bottom and top of lower-tier mobility chains, filling the former with secondary workers and moving the latter to the upper tier trough systematic rotation of labor. On the supply side, the main avenue of adjustment between secondary and primary workers is the rate at which new migrant communities can be expanded and the aging of older communities retarded... This, it will be noted, is not a theory which says anything about a price system, and to introduce it here would require a much expanded format. It should be pointed out, however, that certain of the adjustment mechanisms could be triggered by price changes while others would operate effectively without a price trigger (Piore 1975: 147-148).

What technology gives rise to which mobility chains is seen by Piore to be determined by the relative standardization, stability and certainty of demand for a firm's products. If demand for its product is relatively standardized, stable and certain, a firm will tend to move jobs to the lower tier of the primary segment:

Because such chains tend to involve fixed capital investment, however, there will be a certain irreversibility in the process. It is easier for the economy to move toward lower-tier mobility chains than away from them (Piore 1975: 143).

This, of course, revives the old argument, so vividly discussed in the German labour market literature, about whether a firm can control its environment in general and its markets (including the labour market) in particular. The important question is whether industrial firms have enough autonomy to develop strategies to control their environment, in order to control their core and secondary technologies and the use of their labour force, and what the fundamental conditions of that relationship are (Gensior and Krais 1976: 99). A related question is whether they perceive themselves to have such autonomy in formulating their strategic choices (Child 1975).

We have treated these two segmentation models, one German and one American, in some detail, because we think they do constitute an important step towards the theoretical elaboration of a non-competitive model of the labour market. But we are left with some problems. Are there only three segments or are there more? How rigid are the boundaries between the segments? Are ports of entry and exit really confined to only certain points in certain segments?

A multi-segmented labour market

In an attempt to integrate the various economic, organizational and cultural features of the labour market that have been emphasized by segmental theorists, Mok (1975) suggested a four-part model in which a further bifurcation emerges, this time in the 'secondary' sector.

On the 'vertical' axis is a differentiation of jobs and people in terms of their rewards (and punishments), working conditions, responsibility, autonomy and job security. This is, one could say, the 'industrial relations' or social axis of the labour market. On the 'horizontal' axis jobs and people are characterized by their tasks, the skills required (training) and their place in the hierarchy. This is, one could say, the 'bureaucratic' or technical axis of the labour market (see Figure 5).

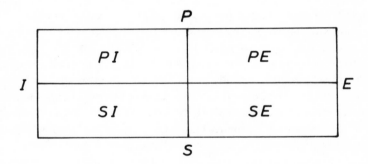

Figure 5. Labour market segmentation on two axes.

Mok does not contend that there are only four segments, nor that the barriers are so rigid as one would think by looking at the 'boxes'. On the contrary, within the boxes there are many segments and the barriers are rather permeable (be it often only in one direction).

The segments of the labour market have come into being because of vertical and horizontal differentiation in the job structure. Jobs in the P-sector have relatively high wages, good fringe benefits, good working conditions, a high degree of job security, a high degree of autonomy and responsibility, while jobs in the S-sector have relatively low wages, bad working conditions, almost no job security and a low degree of autonomy and responsibility. Applied to the firm one could speak of the job structure and the authority structure.

This differentiation comes into being because the labour market is different from other commodity markets in that, if workers fulfil only the legally enforceable aspects of the contract (e.g. go to a certain place to work at a certain time) little production would take place (Bowles and Gintis 1976: 132). The organization of production must be so that workers are motivated to produce and must be controlled by those higher in the hierarchy. That means that workers' goals and orientations must somehow be brought into line with those of management (that is, with what management perceive workers' goals and orientations to be). There are as many perceptions of workers' expectation as there are distinct groups and roles on the supply side: women, young people, foreign workers, the well and not-so-well educated, occupational groups, etc. Enthusiasm and commitment cannot be written into the labour contract, so must be generated or imposed by management (Lupton and Bowey 1974: 72).

Jobs in the I-sector are task specific, need high skills, require on-the-job training and have good opportunities for advancement, while jobs in the E-sector are task un-specific, do not require on-the-job training and do not have opportunities for advancement. It is important to note that the E-sector will be found inside as well as outside a given firm: external jobs exist on the periphery of any work organization. In this case Mok calls these workers marginal workers, even if, as in the case of the PE segment they may include highly trained craftsmen and professionals (cf. Lutz and Sengenberger's craft sub-market!).

Job clusters within market segments
PI: This is a cluster of segments with jobs which are skill specific, need long on-the-job training, have good promotion chances, job security, working conditions, autonomy and responsibility, and relatively high material rewards. The hard core of stable employees are to be found in these jobs. High commitment to the enterprise, as opposed to the occupational market, is demanded of workers in exchange for stability of employment.

PE: This is a cluster of segments with jobs which have a less skill-specific task content, need less on-the-job training and have low chances of promotion, but on the other hand have relatively high material rewards and autonomy in the job. This segment of the labour market is interesting, but at the same time the most difficult one to account for. As we have seen, in Piore's and Lutz and Sengenberger's version of labour market segmentation, the external labour market is not split between 'good' and 'bad', but is rather an unspecified, diffuse labour reserve on which firms may or may not call to fill vacancies. In Mok's segmentation model it is essential that the external market segments straddle the firm's boundaries. While the essential element of externality is the open exchange between job structures, there are marked differences in 'goodness' or 'badness' of jobs in terms of working conditions, material rewards and autonomy. The PE jobs offer better conditions in this respect than the SE jobs, the most unstable jobs of the labour market, with a distinct in-out pattern of the workers.

The PE segment also contains jobs that have lost their potential for promotion chances because of structural changes in organization and technology, especially in the white-collar sector. It could be dubbed the 'cooling-out' segment for frustrated graduates and other higher education white-collars. Quite a few jobs in the lower echelons of the educational system, for instance, belong to this segment. Recent temporary job creation programmes to induct school leavers into the labour force (e.g. in Belgium and the Netherlands) tend to create marginal jobs (and workers) in precisely this PE segment of the labour market (see Chapter 7). Perhaps this cluster of segments should be regarded in a positive way, in that it frees the worker from the tight grip by and the lifelong commitment to the work organization, which is normal in the PI segment of the labour market (Falkenburg and Vissers 1978).

SI: Here are the jobs which are skill specific and which have some on-the-job training, and have some promotion chances, but are further characterized by lack of autonomy and responsibility, little stability, relatively low material rewards and bad working conditions. The SI jobs are those jobs most susceptible to technological changes and a Taylor-like control structure. Many of the jobs for women and young people are to be found in this segment, in specific industrial sectors. These jobs are likely to be hit most when labour is substituted by capital because of high labour costs. Much of structural unemployment may be explained by lack of jobs, often as a result of redundancies, in the SI segment. The jobs in this segment may be especially disadvantageous to some workers, in that they involve a firm hold on the worker by the organization without the concomitant advantages which are usually bestowed on the workers in the PI segment of the market.

SE: These are jobs in which there is low skill specificity, no on-the-job training, little autonomy and responsibility, no job security, low wages and bad working conditions. Instability is high in this segment, which has a direct channel to the labour market outside of the firm. This is the segment of the foreign workers, casual labourers, etc.

The confrontation of supply and demand

The 'hard core' of the job structure is restricted to the PI segment (and to a much less extent to the SI segment), while 'peripheral workers', according to Morse 1969, are predominently to be found in the SE segment and to a much less extent in the PE segment. His data demonstrate the longevity of employment in one job within certain sectors of the work force from which we may derive a crude categorization (see Figure 6).

		PI segment	*SE* segment
Vertical axis: industrial relations (motivational) axis	wages	higher	lower
	working conditions	better	worse
	unionization	higher	lower
Horizontal axis: bureaucratic (technical control) axis	technology	(very) sophisticated	little sophistication
	control	autonomous	rigid work rules
	promotion	much	little
Morse's examples:		*Hard-core industries* oil chemicals gas/ electricity metallurgy	*Peripheral industries* textiles shoes/ leather works glassware food

Figure 6. Characteristics of segments of the labour market.

Morse himself sees the 'time-in-job' criterion as a crude one for the measurement of peripheral workers. As we mentioned in Chapter 1 many itinerant workers, or persistent job-changers, enjoy a high standard of living and are doing no more than 'maximizing their net advantages'. It includes those with employers who are able to create and maintain good working conditions. The other group is composed of the bigger number of workers who cannot gain a toehold in the preferred sector of the economy and must accept employment where they can find it, usually with small employers in the services or trades where wages are low, fringe benefits are few or non-existent, work is part time and employment intermittent (Ginzberg, in Morse 1969: x).

If we take the work place experiences of the employee as a major source of conditioning behaviour, and therefore of perpetuating the supply of unstable labour, we see that many other conditions come into play in determining market behaviour. The life-cycle effects on mobility is another structuring influence but one that must be modified by the evidence of differential career trajectories across different social classes suggested by Piore's evidence. We thus begin to derive a view of a multi-sourced SE segment.

The unemployed, by definition, cannot be characterized by their jobs, but only by their potential or eligibility for a certain segment, due to past experiences, qualifications and aspirations. The external sector in our view is a part of the labour market which exists inside as well as outside the firm, and on the periphery of both, which means marginalization as a process exists inside as well as outside the work organization. That is sufficiently illustrated by the workers 'sent out' by temporary work agencies, who remain part of the organization of the agency while being hired by the client of that agency. They remain on the external market while being inside a firm (Mok 1976).

There is a good deal of evidence of the 'crowding' of high earnings and career prospects in certain industries which are referred to as 'hard-core' industries in Figure 6. In itself the fact that these industries are manned by certain categories of workers and not by others need not signify conscious prejudices against some workers or discriminatory behaviour. Movements in technology and organizational structure may allow a company in say, banking, to adjust its employment conditions to an already established source of peripheral workers, and even may be to improve the conditions operating within the secondary markets. Thus work in banks and insurance companies has become increasingly automated to the detriment of workers in the PI segment of the market but is driving more and more work towards the PE segment. Women–young girls and matured women–are seen to be the more 'natural' occupants of the dead-end jobs thus created. Once the change has been allowed to take place unions tend to agree with management that the new incumbents have few career aspirations. For instance, the prognostications of the Congress of Belgian (Christian) National Union of White-Collar Employees point to the existence of a 'dual labour market' (1977: 133) among white-collar workers, with the lower jobs for women and the 'better' jobs for men, but in the policy recommendations not much can be found to remedy this (1977: 159-170).

Demand

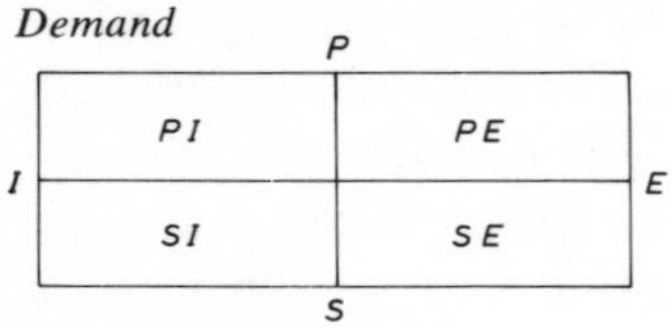

	PI	PE
	SI	SE

Supply

	II	I & II
	II & III	I & III

Bureaucratic criteria:

− tasks and skills
− control
− rewards

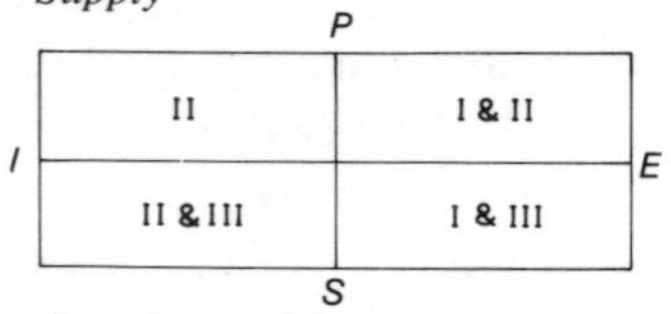

Social stratification criteria:

− class
− status
− power

Jobs

Primary sector (P):
− relatively high wages
− good fringe benefits
− good working conditions
− high degree of job security
− high degree of autonomy, discretion and responsibility

Secondary sector (S):
− relatively low wages
− no fringe benefits
− bad working conditions
− no job security
− low degree of autonomy, discretion and responsibility

Internal sector (I):
− tasks and skills specific
− on-the-job training
− career opportunities

External sector (E):
− tasks and skills unspecific
− general education
− no career opportunities

Characteristics

I. Ascribed:
Sex
Age
Race
Religion
Residence
Socio-cultural background

II. Achieved:
Educational qualifications
Experience
Occupational identity
Union membership

III. Institutionalized:
Job centre
Career guidance
Employment agency

Figure 7. The segmented labour market.

The existence of the SI and PE segments show that personnel and manpower policies in firms (and industries as a whole) are often caught in a dilemma. Mok believes the dynamics of the labour market (caused by the rise and fall of demand in other markets, the dictates of technology and/or by the economic and political situation in general) are such that the number of jobs in the hard-core segment is decreasing or, (under the influence of union action) are at least held constant. The number of jobs in the other segments is increasing, either absolutely or in relation to the 'hard-core' segment. That means that even more employees with less stable behaviour patterns have to be taken into firms.

But although theoretically there would be a choice of job creation in three segments, in practice the firm is confronted with a more structured choice. This job creation process is not an autonomous one, but is dictated by societal as well as economic and technological factors. Loveridge (1972) has suggested that new tasks demanded by changes in technology or organization are more normally regarded as extensions to existing jobs and/or occupations. The existence of unions or professional associations ensure that vested interests other than those of management compete for 'ownership' of the new tasks. Often however they are in fact demeaning or 'dirty' tasks that existing occupations have consciously sloughed-off by inventing complementary but lower-level strata; the 'plumber's mate' exists at many levels of the work organization. In this way existing interests are maintained and a strict control is maintained over new jobs by the occupants of the old ones in the PI segment (Turner 1957).

How viable are the models?

First we should question the extent of ILM's insofar as it is possible in practice to identify them. Doeringer and Piore (1971) suggest that internal markets can be analysed according to three characteristics: their *degree of openness* to the external labour market in terms of the proportion of ports of entry and exit and criteria for entry; their *scope* in terms of size, geography and numbers of occupations; and the *rules for internal* job allocation. Doeringer and Piore (1971) suggest that about 80 per cent of the employed labour force of America works in ILM's whilst the rest are engaged in agriculture or service occupations. The manner in which an ILM is defined seems somewhat inadequate for many purposes. For instance, they include under the heading of structured markets 27 per cent of workers employed in small enterprises, where administrative rules could well be relatively unimportant. These authors used only crude data on size, type of industry and craft union membership. In many ways the emergence of the internal labour market as a focus of theoretical interest is feature of a period in which large scale bureaucratic organization has become characteristic of industrial management. This characteristic (bureaucracy) is not necessarily one that is associated with size of firm or even technology. It may well be associated with a growing 'complexity' in the environment complicated by an increase in governmental and inter-organizational statutes and ordinances (Loveridge 1978).

More precise direction on the *degree of openness* might be gained from Alexander's study of labour mobility in the UK in which he uses turnover data to define differences between manorial (firm-specific) and guild (craft) sub-markets (Alexander 1974). Other studies of turnover such as that of Burton and Parker (1969) presage this proof of the existence of structural markets. But the work of Mackay and his colleagues (1971) indicates the possible presence of national differences. In their study of the British engineering industry they suggested that there was a major difference between American and British practice such that:

None of the case study plants operated a procedure for internal promotion in which seniority was the only guiding principle, and there was no evidence that managements were under pressure from unions or workers to recognise the very informal procedures used to determine such promotion. This contrasts with much American experience, where promotion has become an important issue in labour-management relations, and the criteria used in selecting candidates for promotion have become a matter for collective bargaining (Mackay et al. 1971).

Comparing the findings of Mackay et al. with those of Rees and Schultz (1970), Jain and Sloane suggest 'a tendency to rely on employee referral to a much greater degree and application at the gate to a much lesser extent in North America than Britain, which again might suggest greater care in hiring in North America' (1977: 29). In spite of these differences in the formality the degree of discrimination exercised in British hiring practices was revealed in the research reviewed in the last chapter. It does however suggest that 'statistical' discrimination i.e. through a preliminary review of entrance qualifications often made by a low-status 'gate-keeper' such as a receptionist, is not so likely. The very lack of records *may* possibly work to get an interview for a female or a black job applicant. On the other hand this seems not to have been the direction in which the looseness of British hiring standards have worked in the case studies collected by researchers for the London Business School Race Relations Project (forthcoming). In other words, the structure, though informal, was very real and perhaps *because* it was so informal encouraged interviewers to set their own stereotype of an acceptable recruit i.e. 'somebody like us, who would fit in'.

In the previously quoted study by Brown and Sissons (1975), the authors found few differences in earnings and conditions that might be directly attributed to the structure of the internal market in the manner suggested by Doeringer and Piore, that is in terms of its centrality to the 'core technology' or proximity to an entrance 'portal'. One may, of course, question the ex post facto use of data that was not specifically collected to test the ILM hypothesis and neither researcher denies the existence of a structure of internal rules for job allocation.

In research in two firms carried on in the Netherlands at the University of Nijmegen in 1976-1978 (according to oral information by one of the researchers, F. Huygen), it was found that job structure and authority structure were related in specific ways. In one firm, in the food sector, there was a relatively flat authority structure, with little differentiation among the predominantly unskilled workers. Control was largely decentralized and management relied a great deal on monetary incentives and informal norms to regulate production. Power rested with local supervisors, who were rather autonomous in organizing the production process. Those who had acquired influence in the system set the norms for others, these tended to regulate the distribution of tasks among work people. This resulted in the segmentation of the internal market into 'pleasant' and 'unpleasant' jobs. So instead of a formal hierarchy of jobs according to skill level there appeared an informal segmentation on the basis of 'custom'–the unwritten set of rules based largely upon past practice or precedent (Doeringer and Piore 1971: 23). Those workers with characteristics which made them less powerful (like absence of training or lack of experience) got the least pleasant jobs. Why did lack of training make workers less powerful in such an informal control structure? Because that caused them to be less universally usable in the organisation and thus made them more dependent upon their present low status job.

On the other hand in the second firm, in the engineering sector, there was much more of a formal hierarchy and the organization of production followed closely the demands of the technological system. Here the job structure was far more complex, with many skilled jobs. Control over the production process was much more centralized; careful planning was seen to be necessitated by the high technological content of the tasks and machines, the small-scale production (short runs and high set-up costs) and the dependence on the product demand. This led to a high degree of interdependency between processes and high costs of breakdown or missed deadlines.

The Nijmegen researchers reached the following interesting conclusions:

1. The organization of production follows closely the demands of the skill structure and the applied technology; that is to say the control structure tends to *follow* from the recruitment pattern.
2. There is an internal segmentation of the internal (I) labour market into 'good' (P) and 'bad' (S) jobs predominantly in terms of working conditions.
3. As long as foreign workers are available there is little inclination to try to do away with S jobs; when foreign workers are induced to stay in S jobs by monetary incentives, the higher wages strengthen their will to remain in such jobs rather than seeking their modification.
4. The more on-the-job training is given, the more workers tend to get stuck in the enterprise (firm-specific) market (which causes structural unemployment when older workers have to be relocated).
5. Higher labour costs in these firms did not lead to substitution (of labour by capital) but to reallocation of production activities, depending on the possibilities in the product market.

We have treated this piece of interesting research rather intensively, firstly because it makes clear that organization and technology are not fixed given factors, but tend to be manipulated by the firm's management because of the dynamics of the labour and product market; and secondly because it does point to a more complex structure of segmentation than is usually found in the literature. Every firm is situated at the crossroads of labour market and work organization. The 'external' labour market, as we see it, may be part of the firm as well as of its environment.

However the degree of choice open to the firm in pursuing particular job-creation or manpower policies remains unresolved. The discussion going on between the Munich researchers and their critics, notably Sabine Gensior and Beate Krais, is very relevant (Bolle 1976). How autonomous is the firm? How much and in what respects is it dependent in its labour market decisions on social policy in the environment? How far must the firm adapt its personnel policies to labour market developments, instead of actively planning and directing those policies, if it wants to follow the trends of the market? Perhaps firms that can afford to remain active in one market segment only (like electricity or oil or chemicals) can 'control' their personnel policies? Most of the others (e.g. in textiles, shoes, etc.) may only be able to 'adapt' (Hamaker 1976). The main dilemma for managers is how to combine the levels and nature of aspirations and patterns of expectations found in a particular market segment with incentives to productivity which are effective in both the long and short term. There is however at least some evidence that manpower policies within similar technological and product market contexts *can* vary enormously, as is the case in Mackay's comparison of Britain and America. (That is to say that the crude technological determinism typified in Figure 6 is no more than an implication of likely constraints). In Loveridge's current research (1978) he has found a range of manpower policies may be applied within the same industry. Their distribution is not however a random one but is geared to that of the financial/investment strategy being pursued by the corporation. This is in turn related to the pre-existing structure of skills within their ILM. Whether managers have decided to change this or not relates to a whole series of factors that are currently under investigation. Among them the existence of a strong craft or 'guild' market which provides a continuity of skills and experience related to their current mode of technology appears important: this structure operates irrespective of union 'pushfulness'.

The trend in employment seen by researchers like Martens (1973) to be currently running from the PI to the SE segment is therefore one that is taking place within an existing institutional structure which provides many checks and constraints. It is indeed extremely difficult to demonstrate such a trend for all of the above reasons (including the crudely aggregative nature of occupational statistics). Similarly it is difficult to 'prove' the existence of 'hard-core' industries. Publicly owned utilities such as gas and electricity sometimes provide *safe* but *lowly* paid 'harbours' for stigmatized workers such as the elderly (see Sleeper 1975) but in some countries, like Belgium, they belong to the highest paying sectors of the economy. Other sectors, especially the service sectors, appear to contain both the best and worst jobs.

Nevertheless we would contend that the type of model advanced by Mok enables the incorporation of motivational and technical variables within the organizational context of job creation. It also enables realistic assessments to be made of the 'ratchet-effect' of worker mobility of job dilution across market segments. That is to say that whatever the initial source of stigmatization, institutional barriers act 'as if there were' a discrete market for each of the four segments in which employee services are matched to jobs.

We now have to ask whether policy solutions have to be shaped by consideration of the initial *sources* of stigmatization or in terms of the institutional barriers by which they are maintained. If the former then clearly legal or other intervention has to be at a large number of discrete and unique points. If the latter then a few changes in policy on the part of major institutions such as trade unions and professional associations might modify the barriers facing the aged, the disabled, the young, the black and the biggest group of stigmatized workers, women.

Cultural capital

Before going on to consider manpower policy in these terms we should like to turn away from our previous line of argument to offer one further explanation for the process by which jobs and people move within and between segments. When referring to entrance interviews we mentioned the practice of stereotyping or 'labelling' of applicants on the basis of whether they were like 'us' or not. In a perceptive analysis of the manner in which a new entrant is inducted into the employing organization Schein (1974) talks of the socialization of newcomers into the adoption of certain patterns of behaviour, certain manners of expression, and finally, into the acceptance of (or expressed compliance with) certain organizational beliefs. Some are central to 'getting-on' in the firm and some not so; some jobs in the organization demand greater signs of loyalty than others, and so on. Much depends on how far a worker's skill has become part of his work identity, as Marsden (1975: 38) puts it.

This acquisition of values goes along with the acquisition of knowledge about how the system works within the company, both formally and informally. Some jobs are in a good position to enable the new entrant to acquire this data, others not. Altogether this knowledge of the culture may be more specific, i.e. relating to a single plant, a single company or a single industry or more general, i.e. a good 'knowledge of the world', of the 'right networks', a good presentation of self in terms of the expectation of significant others, etc. This *cultural* capital, as we shall call it, can be at least as valuable as the technical capital contained in skills and knowledge required by the job itself. Obviously seniority in status and experience contributes to this cultural capital, perhaps to a greater degree than towards the technical skills of the role incumbent. In some jobs experience of the way the technical tasks are done in a number of firms may be an asset to a craft or professional worker in early career but to 'get on' he must learn to come to terms with 'the way things are done around here'. For the peripheral worker, he or she may never get close enough to the bottom of a 'mobility chain' for cultural capital to be regarded as important even *if* he or she possesses any.

But for most peripheral workers their lack of cultural capital comes from their social background and early training. Women are taught early to regard business and politics as essentially male preoccupations and so have no interest in gaining access to such social networks (Bott 1957). Ghetto dwellers gain little knowledge of the middle-class mores and social skills required in senior management, and indeed as Willmott and Young (1957) demonstrate, may show a fierce hostility towards these 'unnecessary' accoutrements of power which mark them as 'outsiders' as manifestly as if they carried a yellow star on their backs.

7. Labour market policy and segmentation

Labour market policy defined

Labour market policy, as it is often defined, gives the impression of conscious, active and autonomous behaviour on the part of governments or of governmental bodies, with an eye to the optimal allocation of workers to jobs. Such a policy is usually narrowly described as that of manpower planning especially in American neo-classical literature. It is more often than not connected with the human capital approach which is so predominant in neo-classical thinking on labour market problems. We think this has grave consequences for the persistence of labour market segmentation: 'An active manpower policy is a conscious attempt to intervene in the labour market to raise the resource value of manpower', as a well-known American handbook has it (Jakubauskas and Palomba 1973: 189). 'Active' is contrasted with 'inactive': 'An inactive policy is a situation in which it is not the primary intent of government to influence the resource value of manpower'. These authors also mention the cohesiveness of manpower policy: it is seen to be a logical and consistent strategy for guiding manpower activity.

Such a policy is seen to have the implicit or explicit goal of influencing labour market processes in order to improve the resource value of the individual worker either before or after he or she has entered the active labour force. Broadly defined manpower policy thus deals with the relationship between man and his working environment, seeking to improve his status, income and career opportunities (Jakubauskas and Palomba 1973: 184). Individual choice is constrained by the government only in order to offer a 'better' or more viable range of career opportunities to the individual. But his choice *only* becomes available in the context of achieving the most effective and efficient division of labour within the community as a whole.

Through the provision of an *expected* demand schedule for labour skills (indicative planning) or an *intended* allocation of jobs (positive planning), the manpower planner attempts to avoid wage differentials, economic rents, premiums and other costs arising out of shortages or surpluses of skills relative to predicted needs. For the neo-classicist manpower planning may be seen as a means to adjusting the price of labour to its revenue product; government agencies designed to reduce structural obstacles to mobility between jobs and between disparate careers may therefore be justified in terms of their contribution to the effective working of a free market for other goods and services. More immediately the contribution of such agencies to incomes constraint may be both indirect through the effective matching of skills training to job openings, or more directly through the limitations they are able to impose on the structure of wages and salaries. This is clearly the case in the command economies of Eastern Europe and the Third World; some such effect may also be observed in the co-operation between voluntary and governmental agencies in Sweden and Norway for example.

We begin by setting out some of the characteristics of conscious, active and autonomous action in the labour market. A number of questions arise from this description. How *autonomous* can labour market policy be within a 'mixed' economy? How far is it feasible to adopt a *manpower planning* approach to a freely competitive market at macro level? Does the *human capital* approach express the true nature of the differences between the private and collective costs and benefits of a labour market policy and if it does not, what basis does the theorist have for advising politicians on the means of bringing about 'induced mobility'?

The neo-classical approach adopted by most governmental interventionists in the Western world has been modified to assume the existence of a community welfare function against which the existing and desired job structure may be judged. (See for example Jackson 1972, Van Voorden 1975, Schmid 1976). There is a further assumption that the structure of monetary rewards and social benefits available to individual workers and potential employers can be manipulated to bring about movement between jobs and job locations of the appropriate kind and direction. A more exacting criterion of effectiveness may require that the community should benefit by at least the amount of its investment in human resources over a given time period (Little 1950). This is an implied rather than a generally imposed operational condition for an interventionary market strategy in parliamentary democracies, though not one that would be acceptable to radicals.

Finally we suggest that all forms of planning imply a wide measure of social control. This in turn implies more than a technical understanding of market forces and consumer or community preferences. The realloca- tion of resources required by an active labour market policy is an exercise of power. Because of the very nature of economic environ- ment—its variability and unpredictability—employers and primary sector employees place a high premium on retaining and maintaining present market positions with their accumulated advantages. The achievement of the optimum allocation of labour resources through the short-term manipulation of the price mechanism is therefore extremely unlikely; fundamental changes in the institutional control of education, training and job entry are even more unlikely unless political intervention is undertaken on a very large scale and with the expressed intention of reshaping 'consumer preferences'.

Active, inactive and reactive policies

Van Voorden (1975: 223-225) has made an interesting analysis of the evolution of labour market policy in the Netherlands since World War II. Dutch labour market policy has gone through three stages of develop- ment. The first stage could be characterized by what Mertens of the German Federal Labour Bureau has called a 'reactive' labour market policy, the second stage by what he calls a 'forward-looking reactive' policy, and the third stage by an 'active' labour market policy (Schmid 1976: 167). Van Voorden (1975: 223-224) describes the Dutch situation as follows:

Before the Second World War, labour market policy was mainly confined to fighting unemployment: in that stage goals were neither deliberately and explicitly chosen nor actively pursued. After the war more attention was paid to the formulation of labour market goals. In this second stage the general purpose of fighting unemployment changed to an attempt to achieve optimal labour allocation: the idea of allocating persons to jobs which suit them best. Compared to the first stage with its general, collectively aimed measures, a more sectional or even individual approach becomes apparent. The quantitative problem (large-scale unemployment) in the thirties gives way to the qualitative problem of placing the best man in the best job. A third stage has been noticeable since the early sixties and is known as 'active labour market policy'. Despite several interpretations, two elements are basic to this type of policy.
   Firstly, active labour market policy deliberately operates on both sides of the market. It is explicitly directed towards *demand* (employment) as well as towards *supply* (labour force). Secondly this stage is characterized by a special interest in interventionary measures aimed at ensuring harmonious market developments on both sides of the market.
   Under the influence of the OECD, this active labour market policy has been closely bound

up with the goal of economic growth in the policies pursued by most European countries. The all-round value of this goal is questionable; sometimes it may even bar the pursuit of other more individually oriented goals like job satisfaction, deployment, career perspective and so on. Dutch labour market policy has been increasingly confined to stimulating economic growth and this general economic goal has been persued during a period in which there was room for the introduction of more social and individually aimed goals. The problematic relationship between economic growth and labour market policy is receiving increasing attention in the literature.

Van Voorden's work does raise the important question of whether the current type of labour market policy may be correctly typified as 'active'. Schmid (1976) has remarked that the governmental agencies responsible for labour market policy are now quick to label their policies as being 'active'. As soon as they do more than just register the unemployed in order to pay unemployment benefits they tend to refer to their approach in this manner—when, for example, they practice occupational guidance and counselling, vocational training of adults, placement, etc. In labour market policy literature 'active' means 'goal oriented', and the goals must then be labour market specific, e.g. the reduction of the number of unqualified workers by x per cent in sector y or region z. This stress on *goals*, Schmid says, can lead to the three forms of activity mentioned earlier: active, reactive and forward-looking reactive. Schmid points to the weakness of looking at policy in this way: it neglects the use of power and the existence of separate vested interests in labour market *policies* (that is the process by which these goals have to be implemented). Furthermore 'active' and 'reactive' policies can be seen as two extremes of a continuum, which means each policy may be more or less active or reactive, depending on one's criteria and time perspective. Policies which are active in a short-term perspective may well be reactive in a longer term perspective.

Schmid proposes a policy model in which the central aspect of all labour market behaviour, whether of the state, employer, or employee, is the control function. To develop this model two kinds of theories are necessary:

1. A general societal theory with the power to explain the genesis of problems out of the relationship between production and reproduction functions of the labour market and the organizational and distributive functions of the market;
2. A theory of behaviour which is capable of predicting successful behaviour to solve specific policy problems.

He sees an active labour market policy as only being possible against the background of such analytical models. (Without the predictability given by such models one might expect 'unintended consequences' to be inevitable.)

After pointing out some specific problems which such a policy would have to solve, Schmid asks the question: How active are the labour market policies of Germany and Sweden when compared with each other? To give some examples of the way Schmid treats problem areas: in neither of these countries is the state autonomous in its relationship with private interests. The result is that the state is not capable of influencing the handling of labour market problems such as the allocation and reallocation of factors of production necessitated by technological developments, changes in the national division of labour, demographic developments, etc. All these problems come into being and are solved in the private sector of the economy. Or again: in neither of these countries does there exist a structural policy for the labour market. For instance, there is no active population policy in either country. In view of the fact that rising structural unemployment is to a large extent caused by the quantitative discrepancy between demographic developments and the number of available jobs, this is an important problem.

One might well argue that the current lack of attention to these Malthusian elements of labour market theory reflects the growing complexity of the social context in which such problems appear. Schmid's analysis contains an almost nineteenth-century naivety in its search for universal explanation. However his questions may fulfil a function in that they direct our attention back to the institutionalized setting in which we develop modern choices in the labour market.

As Van Voorden (1975: 223) comments, the desired policy results may be obtained by operations which induce the market to function toward public goals, or by the introduction of extra-market operations which bypass the market process.

Van Voorden distinguishes between two unconscious (or non-state-directed) institutionalized processes: firstly, the developments and changes which occur in the actual places where the parties meet each other. The way in which transactional possibilities are structured exerts considerable influence on the market process. An important example is to be found in the phenomenon of temporary labour, which is rented in a specialized form to employers in need of 'full-time, part-year' labour. This phenomenon came into existence purely because of the workings of the market, without any conscious policy measures. And the resulting marginality of the temporary worker, which confines him or her to certain segments of the market, is an undesired but nevertheless logical result of the phenomenon.

Secondly, Van Voorden says, there is an unconscious institutionalization process involved in the structuring of the labour market, based on differences in capacities, in occupational knowledge, in technical development, and so on. This causes the existence of 'relative submarkets' which may, or may not, result in non-competing groups. The submarkets are 'relative', because the behaviour of parties is based more on preferences and priorities than on characteristics affecting the productive capacity of labour. These preferences and priorities may change over time, which causes the undesired outcome of discrepancies; qualitative and quantitative. Both are important causes of unemployment; qualitative discrepancies between supply and demand may lead to segmentation, first into 'relative' submarkets, but eventually into 'absolute' ones. In the National Programme of Labour Market Research (under the auspices of the Netherlands Ministry of Education and Sciences) three kinds of qualitative discrepancies are distinguished (1975: 38):

discrepancies which do not have an influence on behaviour and attitudes;
discrepancies which influence behaviour dependent upon certain compensatory conditions (like the realization of other preferences);
discrepancies which always influence behaviour and attitudes, regardless of the conditioning.

Qualitative discrepancies between worker preferences and the realities of the employment situation have great relevance for labour market policy because they may constitute one of the most important causes of overt and hidden unemployment. Also, because of the existing structural problems in the economy as a whole, these discrepancies are expected to increase rather than decrease. Are workers willing to enter and re-enter jobs or to remain in those that they have if they experience a large measure of discrepancy between their preferences and their existing employment situation? Hill et al. (1973: 136) have found that the public employment service tends to classify men on the basis of what they are known to be capable of doing, rather than what they think they are capable of, or would like to do. In this the service will be likely to follow the desired outcome of employers, who generally seem to be able to convey their conditions of employment, but not the job content, to the employment officials. There is evidence of this in research done in Belgium (Lammertijn, 1976) and the Netherlands (de Jonge 1977).

In the case of Belgium, Lammertijn has been able to prove that these policy customs are conducive to the persistence of labour market segmentation. Furthermore, as Marsden and Duff (1975: 38) have put it, the question is whether a worker's skills, knowledge and capacities have become part of his work 'identity', and whether the state has an obligation to allow him to retain those skills and identity. Indeed it may be that government agencies are forced to recognise the skills and identities attached to particular occupations by the existence of professional interest groups. In this regard we may note the differences in socio-economic experiences between neighbouring European countries as between different occupational groups.

The agency for temporary workers is a universal phenomenon in some industrial sectors such as construction, and some 'new' occupational markets such as that for stenographers, computer programmers, nurses, and so on. In older markets for skilled manual workers the existence of unions of journeymen (journée-homme) has inhibited the emergence of such agencies in Britain, though not in France, Belgium and Holland. Such differences in experience do not lead us to believe that French, Belgian or Dutch workers are necessarily any less identified with their work role and status than their equivalent worker in the British Isles: in Van Voorden's terms there may be compensatory conditions in these countries to explain their lack of collective identity. On the other hand the balance of power within the labour market may not be conducive to the expression of localized grievances of a task-related nature and groups may therefore be inhibited in their response to market discrepancies.

This institutionalist approach again highlights the crucial fact that labour market policy has to deal with the realities of employment. The employment contract is a power relationship in which the employee puts himself under the control of the employer. Not only wages are involved: no employee sells himself body and soul to the employer, there is always the freedom or autonomy to put a variable amount of effort into the job (Lupton and Bowey 1974). The declared objectives of manpower planners such as Miernyk (and many others) 'to eliminate obstacles to occupational and geographical mobility' (Miernyk 1973) are essentially political ones.

Furthermore these policies are often expressed and presented in a manner which indicates the narrow assumptions upon which they are constructed. Even the most advanced strategies concerning relocation of labour, such as those pursued by the Swedish National Labour Market Board (*Arbetsmarknadsstyrelsen*–AMS) and in Canada by the Federal and Maritime Welfare Systems (Steinberg 1976) lay heavy emphasis on the assumed desire of the individual worker to maximize the net advantages gained by a job move in solely cash or economic terms.

However, approaches to manpower redeployment in these latter countries recognise, more vividly than used to be the case in EEC member-states, that many of the social obstacles to job mobility cannot be overcome by short-run economic measures operating solely within the constraints of existing institutional parameters. The AMS has, for example, embarked upon large-scale training projects for schoolteachers, designed to change expectations about existing sex roles in industry.

By and large however we find that in most countries a manpower approach to the definition of an 'active' labour market policy is adopted, in which an emphasis is placed upon facilitating worker mobility, either between job or work locations, or residential locations. Having accepted the necessity for such movement the judgement of the employee will obviously reflect his or her narrow range of perceived choice. Thus workers who are freely mobile in this manner are generally those who have little to lose and much to gain from a change in location (Lutz and Sengenberger 1974: 37-39). Policies aimed at stimulating mobility may, according to the latter authors' findings, actually reinforce market segmentation, and in so doing, become 're-active'. As soon as a policy maker (not only the government, also private firms) acts on the assumption that he has a certain responsibility for the placement of workers, he exercises control over the worker. This means limiting his use of skills, retraining him, making him move, and so on, squandering a sort of capital, such as social ties and social relationships (Marsden and Duff 1975), which we have referred to as a worker's 'cultural capital'. It is in these aspects that the essential control function of the labour market becomes clearly visible, a control function which is not limited to the work situation but stretches far and wide into the non-work aspects of the worker's life.

Yet even where job relocation policies have been pursued against the background of considerable research into the effects of relocation on the workers' social life and that of his family the success of such a policy is by no means certain (Steinberg 1976: Dymond 1969). There is little in the experience of Western European countries, or in that of Canada and Scandinavia, to suggest that the movement of large numbers of workers either geographically, or through skills training, will guarantee the provision of long-term employment of a 'primary' character within 'core' industries. On the other hand there is fairly conclusive evidence that in times of economic recession employers with operations distributed over a wide geographical area *will* close down plants employing former 'secondary-sector' workers before those in well-established 'primary' areas. Indeed this action often appears to be taken in relation to the period over which the employer is allowed to amortize his initial investment in plant and equipment in order to earn a state subsidy. That is to say that the plants remain open only so long as the costs of employing secondary workers (together with such other costs as may accrue with an unfavourable location) can be offset against government subsidies *and* the premium that may be gained by shifting the plant as soon as the conditions under which the subsidy was given permit the entrepreneur to do so.

For the neo-classical economist these events are perfectly easy to explain in terms of the 'efficient institutional response by firms to the basic market imperfections' (Wachtel 1974). His limited frame of analysis leads him to consign the disabilities of secondary workers or of underdeveloped regions to *pre-market* effects, that is to the generic intrinsic quality of labour. This is a basic source of weakness in the advice which neo-classicists have to offer the policy maker (see for example Phelps-Brown 1977: 177). In the analysis of the institutionalist the problem is seen as being one which stems from the failure of secondary-sector groups of workers to gain control over access to certain valued job markets (Perlman 1922, Webb 1897). Radicals will argue the need for a concerted movement to bring about a change in the social as well as economic milieu of secondary-sector workers but will see the need for greater emphasis in government policy on constraining *employer* actions in the employment, training and movement of labour. One's definition of an 'active' labour market 'problem' is limited to one's frame of analysis—and ultimately to one's ideology.

Conscious and/or desired?

Labour market policy, according to Van Voorden, may be either a conscious (or directed) or unconscious (or non-directed) process, characterized by institutionalization–that is the preservation (stabilization) of norms, values or goals, which in their most far-reaching forms are precipitated in a national structure:

> Two conscious (or directed) institutionalization processes are discerned on the labour market. In the internal institutionalization process the parties involved in the market try to change the market structure by committing parties to some behavioural pattern because of dissatisfaction with the original market results. In the external institutionalization process the parties involved in the market try to change the market structure by committing parties to some behavioural pattern because of dissatisfaction with the original market results. In the external institutionalization process behavioural controls are introduced in the market, aimed at welfare goals, by non-party institutions (e.g. government) with a general responsibility (Van Voorden 1975: 223).

It is necessary to distinguish between conscious or unconscious policies, in the sense of inputs influencing the allocation process and/or the behaviour of the parties, and the desired outcomes or effects of those policies. Conscious policies may have outcomes which are desired by the policy makers but not by other parties in the labour market, and vice versa. If 'the social position of the foreign worker in Belgium is determined by the type of immigration policy conducted by the Belgian government' (Martens 1973: 37), this policy can be called conscious, but the outcome–'foreign workers are marginalized proletarians' (1973: 294) can hardly be called 'desired' by the Belgian government.

It is clear from this example that desired market results are not always reached i.e. that disharmonious relations between supply and demand tend to occur, which leaves some of the parties involved more or less permanently dissatisfied and alienated from the other parties. Segmentation, as an institutionalized pattern of market behaviour is often an undesired consequence of labour market policies. Here perhaps we find the most significant difference between labour market theories. For neo-classicists there is no question that segmentation in its institutionalized form is a market imperfection that may perhaps be the result of a conscious policy on the part of the policy makers (be they governments, employers or representatives of employees), but rarely a desired outcome of such policies. On the other hand among radicals it is quite common to assume that a segmentation policy is not only a conscious policy on the part of employers (and governments in their wake), but also a desired outcome, a 'strategic' process:

Employers turned to strategies designed to divide and conquer the work force. The central thrust of the new strategies was to break down the increasingly unified worker interests that grew out of both the proletarianization of work and the concentration of workers in urban areas. As exhibited in several aspects of these large firms' operations, this effort aimed to divide the labour force into various segments so that the actual experiences of workers would be different and the basis of their common opposition to capitalists would be undermined (Edwards et al. 1975: xii-xiii).

Thus the question is forcefully put to us whether the segmentation process is a strategic process resulting from conscious behaviour on the part of the parties in the market, and desired by at least some parties, or the result of 'functional mechanisms', or indirect and unpremeditated responses from the environmental structure: what Vietorisz and Harrison (1973: 374) would call 'positive feedback':

This process can be explained by positive feedback that connects technical change, labour productivity, and the money-wage bargain in the labour market. The emerging segments are prevented from coalescing by low mobility between them. Low mobility is endogenous to the system and results from divergent education, training, and skills associated with distinct labour market segments. Thus the mobility barriers are themselves maintained by positive feedback. Forces of negative feedback are present but are too weak to prevent 'segmentation'.

Vietorisz and Harrison are of the opinion that divergent developments in the labour market are the result of a type of institutionalization process which Van Voorden would call 'internal', because it is geared to the objectives of one or more market parties and uses instruments which are inherent to the labour market itself: it is at work only in that market and because of the existence of that market.

The dominance of positive feedback and the resulting tendencies for divergent development are inherent in the core institutions of a modern market society. These tendencies are further reinforced by clusters of secondary institutions which arise because segmentation is functional to the system (Vietorisz and Harrison 1973: 375).

According to Vietorisz and Harrison, conscious policies on the part of firms result in the undesired consequence of segmentation tendencies: firms apply labour-saving techniques which cause a bifurcation in the industrial structure: big, capital-intensive firms with relatively high wages, and smaller, labour-intensive, firms with relatively low wages. This they explain by referring to positive feedback mechanisms: high wages lead to labour-saving devices, which lead to higher productivity, which lead to even higher wages. But in low-wage firms this mechanism does not work, because the incentive to substitute labour by capital is absent.

As Van Voorden (1975: 223) comments, the desired market results may be obtained by operations which induce the market to function in line with policy goals, or by the introduction of extra-market operations which bypass the market process.

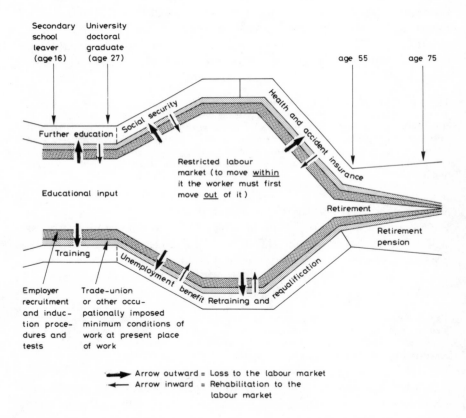

The thickness of the arrow denotes likely permanency of the movement for the «average» worker availing himself of these facilities in the 1970s.

Figure 8. The institutional structuring of labour supply.

Autonomous?

This brings us to the third element of our 'definition' of labour market policy – autonomy. How autonomous can a labour market policy be? Autonomy is used here to mean free from outside pressure. Government and supra-national bodies have to propagate their policy directives through a network consisting of private companies, trade unions, geographically dispersed plants and socially distant groups of managers and workers. Nor are strategies evolved in a vacuum: they emerge out of a series of outcomes from previous strategies and in a milieu produced by the implementation of these strategies. In all of this complex of overlapping and interacting forces there is no more important focus for analysis than the internal labour market: that is the point at which the employment contract is made and implemented. On the other hand this market is bounded by a series of extra-market conditions offering alternatives to employment that have been created by government intervention. The nature of the 'market' resulting from these diverse forces is illustrated by Figure 8, which is adapted from the work of Hesseling (1978). It illustrates the manner in which a worker has to move through a series of governmental or institutional 'membranes' in order to enter or leave the particular labour market in which he finds himself at each point of his career. Without the necessary qualifications he is not able to effect the process of *leaving* the market, and once out of it he may be neither motivated nor qualified to re-enter. We now propose to examine briefly the empirical research into the working of these services and how they relate to the internal labour market.

The employment service

Daniel (1970: 32) rightly observes that 'public employment services are internationally a sitting duck for easy criticism', and one must beware of drawing unfair generalizations from the available evidence. Some observers blame the general lack of success of the employment service (E.S.) on the poor 'image' held by both employers and employees, leading to an unwillingness to use it. Daniel (1970: 33) puts it thus:

On one side it has been seen mainly as dealing with undesirable employees, on the other side it is seen as dealing with undesirable jobs. A vicious circle is set up as many employers who have vacancies above the level of unskilled labour do not inform the office, and people seeking good jobs do not go through the office.

After studying job search by redundant workers in the West Midlands during 1968, Reid suggests:

> The first point to note is that the great majority of involuntary job-changers do contact the E.S., either because they go to the employment exchange or because the E.S. comes to them in the plant... In fact, though, the majority of E.S. contacts considered that the information and advice received in their job search had not been particularly useful (Reid 1970: 10).

In this sample Reid found the proportion of successful placements through the state service to be low (17.5 per cent) on average and greatest among the unskilled (26.7 per cent). Although the quality of the job often represented an improvement on their previous one, subsequent turnover among employment service placements was higher than in the rest of the sample who had found a new job without its aid. From other empirical studies (Lammertijn 1976; de Jong 1977; Blankenburg 1978: 12) we know that public employment agencies have very little possibility of penetrating the internal labour markets of individual firms or unions. This fact severely limits any government in the implementation of an active labour market policy. Without the knowledge that might be provided by firms and unions on the availability of primary sector jobs the employment service is unable to compete with the informed network, the private agency, or the 'labour pool' or bourse, that is controlled by the union or professional association.

The public employment service has undergone a major restructuring in several European countries. For example under its new guise the British Manpower Services Agency has adopted European-style 'job-shops' or manpower centres. The distribution of unemployment benefits, from which it formerly drew both its main function and its public image has been reallocated to the Department of Health and Social Security. A publicity drive is being conducted in an attempt to gather local market information from employers. Under the 1975 Employment Protection Act British employers are being brought more into line with other European states in terms of notice of intended redundancy. These vary within the Community states from two weeks to six months and are usually related to the numbers of workers involved in the proposed redundancy. In this way the local E.S. has a chance to place redundant workers and even to arrange their retraining.

However as Reid concludes, given the nature of the recurrent job changer there is little evidence that training and other aids to mobility have the desired effect. Neither is there any real evidence from his study that a better supply of (existing) information was more effective in producing long-lasting placements than the informal network of the local market.

In the 1966 Sample Census the unemployed in Britain were divided into those who registered at the exchanges, those who were sick and did not register, and those who did not register for other reasons. An analysis of these data undertaken by Standing (1972) suggests that *people out of work tend, ceteris paribus, to register in an inverse relationship with the possibility of finding jobs*, that is to say that people only go to the employment exchange to register when they do *not* want a job. Miners and labourers were most likely to register, professional and technical workers least likely. Regional differences in the propensity to register were also great and point to the conclusion that regions generally regarded as the depressed or less prosperous ones coincide with high propensities to use the services of state agencies.

Over the period of industrial rationalization that took place in British industry over the late 1960s the level of non-registration among the unemployed was observed by Bosanquet and Standing (1972) to increase remarkably. The fall in the active work population could not be explained in terms of the drop-out of married women or older manual workers: in fact the most significant fall was in the 25-44 age group. It seems possible that many of these prime age males passed into self-employment for reasons that related either to lack of other job opportunities or income tax avoidance (some are known to have emigrated). This process of 'dropping out' brings into question many of the assumptions made in creating occupational statistics: Bosanquet and Standing appeal for alternative methods of data collection. However, it remains true that the secondary-external labour market segments are by definition comprised of 'marginal' workers who drift into and out of many forms of totally unrecorded occupations: much of this marginal economic activity is, as a whole, beyond the control of official scriveners and tax collectors.

On the demand side employer cooperation is equally reluctant. Compulsory notification of vacancies would be unpopular and difficult to enforce, and if this is ruled out, the manpower service has to rely on persuasion, and on convincing employers that notification is worthwhile. Perhaps the inability of the E.S. to communicate adequately with personnel departments, or to cater for the needs of the internal labour market, is the stumbling block here. It could be a real contribution to the effectiveness of the E.S. and to its depth of penetration into the internal labour market if its staff included a greater proportion of administrators with knowledge and experience of the selection procedures that actually operate within companies. The internal political process by which job vacancies are specified, advertised and filled is one involving the interaction of line (production) managers, staff (personnel) managers and labour unions or works councils. For example the acceptance of broad job specifications from junior personnel staff without sufficient regard for the tasks which production managers actually need to have performed often appears to give rise to frustration and disappointment on the part of both the newly recruited employee and his or her supervisor. As a consequence production managers interviewed by the authors in Belgium, Britain and the Netherlands reported a lack of trust in the recruitment methods employed by personnel departments. By displaying a more professional concern for their clients (personnel managers) the E.S. official can reinforce their status and function within the management hierarchy.

Training

The training systems of most European countries are characterized by their high degree of centralization. Even in Germany where formal apprenticeship schemes are almost as numerous as those in the United Kingdom they are highly regulated by industrial and state bodies.

This contrasts with the decentralization and, until recently, relatively informal nature of the British system. The Industrial Training Act of 1964 went some way towards changing this state of affairs. Its history is worth a brief consideration, since it serves to demonstrate the effective power of existing institutions. The Act empowered the minister to set up boards for each industry with 'a duty to provide or service the provision of such training courses or facilities as might be necessary for the training of persons in the industry and to make recommendations with regard to the nature, length and standard of training for occupations in the industry' (Clause 2). Clause 4 required the board to impose a levy on employers in its industry with which to finance its activities. The rationale for the levy system was to spread the costs of training across industry so that small companies, who supposedly make up the secondary market for labour, would contribute to the training of skilled workers by bigger, or better, employers. Training of an approved standard was to receive a grant and in this way would provide a cross-subsidy from employers in the secondary sector to those in the primary sector. The market signals were deliberately set so that employers would *have* to pay for training whether they engaged in it or not.

By 1969 twenty-seven statutory boards were established and significant advances had been made towards restructuring apprentice schemes in a modular, and therefore more generalized, form. Within ten years, however, the Employment and Training Act was passed which effectively amended both of the main precepts of the earlier Act: the financing by cross-subsidization and the emphasis that has been placed on the teaching of generalized skills. The Bolton Committee on Small Business had earlier commented 'we are forced to conclude that because of the difficulties [in facilities] described... most [small] firms will be unable to derive benefits from the training board system commensurate with its costs to them' (Committee on Small Firms 1971). A very considerable pressure group had developed on behalf of small companies which receive ammunition from the manner in which many larger companies openly boasted of the 'profits' they were making in training grants. This, combined with the large administrative staffs attached to many training boards, brought the Act into disrepute.

The argument appears as an emotive but successful refusal by 'grass-roots' entrepreneurs to pay for the training which their more skilled employees had received from larger competitors: in welfare economic terms they were continuing to enjoy a 'rent' because they were not paying 'social costs' which had to be borne elsewhere. Some theorists argued that this was not so. They distinguished between 'general' and 'specific' training and argued, in line with Mincer et al. (1962), that each entrepreneur balanced training in a way which reflected his idea of a normative pay-back to a given level of skill specificity (McCormick and Manly 1971). The farmers and small businessmen who argued that their employees left them after getting better qualifications were, they said, right to do so.

The type of training which qualified for training grants was of a general rather than specific type: small employers had to employ craftsmen coming to them with general skills, yet it was experience rather than formal training that was needed in small businesses. The economic rationale of the 1964 Industrial Training Act, with its emphasis on the

Becker (1964) dichotomy between general and specific skills has been criticized by Pettman (1972: 225-239) as being unrelated to the reality of the internal labour market in which beyond a certain level of technical education most skills are highly specific; a fact which was later to be recognized in the 1974 Act. Since that time formal recognition has been given to the local attempts by employees to provide workers with skills sufficient only for the specific tasks required within the firm or internal markets. The basis for the payment of financial grants has been shifted in favour of the small employer.

The practical contribution of neo-classical theory to these problems has nevertheless been limited and the outcomes of the debate inconclusive. The adoption of cost-benefit analyses of placement services, retraining schemes and assisted migration in other countries has however proved useful (Dymond 1969; Beaumont 1976). Such analyses have enabled the identification of worker/employer propensities and an allocation of priorities on the basis of these displayed preferences rather than upon hypothetical models of 'rational behaviour'. Similarly empirical studies of industrial attitudes towards 'skill-dilution' through retraining schemes (Unwin 1970; Hall and Miller 1971; Hughes 1972) also provide evidence of the relative difficulties to be encountered in placing the graduates from government training centres. These types of study describe and categorize the propensities of employers and employees to accept or reject applicants for entry to particular job markets through training and qualification. The fact that such studies have been carried out at all indicates the existence of a 'problem'; normally this problem relates to the existence of an effective barrier to entry for some or all individuals outside the institutional boundaries of the job market.

Social security and unemployment benefits

The traditions of Western industrial countries in respect to state aid for the unemployed varies immensely. In some European countries, Germany and France for example, there is a history of state-imposed obligation on the employer to contribute the major part of the insurance against unemployment, sickness, or incapacity carried by the individual worker. Other countries such as Britain, Holland and Belgium attempted to maintain the principle of contributory benefits contained within the Beveridge Report of 1942. Increasingly this latter principle has been eroded by the complementary objective of sustaining an overall minimum level of income in a period of sustained inflation. The consequence has been an ever-rising state contribution to the national social security fund in all Western European countries. The effect of growing unemployment of a structural or long-term nature has therefore been to increase the amount of 'transfers' from productive to non-productive parts of the sectors of the labour force. The concern that has been expressed at the size and alleged effect of these social security payments has resulted in a growing body of criticism from neo-classicists.

For example Rhea (1976) has attempted to build an econometric model for the Canadian unemployed that incorporated the effects of

1. the period of employment required to qualify for unemployment benefit;
2. the period of waiting before receiving unemployment benefit;
3. the period of unemployment over which unemployment benefit may be claimed.

He suggests an increase in the second element would substantially reduce those claiming unemployment benefit by making short periods of unemployment less rewarding for secondary workers. It would, to use the neo-classical frame of analysis used by Feldstein (1975), reduce the time spent in job-search activity. Marston's work (1975) also points to the fact that workers tend to 'ride along' until their benefit period comes to an end.

But this means looking at unemployment insurance only from the financial angle. We tend to agree with Van Wezel (1972: 184) who points out that unemployment insurance is always only insurance against loss of income, not against loss of job:

in our opinion, the positive promotion of re-entrance to work should be especially emphasized in the design of labour market policy. However, the social fact that certain groups of unemployed (the disadvantaged) stay unemployed because of their slight market-value, can only be overcome to a limited degree by the present labour market policy (Van Wezel 1972: 233-234).

A study by Taylor (1975) suggests that:

unemployment has not drifted upwards because of an increased preference for unemployment as opposed to work. There can be no doubt that the vast majority of redundant workers would have preferred to stay in their old job rather than join the ranks of the unemployed.

His paper simply argues that unemployed workers are likely to spend more time searching for a job in 1975 than they did in 1951, *allowing for differences in the pressure of demand for labour:* 'The increase in unemployment benefit relative to [net] average earnings has permitted the unemployed to search for a job more carefully' (Taylor 1975). However, research by Daniel (1977) suggests that many British workers have learnt to use the social insurance system to maximize the benefits derived from their size of family and the statutorily enforced periods *in* work required for maximum benefits. These are not workers who would normally be considered to be secondary workers, having had considerable periods of regular employment before entering their present period of sustained unemployment.

It is interesting that none of the neo-classical theorists doubt the existence of jobs and believe that a reduction in unemployment benefit will punish the job searcher in a way which will force him to be less discriminative in his *choice* of jobs. Yet the combination of Taylor's data with that of Daniel serves to suggest that the experience of redundancy and the effect of lowered expectation of employment opportunities *may* educate former primary sector workers to take a place in one of the secondary market segments. Certainly British Department of Employment data suggests that the longer a worker remains unemployed the more likely he is to continue unemployed (*Department of Employment Gazette* 1977: 964). A similar conclusion was reached in a research report on long-term unemployed in the Netherlands (Koopmans et al. 1976).

The application of both employment and social security policies may therefore serve to educate employers and employees in a manner that dichotomizes the market still further. The paradoxical effect may be analysed in either neo-classical or dualist terms but the remedies are quite different. The neo-classicist might well suggest that a reduction in security benefits would reduce employer overheads at a time of low product demand and therefore encourage him to take on more workers. The dualist would see the employer as always stopping short of the secondary worker in his recruitment to better paid jobs whatever effect on employment was brought about through downwardly flexible wages. There is plentiful evidence in the research undertaken by the authors to demonstrate that the 'rationalization' of work and the accompanying redundancies leads to an increase in the use of protective practices by the active work force. Employers too, often prefer to increase overtime working or to take on temporary labour, rather than to offer 'permanent' employment to the unemployed.

In times of great unemployment workers lower their demands and expectations of their jobs and employers tend to raise their demands and their selection norms. The extent to which these preferences and selection criteria do indeed change over time has seldom been an object of research. We do know from research done in the Netherlands (Van Wezel 1972; Koopmans et al. 1976) that willingness to work on the part of the workers suffers from the experience of qualitative discrepancies and also that, once out of work, the personal estimation of the re-entry chances has a considerable effect on success in obtaining another job (Reid 1970). Van Wezel's analysis showed that if personal estimation of the re-entry chance is low this adds to the feeling that active job-seeking is senseless. In the 'career' of many unemployed persons, as time goes by and job searches remain without success, there is an increasing resignation to the situation of unemployment (Van Wezel 1972: 231).

Such studies as have been done suggest that unemployment is most socially costly among young people (Manpower Services Commission 1977). It results in three effects: the immediate waste through under-utilization; the long-term impact of frustration and idleness on the psychological orientation towards work among the unemployed; and a long-term misallocation of resources through young entrants accepting work below the level of their academic attainment. It is of course possible that this initial misallocation of human resources may adjust through the working of internal promotion channels and through on-the-job training in future employment, but this adjustment is not likely to correct the combined effects of discrimination by sex or by skin colour when taken together with an initial disadvantage by age cohort.

Many, however, will enter secondary market jobs who would, a few years ago, have been acceptable within the primary market. Even within this latter market the range of occupations offering 'long-range' social mobility to young people from working-class homes will be even more limited than usual. In periods of economic recession localized and family-based information networks take on increased significance in giving some progeny a favoured start over others (see for example the *Sunday Times* sample of 22 May 1977). Economic recession accentuates the economic importance and impact of the 'family of origin' even in advanced industrial societies. Where families act as bridges into formal organizations they may determine the level of entry into the internal career structure of the firm.

National minimum wages

One of the most usual ways to ameliorate poverty is by means of setting a statutory minimum level of earnings. The 'method of legal enactment' was seen by the Webbs as the most appropriate way to keep wages above subsistence level: unions could bargain differentials from a statutorily enforced base. Inefficient firms that could not compete would be driven out of business; thus marginal revenue productivity would always be maintained at a sufficient level to maintain the base rate (Webb and Webb 1897). Whilst the Webbs were prepared to dismiss the 'wage-fund' theory of classical economics it is not so easily dismissed in a climate of zero or negative economic growth. Furthermore the theoretical re-interpretation offered by Keynesian economists does not save the real value of wage minima from the self-eroding 'knock-on' effects of union bargaining.

National minima tend to take two forms. The most important in Europe are those that are bargained or, in France, fixed in consultation with the three main union blocks for a single industry or industrial sector. The second are those that are fixed for a whole economy or for certain defined industries as a means to assist workers who possess the characteristics of secondary sector workers. These latter are, of course, those of whom we refer in the last paragraph and about which this section is written. However both 'bargained' and 'enacted' minima are effective to the extent that they do not set off a chain of consequential claims. For this reason they are regarded as relatively ineffective in North America and the U.K. where local union organization and the practice of 'pattern-bargaining' between ILM's and of 'fractional bargaining' within ILM's result in a rapid erosion of statutorily set standards. It is worth noting the relative longevity of centralized settlements in France, Belgium and Scandinavia as against those in Anglo-Saxon countries, the Netherlands and Denmark, and of those at *Länder* level in Germany. If concepts such as the ILM are to have meaning in policy-related terms then the nature of the institutionalized bridge to industrial and occupational markets has to be established. These appear to vary from one European country to another.

It is paradoxical that legally enacted minima should exist in precisely those countries in which strong localized bargaining makes them least effective. The explanation is perhaps to be found in the desire of liberal politicians to provide a 'countervailing power' acting on behalf of disadvantaged groups in the bargaining process that characterizes the distribution of income in these countries. For example in the UK the industrially based Wages Councils were set up to foster the growth of voluntary association among the employees in chosen industries: 'It was hoped that the statutory machinery... would in time be replaced by voluntary collective bargaining' (Royal Commission on Trade Unions and Employers' Associations 1968). These councils originated in the Trade Boards Act of 1909 as a means of dealing with the evils of 'sweated labour'. They consist of equal numbers of persons representing workers and employers, together with up to three independent members, one of whom is chairman.

At the time of the Donovan Report (1968) there were 57 Wages Councils covering about 3.500.000 workers in about 500.000 establishments. Nearly 2.500.000 of the workers covered were in catering, retail distribution and hairdressing. The Royal Commission found the purpose of the councils to be largely abortive in many instances. Trade-union membership remained relatively low in these industries even though, in almost all cases, the workers were represented on the councils by national trade-union officials. A previous study (Baylis 1964) had suggested that the difficulties of recruiting and organizing membership in these industries were such that unions rarely attempted to grow beyond a core of members in large establishments or among those working for sympathetic employers like the Cooperative Wholesale Society (Co-op). Employers in these industries were also found by the Royal Commission to be reluctant to see them disappear.

A detailed study of the retail distribution trades completed by the National Board for Prices and Incomes one year later showed the Co-op and other companies who recognized unions were the lowest payers among large employers in the industry. The commission criticized on the inefficiency of the Councils in respect to data collection. The report commented that Wages Council industries appeared to be among the lowest paid: 'However there are, it must be noted, other industries not covered by Wages Councils which have low earnings levels and there are pockets of low paid workers in many industries which enjoy relatively high average earnings' (Royal Commission on Trade Unions and Employers Associations 1968: 66). Furthermore:

There is ... a good deal of evidence that statutory intervention does not result in raising the pay of lower paid workers in relation to other workers... Nor does pay in Wage Council industries seem to have improved significantly in relation to that in other industries (1968: 66).

It has been argued by Feldstein (1975) that minimum wage legislation prevents youths and other minority groups from 'purchasing' training by accepting wage levels lower than those offered to experienced primary sector workers. Doeringer and Piore (1975) argue that this would simply lead to the supplanting of more costly workers, often older secondary market workers, with teenagers, and could result in more registered unemployed. It is unlikely that the kind of occupations to which minimum wage legislation would be applicable would offer much by way of training anyway.

Two alternatives to legally enacted minima seem to be suggested from historical experience. The first is that of extending a nationally negotiated settlement to all in similar jobs to those for whom a wage increase has been bargained. This is the traditional manner of agreeing increases in France and Italy where local union organization is weak but leaders may call for one-day demonstrations of solidarity from workers across all market segments, union members or (more frequently) not. It is also contained in the more prosaic British form of Section 11 of the Employment Protection Act of 1975 which allows terms and conditions agreed in one district or company to be extended to another through the use of compulsory arbitration in Industrial Tribunals. This law has been in existence in one form or another since 1940. Its initial effect was to speed the local recognition of newly unionized bargaining units during the Second World War (Bain 1969; Roberts et al. 1971). Little subsequent use has been made of it by low-paid manual workers although it has continued to be a means whereby relatively well paid groups of white-collar workers have gained employer recognition (i.e. the effect of imposed settlements has generally been to cause employers to opt for union recognition and free collective bargaining).

In most of Northern Europe (U.K., Denmark, the Netherlands) attempts to assist disadvantaged groups through statutorily assisted extensions to collective bargaining appear to have met with little success. The reason seems to lie in the unwillingness of employers in the low-paid secondary sector to recognize and maintain the initiative—both substantive and procedural—brought about by statutory or legal intervention. However opposition to the 'levelling up' of disadvantaged groups also comes from strategically placed groups of skilled workers. There is considerable evidence that the 'solidarity' principle adopted by the Swedish Confederation of Trade Unions (LO) in 1951 had the effect of compressing the spread of earnings across all industries (Meidner 1974).

But the wave of unofficial strikes that began with the miners of Kiruna in 1969 and spread to professional and white-collar groups demonstrated the limits to the malleability of the reward structure vis à vis the perceived structure of status and responsibility (Tersmeden 1972).

There appears to be a greater willingness on the part of French and Italian employers to respond to substantive settlements at national level. In the absence of widespread efficient union organization at local market or ILM level it is difficult to obtain sufficient data to know whether the policies of 'national unity' adopted by unions in these countries are uniformly effective in bringing about any real changes at establishment level (Sturmthal 1965).

The second, and perhaps most effective means to alleviating relative poverty, has been through the deliberate use of incomes policy in some European states to reduce earnings differentials. This suffers from the same debility as that of the solidarity principle of the LO: there are political limits to the amount by which a government can redistribute income in this overt fashion without encountering a 'backlash' from the better-off groups.

Job creation programmes

Labour market segmentalists would see the major attack on the sources of disadvantage as coming through the creation of new jobs in the primary sector with reinforcive action on the part of the government in the areas of investment, training and other forms of expenditure designed to favour the movement of workers from the secondary sector into the new jobs so created. The 'Great Society' programme of Lyndon B. Johnson was seen by many American reformers to contain elements of such a redistribution in employment opportunities for blacks and in regionally depressed areas of the U.S. Its relative failure to do so demonstrated two things at least: firstly the difficulty of moving the decision-making parameters of local employers of labour through exhortation or through fiscal measures that are not specifically related to certain courses of action (for example the training grant levy scheme of the U.K.); and secondly that the frustrated expectations created by such aspirational policy formulation can, and did, lead to the formation of pressure groups to bring about the intended goals of the legislation by alternative means.

The type of 'job-creation' programmes currently undertaken by national governments in Europe, under the guidance of the European Community, are generally designed to alleviate the growing problem of structural unemployment, particularly among school leavers. A widespread criticism of these programmes has been that far from transferring secondary jobs upwards to the primary market, they reward the employer for creating peripheral or temporary jobs to the ultimate detriment of long-term or core jobs.

Research done at the Higher Institute for Labour Studies of the Catholic University of Louvain by Cossey and others (Cossey et al. 1977) evaluating the Belgian government's 1976 temporary job creation programme for young people has shown that those who succeed in getting a job within the terms of this programme (administered by the state employment service) do not complain about being kept at the periphery of the actual work force, but are puzzled by the fact that they get only 75 per cent of the salary of their non-temporary colleagues for doing the same work, even though their employers are quite content with their level of productivity. About 20,000 youngsters per year have found a job in that way, but it is estimated that only one third of those people went into jobs that did not exist at the time the law came into force on 30 March 1976.

The Belgian temporary-job law, with its provision that all enterprises with more than 100 employees are obliged to take in jobless young people (under 25) at the rate of one per cent of their work force and to give them an on-the-job training during the six or twelve months of their stay, did succeed in reducing unemployment of young people. The year after the passing of the law unemployment among young people declined by about three per cent, but this average was not equally distributed. The report concludes that the law works in favour of male youths with higher qualifications, because the unemployment figures of young women and of lower skilled young men continued to rise. This supported the researchers' hypothesis that firms take in recruits under the temporary job programme for jobs which they would have filled anyway, but perhaps the process was speeded up by the programme, and accomplished at lower wages. Almost fifty per cent of the jobs filled in this way were jobs for which demand already existed at the time the law came into force or at least were not specially created for the programme, but were nevertheless included in the one per cent rate for the particular firms. So the temporary job programme in one third to one half of the cases, while reducing the number of inactive young people, at the same time stressed the segmentation of the work force by on the one hand filling already existing marginal jobs against even lower wages, and on the other hand creating new marginal jobs which are added to the existing marginal segments.

A major difficulty in enforcing such a law is that the state employment service and its regional and local branches has a very low rate of penetration in the job market. It was estimated by Lammertijn (1975) that only one out of every ten job movements in Belgium pass through the official labour market channels. This means that the services offered by the employment service have a tendency to be limited to job seekers who present problem cases and who have to take whatever jobs are available. The report of the comparative study by Blankenburg and Krautkramer on the possibilities and limits of an active labour market policy by employment offices (1976) confirms this impression. There is very little possibility of adapting the demand side of the market to the conditions appertaining to the supply side without the employment service penetrating the internal labour market and influencing a firm's manpower policy.

Training, job creation and the internal labour market

The viability of a labour market strategy formulated at macro level ultimately depends upon its implementation at micro level. Labour market segmentation results from a complex of 'rational' (economic) and 'irrational' (socio-emotional) factors which operate upon the employment contract. For most neo-classical theorists this transaction is represented by the 'marginal cost: marginal revenue product' equation; the institutional context of the firm remains 'a black box'. Even work such as that of Mabry (1973) takes the existence of work and job structures as being non-problematic, as indeed does most of the body of theory existing in organizational sociology and psychology. The question of control, power and authority as a problematic in the creation and maintenance of particular jobs and job structures rarely enters the literature of manpower planning.

On the other hand the institutional school of economists, largely represented by the faculty and alumni of schools of industrial relations, have concentrated their analysis almost exclusively on the process of collective bargaining, rather than upon 'job regulation' per se. This has resulted in a void in our knowledge of the process by which a given marginal propensity to invest leads to the creation of jobs of this kind, in that region: a process in which the entrepreneurs' knowledge of labour practices in that region may be extremely influential in determining his ultimate decision. Continental scholars have realized this gap rather better than their Anglo-Saxon contemporaries. A survey of two thousand West German firms monitored the measures taken by employers to cope with falling product market demand in the economic crisis of 1973-1974. The researcher, Schultz-Wild, found that a firm does not react immediately to each and every change in demand, but tries to apply external and internal market strategies, as well as trying to bring flexibility into the use of its manpower within the rules set by agreements with unions and by the law.

In times of crisis the firm tends to find solutions to its manpower problems on the internal labour market. In the first instance a firm tries to:

1. *stabilize* its work force–if that does not work, what measures do firms take to adapt their work force to the crisis? These measures mainly concern:
2. *selection*: Which categories of worker are affected by the crisis?

As regards *stabilization* of the work force there are two main problems to be solved:

1. How to use workers in the production process given the existing organization and technology;
2. What to do with workers who are at the firm's disposal in career terms (Schultz-Wild 1978).

The author discovers several patterns of adaptation to changes in the labour market. For different firms there are various possibilities for screening internal labour markets from the influences of the environment, or, to put it differently, to establish a balance between supply and demand within the ILM. The time period over which changes in the environment takes place seems critical. He divides companies into three types:

1. *Seasonal work* such as in building and catering. In this case stabilizing the work force is rarely possible, delivery time is immediate or very short. These firms have to operate on the external market, especially on the unstructured '*Jedermannsteilarbeitsmarkt*' (Lutz and Sengenberger 1974), or the marginal 'reserve army'. Here redundancy and/or reduction in working hours are relatively easy.
2. *Firms with strong ILM's*, such as in electricity, public services, and so on. Here workers mostly have firm-specific qualifications and a strong commitment to the firm–built up in times of scarcity of labour–through career opportunities, pension schemes, etc. A fall in the product demand will scarcely be felt within the ILM, and will at most lead to measures stretched out over long periods (e.g. a temporary reduction in working hours). Redundancy is here almost impossible, or needs special legitimation, or is reached slowly and over time by natural causes and 'golden handshakes'.
3. A third type of adaptation strategy is to maintain part of the work force as a stable element and part as a flexible element. This split in the work force can be brought about functionally or geographically. 'Secondary'–type workers are easily dismissed or reshuffled internally (see Mendius and Sengenberger 1976).

The functional link made by economists between capital investment and job creation (with its concomitant training needs) may thus be traced through the organizational process of decision making within companies. An understanding of the training and educational needs of a regional and national economy must contain some knowledge, or assumptions, about the nature of management recruitment needs and the manner in which they are formulated and met by the institutes of education and training. The lead time required to change any long training programme, that is the time required between the decision to change its content or format and the production of the first graduate from such a modified course, may be as long as seven years (in the case of a university graduate for instance). The formulation of the needs of industry by businessmen might well add to this lead time quite considerably.

In fact the empirical study of management decision-making suggests that the decision to invest in new plant and to embark on the series of complementary operations such as job restructuring and training, tends to be of a 'marginal' kind and short term in its projected payback period–a 'suck it and see' approach (Braybrooke and Lindblom 1963; Mintzberg 1975; Loveridge 1978).

Even in large corporate structures using operations research techniques and sophisticated methods of probability forecasting, senior executives are forced to make value judgements. The degree to which uncertainty affects managerial decisions will be related to the perceived variability within the firm's environment. This includes changes in both the product market and the internal work flow, both of which may vary in periodicity, range, scope, and content (Child 1973).

The constraints placed on an employer's actions by virtue of his position in the decision-making hierarchy of the firm will also affect his perception of the needs of his organization and how they can best be fulfilled. Research carried out by Loveridge and his former colleagues at the London School of Economics suggests that changes in task considered to be 'minor' or 'experimental' were incorporated into line jobs by an incremental process of decision making at the level of first or second line management (Roberts et al. 1972: 320). They only emerged as 'problems' in terms of job grading when resort had to be made to the external labour market: otherwise transfers within the internal labour market of the firm could satisfy a firm's needs over a considerable period of time. Even relatively major capital investment projects could be undertaken on the basis of internal retraining with very little concomitant regrading.

Decisions which involved staff management–such as personnel managers–in a co-ordinative rather than service function–were likely to be those which concerned the ex post facto rationalization of a series of such lower level decisions. This was accomplished by the formation of a new grade and the placing of some formal qualification upon entrance to the grade. The chosen qualification was a product of the existing range of formal certification and, by this time, the aspirations of the trade unions and/or quasi-professional institutes. The occasion for this decision will normally be when through the engagement of labour from the external labour market, the employer is forced to consider an occupational reference group as being relevant to the pay and conditions of his present employees doing a similar job to those outside the company. By this time the matching of vocational training objectives present in the external system may be only loosely related to the characteristics of the job as it has become defined in a cluster of tasks within the work organization. Institutional forces, including the vested interests of educationalists, make it difficult to change the pattern of external (vocational) education and training in the short run to meet the emerging (specific) needs of the firm.

At senior executive level the view of management is formed in a milieu that is usually somewhat divorced from the immediate job creation process. Time horizons are usually somewhat longer but his considerations must be mainly directed towards the much broader external operating environment comprised of the community and his company's competitors and associates. As the organization grows larger his first-hand knowledge of current product or operations management tends to become somewhat slight.

Decisions at this level are generally taken in relation to long-term financial criteria. For example decisions *to close down plants* are generally confirmed by the Board of Directors: they generally have a much more definitive and direct effect on employee status (that is by making them all unemployed) than have investment decisions which *bring jobs into being*. (These latter are much more affected by the configuration of control that exists within the workplace, e.g. union or professional influence on line managers.) Board intervention in the area of manpower policy varies according to the type of company in which it takes place and the amount of government intervention involved through statutory requirements in respect to the qualification, career, working conditions and participation of employees (Loveridge 1978).

Research carried out by the sociology department of the University of Antwerp (De Ceuster 1978) suggests that in this management decision-making process different segments of the market are being tapped and, coincidentally, moulded by the outcomes. Line managers will tend to select and train employees from the PI sector of the labour market (see Chapter 6). More senior plant managers and professional managers in staff functions recruit from the PE sector. Personnel departments go outside for labour in the SE sector mainly to fill jobs in the SI sector of the internal labour market. Even here the portals are heavily screened by institutionalized controls. Jobs may be filled by simply advertising them *internally* so that outside the firm only relatives and friends of existing employees know of their existence.

These types of empirical studies not only enable a more sophisticated understanding of the operation of market and political forces, but also contribute to the interpretation we give to data based on questionnaire surveys of either personnel managers or senior executives. Often the

demand schedules constructed from such surveys provide the basis for
manpower forecasting at governmental level. Unless such data are
placed against the context in which the data was generated it seems
unlikely that their meaning can be correctly understood. For example
Loveridge (1972) has pointed out:

For the manpower planner, the establishment of a demand and/or supply function for a
given group of employees is paramount. Yet forecasts of demand for similar groups are
often widely disparate not only from the eventually achieved levels of recruitment, but also
from estimates made by other forecasters. One of the major problems is that of definition.
This is not simply a lack of data, but of who is defining the occupation and for what
purpose. In the L.S.E. study it was found that several employers awarded technician and
technologist status to those who aspired to it as a short-term sop to their ambition, or, on
yet other occasions, as a sop to the administrative needs of the Industrial Training Board.

   In the long run, however, the employer's priorities have to relate to the skill mix required
to meet any exigency facing his firm. He, therefore, places a considerable premium on
flexibility in the use of labour within his plant and the specificity of skills to his own uses in
order to minimize outside competition for his staff. In periods of rapid organizational and
technological innovation the level of interdetermination in the allocation of skills, and even
in the nature of the skill or knowledge required to perform certain tasks, increases. Faced
with the need to take decisions in order to match product market innovation the employer
tends to exploit available resources. In the first instance long established means of supply
tend to be used. Such institutions once used for the new purpose may continue to serve long
after they have outlined their effectiveness. For example, the first industrial technicians
were recruited from a craft apprenticeship. This still remains a major source of supply until
the present day with little adaptation in content to serve the new purpose (Loveridge 1972).

The bureaucratization of policy making

The laws of work and of social security have a long history in all Western
European countries. In each one of them the pressures of the early
Industrial Revolution caused an erosion or total breakdown of historical
arrangements. In England the body of labour legislation that had
preserved the structure of labour regulation and social security since
Elizabeth I came under increasing stress in the eighteenth century and
was largely repealed in the early 1800s. The laisser-faire strategies of
early British entrepreneurs destroyed the remnants of a relatively
homogeneous framework of working conditions, wages and social security, just as they destroyed the hierarchy of 'natural' privilege and
responsibility upon which it was based.

   In some other European countries the transition to a modern basis for
labour market policy was much more direct than in the United
Kingdom–Perry suggests that the 1964 Industrial Training Act was the

first major interventionary move by the British Government to control occupational entrance since the Statute of Artificers in 1563 (Perry 1976: 13). The system of occupational control by 'voluntary associations' which grew up in nineteenth-century Britain contrasts with the relatively centralized system of co-ordination and control in most other European countries. This is especially true of vocational training and education. It is important to call these facts into mind in any discussion of the application of a general theory: the formulation of policy should be carried out within the context of the institutions that exist to implement them and against a knowledge of the background of the present position within each country.

Nevertheless we see a move towards some outward resemblance of homogeneity in the formulation of labour market strategies in the member states of the European Economic Community: a congruity which owes a great deal to the co-ordinative and innovative role played by the Social Secretariat of that body. Yet in the design of the formal structures for the administration of labour market policy we encounter all the familiar problems of large administrative bodies: to centralize or to disperse controls? To specialize or to generalize the tasks of administration? Van Voorden (1975) describes the increasing professionalization of services within the Dutch labour market agencies. At the same time he suggests that pressure groups such as trade unions are being incorporated into the administrative structure of these agencies. Clearly the dangers of increasing bureaucratization combined with the insidious incorporation of 'independent' pressure groups is very real: the more so in mainland Europe where such pressure groups are themselves highly centralized in their control structures.

On the other hand the need for specialized attention to each aspect of an 'active' market policy is obviously very real; as is the need for an integrated and co-ordinated approach. Jain and Sloane (1977) have suggested the existence of five different approaches in Europe:

1. the fair employment concept designed to eliminate discrimination at work and in preparation for work;
2. the income distribution focus or the solidarity principle;
3. the job-creation approach to segmented labour markets;
4. the selective underpinning of less competitive groups:
5. the isolation of specific characteristics such as physical disability for special treatment.

These measures are implemented through a variety of means. The existence of industrial tribunals or labour courts is designed to ensure the implementation of anti-discriminative legislation in some countries; in other areas of policy it is the responsibility of rival pressure groups to impose constraints upon each other.

The argument put forward by segmentalists that the operation of all such diverse measures is at best self-negatory and at worst acts only to reinforce existing barriers to entry can only be countered on the basis of the longitudinal monitoring of their operation in different environments. This we would argue is only likely to be effective at the level of the firm: because it is at this level that the struggle for control over the work process is carried out between the parties. The assumption that occupational categories are neutrally descriptive taxonomies which provide a suitable basis for manpower forecasting seems an excessively naive one. Even when, as is suggested by the European Community's directive of 14 November 1973 on equal pay, job evaluation is imposed on a national scale, the equation of effort and reward made in the workplace is subject to interpretation by those within the situation (Behrend 1959; Teulings 1976: 270).

On the other hand the partial analysis presented by the neo-classicists has contributed to an ad hoc approach to national legislation which can only have added to rather than reduced the complexity of the framework of legislation and regulation impacting upon the firm and upon the internal labour market. There may well be a strong argument for returning to the fundamentalist position of Schmid (1976), but certainly there are grounds for being extremely suspicious of arguments such as those that Rhea (1976) advances in relation to social security or that have been advanced by human capital theorists in relation to training. (Table 7 is designed to show some of the diverse factors acting upon the supply and demand for training).

Much more may be gained by adopting an approach which encompasses all of these factors in a feedback model of *family* (rather than individual) deprivation as Jackson attempts to do (1972) and to match this with an input/output matrix of social welfare. However even this attempt fails to account for the effect that institutions, such as those concerned with retraining, have on the market as a whole. Jackson assumes, as do most economists, that resources are freely transferable between uses and that vested interest, and therefore conflict, does not exist.

So long as labour market segmentation is approached under a series of

Table 7. Some factors affecting the supply and demand for training and education.

Factors underlying supply curve	Factors underlying elasticity of supply	Institutional facilities bringing about «equilibrium»	Factors underlying elasticity of demand for labour	Factors underlying demand curve for labour
Population: size, geographical distribution, propensity and ability to move *Age and sex*: (stage of life cycle) Genetic 'ability' Family of origin Conjugal family Community Individual perception of labour market: how it exists (available openings; relative rewards – extrinsic/intrinsic) *Reward output*: consumer goods, prestige, deference, lifestyle	Definition of own 'project' (i.e. short-term and long-term normal 'income' = f ('personal success')) Occupational interest group *Employee orientation to work*: (1) craft/'cosmopolitan'; (2) bureaucratic/local; (3) instrumental/residual	*Very short term*: no training: 1. Labour 'pool' 2. Labour exchange *Short term*: training 3. On-the-job training 4. Local short courses *Longer term*: Training/education 5. Apprenticeship 6. Professional training *Very long term*: education 7. Secondary school 8. Technical college 9. University *Skills*: knowledge/tasks — Generally poor / Generally good; particularistic – specific and manipulative; *Universalistic* at varying degrees of specificity and abstraction depending on sensitivity to demands of users; Universalistic broad and generalized base for further specialized training	*Employer's needs* f (subjective definition of organizational 'success') Employers' association *Employer orientation to work*: (1) Market-directed, (2) Employee directed, (3) Task-directed *Reward output*: human 'capital', life chances, earnings, differences, career opportunities, e.g. market power	Choice of product markets Choice of technology Forms of skills Task division Role structure Types of occupation offered: (1) bridging occupations, (2) closing occupations, (3) preparatory occupations, (4) career-step occupations, (5) incremental hierarchy, (6) residual

Source: Seminar paper presented by R. Loveridge at the London School of Economics, May 1969.

discrete policy headings–social welfare, training, job security, and so on–it is possible to see this conflict as being confined to narrow issues. By adopting a broader view radical economists have attempted, however crudely, to delineate the boundaries of a wider basis of structural conflict within society. Whilst holding an internal logic, which gives them consistency and rigour of argument, the partial-equilibrium theories of neo-classicist analysts may appear to have as much general validity as that of the beliefs held by the ancients on the closed nature of their universe. These pre-historical beliefs were conditioned by the closed nature of the communities of Ancient Egypt or Early Greece. They would, of course, prove woefully inadequate in getting a man to the Moon, just as partial equilibrium analysis offers little guidance on the operation of a dynamic and integrated labour market strategy.

8. The labour market as an arena

Distributive justice and labour market policy

Work done in the Netherlands by researchers of the Catholic University of Tilburg (Van Wezel et al. 1976) and by the Scientific Advisory Council of the Dutch government, the Dutch 'think tank' (W.R.R. 1977), in their report on active and non-active members of the population, has pointed to an interesting assumption underlying much labour market policy. A segmentalist model of the working population is generally taken for granted, but this perspective is rarely extended to take in the differentiated view of work and work activities held by the workers themselves. Both reports contend that although work is still the most favoured way to earn one's living, a growing proportion of the population does not actually work any more. In the Netherlands in 1968 there were seven active people against each non-active one, in 1975 there were only four active people against each non-active one. (Active people being those who actually participate in the labour process and who receive remuneration for doing so. Non-active persons are those persons in the total population who are not active as defined above, like the jobless, the disabled and the sick.)

The relationship between the active and the non-active population is regulated by distributive mechanisms, like the social security system, the system of rewards and their distribution, manpower policy, and in the long term the structure of the economy and the educational system. The process of expulsion from the active population does not occur haphazardly, it is a selective process, which hits some groups like women, the young, the very old, foreign workers and handicapped persons more than others. Those groups are more vulnerable than others because they do not come up to the standards which are being used as regards the distribution of the limited amounts of work available to all. In that respect people use social as well as economic standards to measure justice as regards work activities. According to those standards not all groups in society have the right and the duty to work to an equal extent

(Van Wezel et al. 1976: 99). For example, measures to promote the provision of jobs are considered more applicable to men than to women, more to older, experienced people than to very young ones, more to men with families than to single people, and so on.

The central importance of work can, according to these authors, also be ascribed to the fact that there are no adequate alternatives to work as a meaningful way of participating in society. As a result, those who are forced to be 'inactive' make a rather negative appraisal of their situation. In this respect they perceive the mechanisms of the labour market as distributing injustice rather than justice. This is strengthened by the fact that people often become inactive involuntarily because they do not have the opportunity to participate in the labour process in the way they want.

One of the reasons for this is the spectacular increase in the level of educational qualification of the working population, which leads to higher expectations in the content of work and an increasing dislike for the inconvenient aspects of work (dirt, noise, smell, and so on). A Dutch investigation, done by Dr. H. Zanders and modelled on the Ann Arbor 'Quality of working life' studies, found that the proportion of respondents claiming their skills were under-utilized increased with level of education (17.9 per cent for those with primary school only, to 46.8 per cent for university graduates), and was found to be highest in industry and lowest in public utilities. Unfavourable working conditions were pinpointed by respondents as the most important problem area (Zanders et al. 1977: 84, 162-163). The Tilburg researchers point to the fact that extrinsic factors, like wages and working conditions, are the most decisive factors in the job choice and recruitment process of workers. Intrinsic factors, like utilization of skills, about which exchange of information seems less possible during the initial induction phase, seem to gain in importance thereafter (Van Wezel et al. 1976: 39-40). Several kinds of reactions are possible which may or may not lead to inactivity. Sickness absenteeism and change of job are feasible individual responses, strikes or 'go-slow' are collective responses: both lead to longer or shorter periods of inactivity.

As more and more workers opt out of the active population to join the ranks of the inactives, there clearly arises the difficult choice for labour market policy whether to accept the increasing inactivity or to try to stem the tide and try to reduce the number of inactive persons in the population. This choice has important consequences. The phenomenon of inactivity not only draws heavily on collective economic resources, especially social security benefits, which (according to the authors) have reached the limit of what can be borne by the active population in some European countries, but also the psychological readiness of the active population to bear the burden of the growing number of inactive persons. This problem becomes more and more a problem not only of the financial capacity of a nation but also of its social solidarity (W.R.R. 1977: 5).

In the formulation of labour market policy in the Netherlands the job market and the wage market tend to be treated separately; the level at which wage levels are formulated (the macro level) is quite different from the level at which the problems of the returns from work are determined (the micro level). Thus far, most industrial conflicts have been about the returns from work, but Van Wezel and his co-authors predict that in the near future the active population will increasingly resist paying for the inactive ones and that, perhaps more important for the future of our system of industrial relations, many of the industrial disputes of the future will be between the active persons themselves, competing for the scarcely available agreeable jobs of high intrinsic quality and without inconveniences.

Feelings of distributive injustice will come to the fore as disadvantaged groups become conscious of their inferior position and what they can do about it, either individually or collectively. In this respect a reorientation of the policies of trade unions and employers' associations may be necessary. Trade unionists have already turned to the possibility of bargaining about the quantity and quality of manning levels. Employers' associations want to reduce the number of inactives by imposing stricter controls on security benefits, a more stringent application of the notion of suitable work, and revision of the criteria for inability to work. But in general these changes act to protect workers in the PI sector of the economy. Redundancies are largely directed at workers in the SI sector. Although administrative staff and middle management have also been exposed to the effects of 'rationalization' in the numbers employed, in general the result of all recent legislation enacted within member states of the EEC has been to increase the job security of workers in the PI sector.

The effect of long-term structural unemployment may be reinforcive over time, not only in terms of the effect on the individual ego, but also collectively. We have previously suggested that the stock of 'cultural capital' owned by a group or individual gave it a certain advantage in knowing how 'the system works'. It is virtually impossible for newcomers to a workplace to exercise influence until they have achieved the credibility that knowledge of the technical and social structure of the firm brings with it. This cultural capital may extend outside the work organization to knowledge of the trade, markets, communities, and so on. This knowledge can only be accumulated by people who are actually *at work*. Regaining a place in the work community after a long spell of unemployment is often made difficult, if not impossible, by the deterioration that has taken place in the cultural capital of the individual–he has no knowledge of the system and no contacts from whom to replenish his knowledge. Hence the group that maintains its grip over employment opportunities gains in relative power, as the unemployed lose their knowledge of the system. This occurred in the 1920s and 1930s in Britain and France. The circumstances of World War II served to reduce these disparities in work experience: in the 1980s it seems likely that they may grow greater.

Competition or conflict?

The characteristics of the macro system described in the Dutch reports may be seen as the result of a conscious design of employers who have manipulated the market to create occupational sexist and ethnic divisions (Morse 1969; Edwards et al. 1975) or the result of the unconscious workings of the capitalist system (Doeringer and Piore 1971; Bosanquet and Standing 1972). Whatever has been the cause, and the latter process seems the more likely, the result is the same. Free competition has tended to give way to monopoly bargaining on both sides of the labour market. The increasing incorporation or co-optation of trade unions and professional bodies into the administrative structure of labour market agencies has ensured, not an absence of conflict, but rather its expression in a bureaucratically legitimated form–and often directed at issues that are themselves matters of procedure rather than of substance.

How far can the labour market administration influence the demand for labour? To achieve the goal of government labour market policy it is necessary to apply and coordinate not only measures to improve the supply of labour but also those which influence the demand for it. In the Federal Republic of Germany the terms of reference of the labour market administration are largely limited to managing the supply side, whereas in Sweden they traditionally include also measures to influence demand (location of industry, investment for employment, building permits). Where the terms of reference of the labour administration are limited the question arises how far measures of labour market policy are coordinated with other measures of economic and regional policy. Where the labour administration's scope is wide, on the contrary, problems arise over the overload of the administration with political conflicts and a clash of interests (Blankenburg and Kraut-kramer 1976).

Who are the gladiators?

But underlying these institutional and institutionalized conflicts there is the fundamental conflict focused upon the regulation of work itself.

Instead of viewing the labour market as a mechanism for the adjustment of disequilibrium between labour supply and labour demand, we view it as an arena within which individuals attempt to satisfy material, psychological, social, and cultural needs, and achieve personal goals, within the perceived limits of a specifiable occupational structure, whether national or local (Martin and Fryer, 1973: 22).

We differ with this description of the market only insofar as we believe that the specification of occupational boundaries is often one of the most important areas of workplace and labour market conflict.

For the utilitarians the spontaneous division of labour gave rise to a natural identity of interest whose harmony 'becomes ceaselessly more perfect through the multiplication of specialities' (Halevy 1955: 118). But, in the views of Freedman (1976: 115):

This very profileration of specialities lies at the heart of systematic market imperfections. Classical economists believed in the atomistic effects of the division of labour, and neoclassicists have simply carried this belief along as part of their theoretical baggage. It turns out, however, that as economic activities become more diverse, more and more occupations emerge, differences among industries contribute additional distinctions, and the 'spirit of corporation' becomes manifest in ever more imaginative disguises.

Marginal workers often have little or no occupational identity. In a study of stigmatized occupations in Britain, Saunders (1976: 429) concludes:

Vagrancy and transiency are to a degree attributable to the seasonality in the industry, but is primarily a function of the homelessness and rootlessness of the low crystalliser, participating in one or more of the stigmatised occupations.

In this description he refers to the process by which a number of attributes of a given occupation, including the life-style of its occupants, crystallizes to give the work-role an identifiable status in society (Lenski 1954). The permanent *indeterminacy* and precariousness of status surrounding most marginal occupations (Mack 1956; Goffman 1968) is seen by Saunders to account for stigmatization. In other words no group of employees or employers have found it worth 'closing' the occupation and thus giving it a formal identity through training or licencing arrangements of either a generalized or localized kind.

The task content of these occupations is generally intrinsically monotonous and dirty, giving little opportunity for the expression of skill or personal potential. Such jobs are only undertaken as a means to the end of economic survival. Paradoxically they often exist in service industries side by side with highly professional occupations. In part this is a function of the division of labour, the surgeon or chef de cuisine cannot offer his highly esoteric contribution before a hierarchy of retainers have prepared the consumer for the pièce de résistance. But the existence of this social hierarchy also insulates the maestro from the customer and consumer of his labours. Senior members of the hierarchy are encouraged to have a strong 'moral' involvement in their service work, but their most junior colleagues have no more than the most 'calculative' view of their work.

Interest group formation

A possible categorization of disadvantaged employees appears to emerge from our analysis of the market and legal-political forces which work to create their situation. The sub-segments of the secondary market might be by tested groups within the market having more or less strategic identity. We suggest four categories:

1. The individually disadvantaged: those whose source of economic disability is peculiar to their personal situation. They comprise a group which is too heterogeneous or too small in numbers to have any effective monopolistic impact upon the workings of the market even if they were able to seek a 'shelter' in protective legislation or in a pressure group (see Freedman 1976: 113-129). Some groups of handicapped people fall into this category.
2. The collectively disadvantaged who conceive of their situation in personal terms and who are unaware of any means of rectifying this *personal* situation: these are the stigmatized group of people upon whom the dualists concentrate their analysis. They comprise workers who, because of their short-term time horizons, have extremely

explicit and localized reference groups and are unaware of others in a situation similar to their own, or more likely, are unable to conceive of any means of legally obtaining any redress. The exigencies presented by their immediate survival needs appear to be paramount in determining their behaviour patterns.

3. The collectively disadvantaged who have become aware of their existence as an 'economic community'; a group that is aware of the existence of a 'public good'—the concept of public good or common good is central to the study of welfare economics. It is here defined as any good such that, if any person X, in any group $X1$, $X2...Xn$ consumes it, it cannot feasibly be withheld from others in that group. In other words, those who do not purchase or pay for any of the public or collective good cannot physically or socially be excluded or kept from sharing in the consumption of the good, as they can where individually attained goods are concerned. The achievement of any common interest means that a public or collective good has to be provided on a *group* basis or as Olson puts it, 'the very fact that a goal or purpose is common to a group means that no one in the group is excluded from the benefit or satisfaction brought about by its achievement' (1968: 130). We describe the *realization* of this economic interdependency within a group in the term 'economic community.'

4. The collectively disadvantaged who have become aware of their existence as a 'political community' or pressure group; a group that has become aware of the legal-administrative means of acquiring a 'public good'. It applies to a greater or lesser extent to members of trade unions, trade associations and professional bodies. In each of these groups there are politically active individuals or nuclei from whom most initiatives stem and by means of which the dispersed and heterogeneous members of this category attain a bridge to the legal-administration infrastructure of the state, industry or employing body and also acquire an identity and significance within it. (Here it may be noticed that our definition of 'political awareness' differs from the Marxist definition of 'political consciousness'—*Klasse für sich*—in that we do not assume the existence of a collective *consensus* as to political *objectives*. We are only recognizing a *concurrence* of individual views of self-advancement around a collective strategy. The crucial difference between an economic awareness of the existence of a common good and the coming into being of a political awareness is

that of acquiring knowledge of and/or access to the political means of allocating economic resources and in particular to job opportunities. The existence or non-existence of a 'political consciousness' in the Marxist sense is not seen to be significant to the operation of labour market strategy in European countries, member-states of the European Community within the forseeable future. (Should it ever come into existence on a scale that would affect Community policy there would presumably be no need for academics to interpret its meaning.)

The advantages of recognizing this form of political-economic taxonomy are several:

1. It recognizes the possibility of a sequential movement and even the existence of a cycle in the formation of collective practices and institutionalized regulations which form barriers to mobility between labour market segments.
2. As we have said earlier, Doeringer and Piore's model is, like the neo-classical model, based on a 'slice out of time'. It is of the classical comparative-static form which contains no explanation of how the internal labour market and the concomitant environment in which the firm came into being change from one state to another. There are a number of factors discussed in this book that may be seen as contributing to the growth or decline of segmentation in the labour market. They include the growth of the large employer and the organizational structure and methods used by different types of employers as well as the differing orientations to work displayed by the employees in their approach to the employment transaction.
3. It is extremely difficult to generalize about social trends in a cross-cultural manner without a similar data base relating to possible sources of causality within each country. Yet the very differences in culture that give rise to the observed differences in labour market behaviour in each country are themselves affecting any possible sources of structural causation. The four-part categorization of collective behaviour, crude as it is, can be seen to present a means of organizing the empirical data across all of the categories we have studied.
4. Since statutory legislation has to be worked out in terms which are determined by the group forces described above, it is as well to take into account the political means to the *implementation* of policy in any

framework which has to be used for the policy decisions. In particular it is important to recognize the *processes* by which market segments become institutionalized and occupational and other groups come into existence. The role of group *protest*, which is creating major discontinuities in market practices, is completely ignored in both the dualist and radical models. Yet it seems likely that any major abrupt change in the structure of individual expectations experienced on a collective basis leads to a new volatility in group behaviour (Crane 1958; Smelser 1964). Thus the initial reaction to the improved opportunities for blacks in the U.S. provided by President Johnson's legislation of the mid-1960s was a collectively experienced frustration at that group's inability to obtain its de jure rights. The currently experienced militancy among women's groups in most Western states is largely directed at *realizing* the de jure rights contained in newly drafted but as yet ineffective statutes.

Another example of the effect of legislation in bringing about group consciousness is provided by the effect that statutory rights to union recognition among white-collar employees in the U.K. and Canada (Bain 1966, 1971) has had on the rate of unionization, or later by the effects of the Bullock Report (1977) in the U.K. The prospects of all organized groups of employees being offered representation on the boards of large organizations appears to have caused a significant increase in the level of collectivization among British managers. It may be seen that in the latter case of white-collar (PI) employees, legislation effected a (government) desired change in attitudes towards the adoption of a pressure group identity and strategy. In the former case the development of group strategy towards increased militancy among blacks and women was *not* the intention and only occurred because statutory legislation seems to have raised the political awareness of employees.

To be effective in bringing about change, these groups have to acquire status and influence with employers. Experience suggests that employers prefer to treat labour market problems on an individual basis for as long as possible. Examples of what happens when unions make a concerted effort to 'break into' industrial markets in which workers possess secondary market characteristics are to be found in both North America and the U.K. The most famous recent case has been that of the grape pickers in America, when Mexican immigrant farm workers attempted to form locals of the Farmworkers Union in Californian vineyards. A similar, but less dramatic, battle for union recognition has been going on in the British hotel and catering industry over the last ten years.

Doeringer and Piore (1971: 160-162) suggest the use of fiscal measures such as a tax on labour turnover as a means to adjusting consumer preferences among employers. Indirect measures are often unpredictable in their effects: we are inclined to accept the neo-classicists belief in 'economic man' in this respect, and even in a monopolistic market there is usually a wide choice of action which may be taken in response to a change in price brought about by a manipulated tax system.

We believe that the maintenance of anti-discriminative legislation demands the direct intervention by the executive and judiciary on a fairly continuous basis. One may doubt the practicability of this policy as a long-term condition. It would seem more likely that legislation designed to support the birth and growth of self-sustaining blocs of 'countervailing power' representing groups of disadvantaged workers is a more realistic strategy to pursue (Galbraith 1967). There will however be some groups for whom continuous support will be required into the foreseeable future. For these groups the positive sanctions and educative functions of public service agencies are particularly important in generating a change in communal attitudes.

Strategies of aid and enhancement

Disparities in the impact of legislation on the demand side of the secondary market are likely to be matched on the supply side by widespread ignorance among potential workers and an inability to use the administrative procedures set up as a result of its enactment. Even among the economically and politically aware it may be necessary, as Olson points out, to maintain a system of localized 'side-payments' in order to secure their continued support for new or existing procedures of job regulation. Given the explicit nature of the frame of reference used to evaluate their market situation, disadvantaged workers have to obtain very short-term positive feedback, in terms of rewards offered, for changes in their economic and social behaviour. But one might add that by the same token, these rewards must be clearly identifiable with the changes in behaviour required of them. Thus Olson implies that meso-level interest groups such as trade unions only remain in being as 'voluntary' associations through the maintenance of a series of semi-autonomous cells or 'closed shops' sensitive to the 'side-payments' required in order to keep members loyal to the broad social goals of the wider organization (Olson 1968). In the same way any educative strategy developed by a state or supranational body must contain an operational element designed to change attitudes and behaviours at the micro level through a system of positive inducements as well as punitive sanctions.

This type of strategy contrasts with the present operation of many aspects of labour market agencies in Western Europe. The concern of these agencies in the allocation of training grants, social security payments, and so on, appear most often to give greater priority to receiving a short-term positive feedback to the agency administering the grants (on behalf of the taxpayer) than upon building a basis for an 'economic community' among minority groups. As well as the desire of social administrators to meet their 'short-term' 'efficiency' goals there is a longer term objective to 'integrate' disadvantaged workers into the broader community built around the PI sector of employment. Research into the sub-markets that constitute the external or secondary sector of employment has hitherto been largely concerned with isolating sources of disadvantage and data relating to the extent of this disadvantage. For example the research carried out in the Netherlands and in the U.K. by social welfare agencies has demonstrated the relative deprivation of immigrants with respect to earnings, job opportunities, housing and other indices.

What seems to us to be lacking in Europe is research of an anthropological nature which seeks to isolate lines of communication and the process of exchange that moves along these networks. In this manner, the static, or comparative static, models provided by both neo-classical and dualist analysts might be augmented and even amended in the light of new knowledge. (Since these peripheral markets seem to occur at all levels of the economy it might have a theoretical significance that goes beyond our present field of study.)

We have concentrated on the statistically identifiable 'marginal worker', but in Chapter 6 and again in this chapter we have brought out the growing extent of unidentified 'drop-outs' among the prime-age members of the work population. We know very little about this group or the part it plays in the economic life of the industrial nation. In less developed economies such as Spain and Greece a large proportion of the population are either self employed or work for small jobbing enterprises, many of which are of a fairly ephemeral nature. But it is equally true that the most industrial societies are filled with individuals acting as entrepreneurs for short-term profit. For example an ongoing study of 'poor whites' and black communities in Detroit has demonstrated a high division of labour and concomitant interdependency between the two communities (Ann Arbor 1976). None of this economic activity is officially recorded since it takes place within the registered 'unemployed' or is of a 'moonlighting' form which is never declared as earned income for the purposes of taxation. A number of other American studies testify to the existence of such markets in urban centres. Any tourist on holiday in a European city is subjected to continuous offers of services from such casual markets. In particular industries, such as those already cited, the presence of the self-employed casual labourer makes possible the arbitrary workings of seasonal or other forms of fluctuating product markets. The identification of these formal activities may indicate exploitation on a much larger scale, such as organized prostitution, dressmaking, or scattered but 'normal' casualness, such as occurs at any agricultural town's market-place.

Responses to the isolation and alienation experienced by disadvantaged workers may therefore be seen to differ significantly. The entrepreneurial response is an aggressively innotative one, generally based on the group solidarity of the traditional (immigrant) family and/or community. Merton (1950) suggests other possibilities causing 'underachievement' in industrial societies–apathy, retreatism, crime, and so on. The nature of the integrative strategies pursued by government agencies have to be sensitive to such responses from the groups that they seek to aid. The aggressively innovative member of an entrepreneurial family may enhance his material well-being and sense of security by joining a motor-car assembly line, but perhaps he does not perceive of long-term security as a primary goal.

The system of values that has given rise to market segmentation has been complemented by the evolution of another set of attitudes and beliefs held by the 'disadvantaged' themselves. In a free market situation (particularly that of Britain and America) interest groups have generally followed an evolutionary path from their early attempts at 'mutual insurance'–or the maintenance of a particular life-style–to the crystallization of mutually shared goals for which the group was prepared to bargain with the employer community–to the legitimation and extension of these achievements through legal enactment (Webb 1897). In bypassing this 'natural' evolutionary path of group formation the imposition of anti-discriminative laws offers little guarantee of their acceptance or implementation by the groups they were intended to aid.

It is to be expected therefore that a restructuring of the legal framework of employment to the advantage of minority groups may not be immediately effective and that responses will relate to the degree of political awareness and group consciousness present within the segment of the market at which the statute is directed. Furthermore if we are to assume that employers were behaving in a consciously rational manner in respect to their existing employment practices, albeit unconscious of their macro effects, then changes in their behaviour will be extremely difficult to effect without imposing punitive sanctions. The costs of such sanctions will inevitably be passed on, in whole or in part, to the community as a whole. It is therefore important to obtain a high level of political commitment to these unpopular outcomes before entering into major legislative changes. To do otherwise is to undermine the legitimacy of this method of change as well as the change itself.

In putting the law into practice however it seems necessary to view the process from a background of information on the workings of segmental markets (including the 'illegal' variety described in this chapter) which we presently do not possess. We have agreed that the narrow approach adopted by neo-classical economists and the limited nature of their data base has inhibited the generation of a wider body of theory. This theory should incorporate the sources of stigmatization and the broad social functions it serves within wider society. These functions are seen to be related to the configuration of power that exists within the workplace and labour market itself.

The evolution of labour market theory

In this book on the development of labour market theory we have attempted to trace its source through classical interpretations of labour as the ultimate source of economic value through its demotion by neo-classicists to that of a commodity deriving its value from the price paid by the consumer of its ultimate product. In Figure 1 we illustrated this path along the dimensions of objective/subjective relationships between parties in the labour market and the collectivist/individualist strategies pursued by them. We suggested that classical (supply-oriented) models suggested an objective tendency towards collectivism:

neo-classical (demand-oriented) models drove one back to atomistic and ego-centred explanations of market behaviour. The twentieth-century movement towards monopoly and towards institutionalized control of the labour market can be interpreted as falling into the upper right-hand quadrant of Figure 2 that is to say subjective collectivism.

We have ourselves suggested that the labour market may be interpreted as an arena from which a structure emerges as a consequence of the political-economic forces at work within it. That is to say that we tend to reject a theory which attributes a neutrality to the workings of the market or to a 'system of rules' (Flanders 1966) by which positions and rewards are allocated. Rather we see the maintenance and reinforcement of market advantages or disadvantages as being inherent within 'free-market' or capitalistic institutions. However, we do not see the removal of these institutional barriers as an operation that can be carried out only through the 'objective' restructuring of the political-institutional boundaries to market segments. Rather we suggest approaches to reform that start from a basis of concern for the interests, values and belief systems operating within the social groupings represented in labour market segments. Structural modifications of an objective nature must be made to coincide with changes brought about in the orientations of the parties themselves. Only through the mobilization of individual support for the collective changes required to modify present sources of disadvantage will such changes be made permanent.

Annotated bibliography

Classification of the literature

(A) = Economic theory
(B) = Segmentation theory
(C) = Empirical studies of the labour market
(D) = Sociological or administrative studies

B. AARON

'Employer and union responses to anti-discrimination legislation', paper presented to the Conference on International Trends in Industrial Relations, McGill University, Canada, May 1976, (C).
    One of several studies of the effect of anti-discriminative law in the United States.

B. ABEL SMITH AND P. TOWNSEND
'The poor and the poorest', Occasional Papers on Social Administration, No. 17, London: Bell and Son Ltd., 1965, (D).
    Survey demonstrating existence of large number of deprived families in the United Kingdom whose expenditure regularly exceeded their income, for whom little provision was made by the existing state schemes.

J. ADDISON

'Gleichberechtigung: the German experience', B.O. Pettman (ed.), Equal pay for women, Bradford: MCB, 1975, pp. 99-128, (C).
    Statistical test of pre-employment and post-employment discrimination in Germany (see text).

'Information flows: the employers view of the market', Applied Economics, Vol. 8, No. 1, March 1976, pp. 37-57, (C).
    Empirical study of ways employers monitor labour markets at plant level.

'The Institutionalist analysis of wage inflation: a critical appraisal', Research in Labour Economics, Vol. 1, No. 1, 1977, pp. 333-376, (B).
    A neo-classical explanation of the market effects of political-institutional structures.

'Discrimination in labour markets: theory with evidence from Britain and the U.S.', International Journal of Social Economics, Vol. 4, No. 3, 1977, pp. 159-191, (B,C).
    Market segmentation through discriminative practices expressed in an econometric model.

'The labor market and collective bargaining', California: Goodyear/Prentice Hall, 1978, (B).
   A comprehensive and rigorous presentation of the institutional and segmental arguments in a neo-classical framework with chapters devoted to both schools.

A. ALDRIDGE
Power, authority, and restrictive practices, Oxford: Basil Blackwell, 1976, (D).
   An interesting synthesis of the literature on 'restrictive practices' which gives insufficient attention to work-norms outside of the Anglo-Saxon culture.

A.A. ALCHIAN
'Information costs, pricing and resource unemployment' in E.S. Phelps (ed.), *Microeconomic foundation of employment and inflation theory*, 1970, (C).
   Statement and attempted verification of neo-classical view on subject of information search.

J. ALEXANDER
'Income, experience and internal labour markets', *Quarterly Journal of Economics*, Vol. 88, February 1974, pp. 63-85, (B,C).
   Develops Kerr's three sector model of the labour market viz: open and unstructured markets, guild or craft markets, and manorial or enterprise markets.

A.H. AMSDEN and C. MOSER
'Job search and affirmative action', *American Economic Review: Papers and Proceedings*, May 1975, (B, C).
   Empirical development of effect of unemployment payments on job search among disadvantaged.

P.J. ANDRESANI
'Discrimination, segmentation and upward mobility: a longitudinal approach to the dual labour market theory', Mimeographed, Temple University, Philadelphia, 1976, (B, C).
   Part of a much quoted dissertation which uses regression analysis on aggregated data to demonstrate the existence of a dual labour market.

K.J. ARROW
'The theory of discrimination' in Ashenfelter and Rees (eds.) *Discrimination in labour markets*, (B).
   Neo-classical treatment of discrimination as a pre-entry labour market phenomenon.

A.B. ATKINSON (ed.)
Economies of inequality, Oxford: Clarendon, 1975, (B, C).

The personal distribution of income, London: Allen and Unwin, 1976, (C, D).
   Two of the more rigorous examinations of the sources of economic deprivation.

R.T. AVERITT
The dual economy, New York: W.W. Norton, 1968, (B, C).

Introduces the concept of 'core' and 'peripheral' economies to distinguish between sources of stable or unstable careers for workers.

M. Baethge

Ausbildung und Herrschaft. Unternehmerinteressen in der Bildungspolitik. (Education and domination, Employer interest in educational policy), Frankfurt a. Main: EVA, 1970, (B, C).
Educational objectives are to a great extent determined by the desire to retain existing patterns of domination, to a much lesser extent by the wish to have young people join the labour market with the right kind of qualification.

E.C. Banfield

The unheavenly city, New York: Little, Brown, 1968, (C, D).
An original exposition of the 'culture of poverty' explanation of deprivation.

M.J. Banton

The coloured quarter, London: Jonathan Cape, 1955, (D).
Early study of racial discrimination in the U.K. which reveals instability of employment among blacks.

Police-community relations, London: Collins, 1973, (D).
Demonstrates extent of unconscious and conscious administrative discrimination against groups such as the families of convicts.

R.D. Barron and G.M. Norris

'Sexual divisions and the dual labour market' in D.L. Barker and S. Allen (eds.), *Dependence and exploitation in work and marriage*, London/New York: Longman, 1976, (B, C).
The dual labour marker is defined according to four criteria: the division between higher paying and lower paying sectors, restricted mobility across the boundaries of sectors, higher paying jobs are tied to promotional ladders while lower paying jobs are dead-end jobs and higher paying jobs are relatively stable while lower paying jobs are not. Women are confined to sectors which are relatively low paying, are less secure, have jobs with little demands for specific skills and are less instrinsically rewarding. Women are the main secondary work force in Britain. Dualism in the labour market is kept in existence as the result of the forces of supply and demand in a capitalist economy, to save scarce labour power and to prevent solidary relations between workers from developing.

G.S. Becker

The economics of discrimination, University of Chicago Press, 1957, (B, C).
An early attempt to explain differential earnings and career opportunities with neo-classical instruments.

Human capital: a theoretical and empirical analysis, with special reference to education, New York: Columbia University Press for National Bureau of Economic Research, 1964, (A,C).
The most comprehensive statement of the classical view of education and training as an 'investment' in human capital undertaken with a view to the expected returns to such investment. It brings out problems such as the open-endedness of the payback period on

such investment for a private or public investor, the separation of the effects of experiences and training from 'seniority in the job', and the high correlation between 'natural' ability and the tendency for people to continue their education or simply to learn on the job.

'A theory of the allocation of time', *The Economic Journal*, Royal Economic Society, September 1965, pp. 493-517, (A, B).
  An attempt to relate labour force participation of all kinds (hours of work, productivity, transportation, division of labour, overtime, etc.) to the marginal rate of earning.

'A theory of marriage: part I and part II', *Journal of Political Economy*, July/August 1973 and April 1974. See also 'A theory of the allocation of time', *Economic Journal*, September 1965, and R. Gronau, 'The intra-family allocation of time: value of housewives' time', *American Economic Review*, September 1973, and A.S. Leibowitz, 'Education and home production', *American Economic Review*, May 1974, (A).
  These authors maintain that household chores tend to be time-intensive activities. The rational division of labour is that which places the individual for whom the opportunity cost of a career is lowest in the specialist domestic role. One does not have to be a feminist to recognize the circularity of this argument! Furthermore the way in which the role is performed is *not* inviolate and has been shown to change radically in different social and psychological contexts.

K. BEHRING and B. LUTZ

'Betriebsstruktur als Bestimmungsgrösse der Nachfrage auf regionalen Arbeitsmärkten', in: *Mitteilungen aus der Arbeitsmarkt und Berufsforschung*, no. 2, pp. 30-45, 1970, (B, C).
  The relationship between structural aspects of regional labour markets and demand for labour.

R.M. BELL

'Changing technology and manpower requirements in the engineering industry', Engineering Industry Training Board Research Report No. 3, Sussex University Press, (C).
  One of the better attempts at macro-level forecasting coming from the Training Boards described in the text. Now this work is carried on in the U.K. by 'Little Neddies'.

P. BERCKMANS, P. GEVERS and A.L. MOK

Adekwaatheid van arbeidsmarktinformatie (Adequacy of labour market information), Leuven: Acco, 1975, (C).
  Belgian governmental labour market policy is severely handicapped by the inadequacy of labour market information systems, on the statistical as well as on the institutional side. Proposals for the restructuring of the Belgian employment agency and for relevant statistics are made.

I. BERG

Education and jobs: the great training robbery, Penguin Books, 1973, (C).
  A wide-ranging critique of the mismatch between the supply and demand for trained labour.

B.R. BERGMANN

'The effects of white incomes on discrimination in employment', *Journal of Political Economy*, Vol. 79, March/April 1971, pp. 294-313, (C).
Discrimination concentrates Negroes into certain occupations while virtually excluding them from others. In the occupations to which Negroes are relegated, marginal productivity may be lowered by the enforced abundance of supply. A model embodying this 'crowding' hypothesis is used to estimate the effects on white incomes of a reduction in discrimination. Whites with only an elementary education might have a once-for-all loss in the order of 10 per cent; on all other whites and on national income the effect is estimated to be trivial. Formulations by Becker and Thurow concerning Negro marginal productivity and wages are criticized.

B. BERNSTEIN

'A socio-linguistic approach to social learning', in J. Gould (ed.), *Penguin survey of the social sciences*, London: Penguin Books, 1965, (D).
Focusses on the role of languages and its usages in providing boundaries to different social classes and life chances.

W.H. BEVERIDGE

Full employment in a free society, London: George Allen and Unwin, 1944, (B, C).
A restatement of the Beveridge Report (1941) setting out the theory and proposed structure of a universal social and health insurance scheme for Britain which later became known as the 'Welfare State'. (See also the appendix by N. Kaldor on the sources of unemployment.)

H. BEYNON and R M. BLACKBURN

Perceptions of work. Variations within a factory, Cambridge University Press, 1972, (D).
Case study of workers in a food processing firm in Britain. Perceptions of workers are determined by their orientations to work as formed by their experiences in the work situation as well as outside of the factory gates (family, friends, local labour market, etc.). There is considerable variation in these orientations among men and women, shift workers, etc., much depending on their position in the internal and external labour markets.

H.G. BIRCH and J.D. GUSSOW

Disadvantaged children: health, nutrition and school failure, N.Y.: Harcourt, Brace and World, 1970, (D).
Provides indices of disadvantage such as inadequate housing, low educational attainment, poor parental control etc.

P.M. BLAU

'The flow of occupational supply and recruitment', *American Sociological Review*, August 1965, (D.)
An examination of occupational flows with a view to ascertaining the extent of social mobility between classes.

M. Blaug

'The connection between education and earnings: what does it signify?', *Higher Education*, Vol. 1, No. 7, 1972, (B, C).

'The empirical status of human capital theory: a slightly jaundiced survey', *Journal of Economic Literature*, September 1976, (B, C).
Statements of the author's critique of the tautological nature of human capital theory as based on the formal qualification and experience of the holder of 'human capital'. It is supported by evidence of the irregular association between earnings and status across several occupations and ethnic labour markets in a manner which discounts the cause-effect hypothesis contained in human capital theory.

M. Blaug, M.H. Peston and A. Ziderman

The utilization of educated manpower in industry. A preliminary report, Edinburgh and London: Oliver and Boyd, 1967, (C).
An attempt to assess the distribution of qualified labour in the U.K.

E. Blankenburg

'Task contingencies and national administrative culture as determinants of labour market administration.' Berlin: International Institute of Management, 1978, (C).
A comparative study of local labour market administrations in Germany, Great Britain, France, Italy and Sweden. To account for difference beyond the organizational boundaries of the national administrations, the term 'administrative culture' is introduced.

E. Blankenburg and U. Krautkrämer

'Possibilities and limits of an active labour market policy by employment offices.' Berlin: International Institute of Management, 1977, (C).
Preliminary report of a comparative study of the workings of the public employment services in Sweden, France, Great Britain, Italy and the Federal Republic of Germany.

B.F. Bluestone

'The tripartite economy: labour markets and the working poor', *Poverty and Human Resources*, July/August 1970, (B, C).

'The fate of the poor' in S.H. Bear and E. Barringer (eds.), *The State of the Poor*, N.Y.: Winthrop, 1970, p. 127, (B, C).

'Economic theory, economic reality and the fate of the poor' in H.L. Sheppard et al. (eds.), *The political economy of public service employment*, New York: Heath, 1972, (B, C).
All articles set out the radical explanation of labour market segmentation by reference to empirical descriptions of urban poverty.

A.W. Blumrosen

'Strangers in Paradise: Griggs and Duke Power Co. and the concept of employment discrimination', *Michigan Law Review*, November 1972, (C, D).
The concept of discrimination in American law has evolved from one of 'prejudicial treatment' to one of 'unequal treatment' and, in the Grigg's and Duke Power Co. judgement to that of 'indirect discrimination'. What is important is the *effect* of an act by an employer or union rather than the reasons underlying it.

M. BOLLE (ed.)

Arbeitsmarkttheorie und Arbeitsmarktpolitik (Labour market theory and labour market policy), Opladen: Leske/Budrich, 1976, (B, D).
   A collection of papers from a seminar held at the Free University of Berlin in 1975 which attempts to integrate economic and sociological points of view and from thereon critizises Federal German labour market policies for stimulating the marginalisation of certain categories of workers (see the annotations of the articles of Freiburghaus, Gensior/Krais and Schmid from this volume).

A. BORROW

'The development of occupational motives and roles ' in L. W Hoffman and M. L. Hoffman, (eds.), *Review of Child Development Research*, Vol. 2, London: Russell Sage Foundation, 1966, (D).
   Relates job-movement and career pattern to early socialisation.

E. BOULDING

'Familial constraints on women's work roles' in:M. Blaxall and B. Reagan (eds.), *Women and the workplace. The implications of occupational segregation*. Chicago/London: University of Chicago Press, 1976, (D).
   Analyses the role of women in the labour market in view of the triad 'breeder-feeder-producer'.

N. BOSANQUET and R. H. STEPHENS

'Another look at low pay', *Journal of Social Policy*, July, 1972, (C).
   One of a number of articles by Bosanquet on the workings of the State and institutional structure in a manner which reinforces rather than alleviates the problems of low paid workers.

N. BOSANQUET and P. B. DOERINGER

'Is there a dual labour market in Great Britain?', *The Economic Journal*, 33, 1973, pp. 421-435, (C).
   An attempt to assess the statistical basis for asserting the existence of a secondary labour market in Britain. Concludes that while this evidence exists in an aggregated form, the boundaries of market segments are defined in culturally specific terms. This means that access and egress to internal markets (at micro-level) is obtained through different types of institutionalised 'portals' within each country.

J. K. BOWERS, P. C. CHESHIRE and A. E. WEBB

'The change of relationship between unemployment and earnings increases: a review of some possible explanations'. *N.I.E.R.*, November, 1970, (C).

J. K. BOWERS, P. C. CHESHIRE, A. E. WEBB and R. WEEDEN

'Some aspects of unemployment and the labour market, 1966-71', *National Institute Economic Review*, November, 1972, (C).
   Two of early articles exploring the changing nature of structural unemployment in the 1970s.

A.M. BOWEY

'Labour stability curves and labour stability index', *British Journal of Industrial Relations*, Vol. VII No. 1, March, 1969, pp. 71-83, (C, D).
Example of the contingency school of industrial sociology that has evolved from the work of Lupton (1963), see below.

S. BOWLES

'Schooling and inequality from generation to generation', *Journal of Political Economy*, May/June Supplement, 1972, (see below), (C).

S. BOWLES and H. GINTIS

'The problems with human capital theory–A Marxian critique', *American Economic Review*, May, 1975, (see below), (C).

Schooling in capitalist America. Educational reform and the contradictions of economic life. London/Henley: Routledge and Kegan Paul, 1976, (B, C).
The possibility of successful educational reform is severely handicapped by the segmental tendencies of a capitalist economy. An important reason is that employers and other social elites use the schools for the legitimation of persistent inequality in economic positions: they have also used the educational system to bring about the profitable reproduction of the right type of worker consciousness and behaviour. Parents, students, worker organizations, women, ethnic minorities and others compete to use schools for their own objectives.

H. BRAVERMAN

Labour and monopoly capital, New York: Monthly Review Press, 1974, (D).
An influential restatement of the Marxist thesis of the increasing specialisation of labour under monopoly capitalism which draws off recent evidence of this process in America.

A.L. den BROEDER

'Problemen en principes van het arbeidsmarktbeleid', *Beleid en Maatschappij*, December, 1973, pp. 63-72, (D).
Labour market policy should pay more attention to the function of the labour market as a distributive mechanism.

L. BROOM and J.H. SMITH

'Bridging occupations', *British Journal of Sociology*, December, 1963. Reproduced in B.C. Roberts and J.H. Smith, *Manpower policy and employment trends*, London: Bell, 1966, (B, C).
A typology of occupations according to the function they play for their occupants (see text).

R. BROWN

'Women as employees: some comments on research in industrial sociology' in D.L. Barker and S. Allen (eds.), *Dependence and exploitation in work and marriage*, London: Longman, 1976, (D).
Suggests that studies of the role of women in the place of work have neglected their disadvantaged position in the labour market.

W. Brown and K. Sissons

'The use of comparisons in workplace wage determination', *British Journal of Industrial Relations*, Vol. XIII, No. 1, 1975, (C).
Movements in earnings within two local labour markets are compared (viz. Fleet Street, London and Coventry engineering). The authors conclude that the explanation for both movements are to be found in shop-steward bargaining on a 'patternal' and 'contoured' basis.

R. Bunting

Employer concentration in local labour markets, The University of North Carolina Press, 1962, (C).
An investigation of the hypothesis that monopsony (the control over wage levels by one employer in a local labour market) is associated with high degrees of concentration (i.e. a few employers hiring the larger proportion of the potential labour force).

J. Bundervoet et al.

'De bediende. Een fascinerend profiel.' (The white-collar worker. A fascinating profile), Antwerpen: LBC, 1978, (C, D).
Empirical research on the white-collar worker in Belgium.

G.C. Cain

'The challenge of dual and radical theories of the labour market to orthodox theory', Institute for Research on Poverty, University of Wisconsin-Madison, 1975, (A). See also:

'The challenge of dual and radical theories of the labour market to orthodox theory', *American Economic Review*, Papers and Proceedings, May, 1976, (A).

'The challenge of segmented labour market theories to orthodox theory: a survey', *Journal of Economic Literature*, (December, 1976), (A).

G.C. Cain and H.W. Watts

'Towards a summary and synthesis of the evidence' in Cain and Watts (eds.), *Income maintenance and labour supply: econometric studies*, New York: Markham, 1973, (B, C).
The authors examine the dual and radical critique of neo-classical analysis and in particular the charge that it failed to explain anomalies in the empirical workings of the market. The discussion of the dialogue between the new and orthodox economists leads to a conclusion that the neo-classical framework may be extended to explain the phenomenon conceptualised in dual-market theory.

M. Carter

Into work, London: Pelican Books, 1966, (D).
Study of job-selection in urban working class community: emphasises narrow range of perceived choice.

F.H. Cassell, S.M. Director and S.I. Doctors

'Discrimination within internal labour markets', *Industrial Relations*, October, 1975, (B, C, D).
Interesting empirical evidence of job-structures in selected American plants.

S. CASTLES and O. KOSACK

Immigrant workers and class structures in Western Europe, London: Oxford University Press, 1973, (B, C, D).
   Analysis of immigrant labour in several European countries and of the attitudes and policies of employers, unions and governments towards this phenomenon from the radical point of view.

E. CHAMBERLAIN

The theory of monopolistic competition, New York, 1933, (A).
   With Robinson (below) the first successful attempt to re-state the theory of the firm evolved by Marginalist economists in terms which accounted for the downward sloping demand curve facing companies in 'unique' product markets. Also advances new equilibria conditions involving equation of marginal and average revenue product.

B. CHIPLIN and P.J. SLOANE

'Male/female earnings differences: a further analysis', *British Journal of Industrial Relations*, Vol. XIV, No. 1, March 1976, pp. 71-81, (B, C).

Sex discrimination in the labour market, London, Macmillan: 1976, (B, C).

'Personal characteristics and sex differentials in professional employment', *Economic Journal*, December, 1976, (B, C).
   A series of pieces arguing that post-employment discrimination, that is wage not career discrimination, is more important than the reverse.

A.V. CICOUREL

The social organization of juvenile justice, London and New York: John Wiley, 1968, (D).
   Study of manner in which young criminals are 'labelled' by the police and their community.

COMMUNITY RELATIONS COMMISSION

'Multiple deprivation and minority groups', London: CRC73/113 (Mimeo), 1973, (D).
   Summary with evidence of sources of social deprivation in the U.K.

H. COSSEY et al.

'Evaluatie van de stages voor jongeren in ondernemingen' (Evaluation of job creation programmes for young people), Leuven: HIVA, 1977, (D).
   Empirical investigation into the results of the job creation programme in Belgium (law of 30-3-1976). This programme made all enterprises with over 100 employees take in jobless young people (under 25) at the rate of 1% of their work force for a period of 6-12 months and give them on-the-job training. The investigators found that only in a minority of cases were new jobs specially created for the young jobless; most went into existing jobs which had to be filled anyway (at 75% of normal wages). The law tends to work in favour of male youths with higher qualifications, and in that way strengthens already existing tendencies towards segmentations of the work force.

J.M. COUSINS

'Values and value in the labour market', Durham: University of Durham (mimeo), 1976, (D).

A review of the literature surrounding the 'action frame of reference' approach to labour studies.

COVENTRY AND DISTRICT ENGINEERING EMPLOYERS FEDERATION

'Labour relations and employment in the E.E.C.', Coventry: C.D.E.E.F., 1972, (C, D).
A review of earnings and conditions across the metal manufacturing sectors of the E.E.C. member nations.

D.R. COX and W.L. SMITH

Queues, New York: Wiley, 1961, (B, C).
An explanation of how labour allocation can take place through the expected cost of standing in line for a job: a cost which discourages excess demand.

W.W. DANIEL

'A national survey of the unemployed', London: Political and Economic Planning, 1968, (D).

'Strategies for displaced employees', London: 1970 Political and Economic Planning Broadsheet 517, (D).

'A national survey of the unemployed', London: Political and Economic Planning, 1973, (D).
Three of several empirical studies by this author on groups which may be considered part of the secondary segment of the labour market or potentially so. See also the cited work on the use of social security benefits by unemployed persons (forthcoming at time of publication).

DANISH NATIONAL INSTITUTE OF SOCIAL RESEARCH
STUDY OF LABOUR MARKET MOBILITY IN DENMARK

Arbejdskraftens Mobilitet 1-5, Copenhagen: Teknisk Forlag, 1974-1976, (B, C).
The five reports are:
1. A study of the literature on labour mobility.
2. Labour mobility. Pilot study.
3. The scope of labour mobility.
4. The mobility process.
5. The consequences of mobility.

R. DAVIE, N. BUTLER and H. GOLDSTEIN

From birth to seven: a report of the National Child Development Study, London: Longman, 1972, (D).
Comprehensive study of effect of domestic and community life on children of disadvantaged groups.

P. DE CEUSTER

Arbeidsbeleving en interne arbeidsmarkt. (Experience of work and the internal labour market), Leuven: Acco, 1978, (C).
Report of a sociological investigation by the Department of Sociology of the University of Antwerp, into the Belgian branch of a multi-national oil company, Esso Belgium.

Based on the results of a research project which was carried out in an oil refining company, this report explores the relationships between the organization which is characterized as an internal labour market, and the way its members experience their work. It appears that in the case of certain occupational groups these relationships are so deviant from the over-all pattern, that the notion of internal labour market cannot apply anymore to the entire organization.

H. DELEECK

Ongelijkheden in de welvaartstaat. Opstellen over sociaal beleid. (Inequalities in the welfare state. Essays in social policy). Antwerpen-Amsterdam: Nederlandsche Boekhandel, 1977, (D).
A collection of articles on the qualitative and quantitative aspects of social inequality in the sphere of income and social security in Belgium and some other European countries. Deleeck points at a 'Matthew-effect' in social policy, meaning that there are certain mechanisms at work in the welfare state by which the higher social groups in society benefit disproportionately from the advantages of social policy.

P.J. DHRYMES

'A model of short-run labour adjustment' in J. Duesenberry et al. (eds.), *The Brookings model: some further results*, Chicago: Rand McNally and Co, 1969, (B, C).
A neo-classical explanation of movements in the American labour market.

V.K. DIBBLE

'Occupations and ideologies', *American Journal of Sociology* Vol. 68, Sept. 1962, pp. 229-241, (D).

M. DOBB

Wages, Cambridge University Press, 1928, (B).
Attempt to provide a framework for classical and neo-classical approaches to wages based on 'pre-Keynesian' view of wage-fund theory. Later revised to incorporate Keynesian concepts of aggregate demand.

P. DOERINGER and M. PIORE

Internal labour markets and manpower analysis, Lexington (Mass.): Heath, 1971, (B).

'Unemployment and the dual labour market', *Public Interest*, Winter, 1975.
The internal labour market is defined as an administrative unit in which the price of labour power and its distribution is determined by rules and procedures which protect workers against the external market. Internal markets may be firm specific but not necessarily, they may stretch across sectors and occupations. Factors causing internal markets: task specificity, on-the-job training and 'custom'. An internal labour market has distinct ports of entry and a job ladder, which can be climbed only by workers possessing certain characteristics (like seniority).

J.W.B. DOUGLAS

The home and school, London: MacGibbon and Kee, 1964, (D).
Classical study of educational deprivation suffered by working class children because of disjuncture between their language and habits and those of the school as a middle-class institution.

B. DUNCAN

'Education and social background', *American Journal of Sociology*, 72,4, January 1967, pp. 74-81, (D).
Demonstrates empirical relationships between academic achievement and family background.

J. T. DUNLOP

Wage determination under trade unions, New York: Macmillan Co., 1944, (B, C).
An argument for treating labour markets as bargaining arenas shaped by institutional responses to market forces rather than individual choice.

The task of contemporary wage theory, in George W. Taylor and Frank C. Pierson (eds.), *New concepts in wage determination*, New York: McGraw-Hill, 1957, (B).

J. T. DUNLOP and B. HIGGINS

'Bargaining power and market structures', *Journal of Political Economy*, Vol. 50, pp. 1-26, (B, C).
Development of wage determination as institutionalised process of union bargaining strategies.

R. EASTERLIN

'Population, labour force and long swings in economic growth', *The American Experience*, Columbia University Press for National Bureau of Economic Research, 1968, (C).
Attempt to relate long term economic growth to changes in employment.

F. Y. EDGWORTH

'Equal pay to men and women, *Economic Journal 32*, December, 1922, pp. 431-57, (B).
Possibly the first systematic neo-classical treatment of discrimination for 'irrational' motives.

R. C. EDWARDS, M. REICH and D. M. GORDON (eds.)

Labour market segmentation, Lexington (Mass.)/Toronto/London: Heath, 1975, (B, C).
A collection of articles in the radical tradition and largely based on observation of marginal employment in American city ghettos.

C. F. EPSTEIN

Woman's place, Berkeley: University of California Press, 1971, pp. 20-22, (D).
Analysis of woman's role in American society.

S. ERBES-SEGUIN

'Les deux champs de l'affrontement professionnel', *Sociologie du travail*, 3, 1976, (D).
Approaches to the study of industrial relations must account for two fields of conflict, the socio-economic and the institutional.

F. FALKENBURG and A. VISSERS

Theorie van de dubbele arbeidsmarkt. (Review of the literature on the dual labour market), Tilburg: IVA, 1978, (B).

A review of the literature on dualism in the labour market, especially that which appeared in the Netherlands. But the report gives more than that. It also contains the results of a secondary analysis of some of the research done at the Catholic University of Tilburg (by Van Wezel and Zanders). They point at distinct segmentation tendencies in the Dutch economy, geographically as well as sectorially.

A. FECHTER

'Public employment programs: an evaluative study', Working Paper 936-41 of the Indiana Urban Institute, September, 1974, (C, D).
Interesting account of American experience of interventionist strategy.

M.S. FELDSTEIN

'Lowering the permanent rate of unemployment', U.S. Joint Economic Committee, (C, D).
Suggests that much of the new unemployment is voluntary in the sense that workers who are laid off from their jobs involuntarily, pass up opportunities to take other jobs because they wish to extend their leisure or because the insurance payment constitutes a satisfactory income.

M.A. FERBER and H.M. LOWRY

'The sex differential in earnings: a re-appraisal', *Industrial and Labour Relations Review*, Vol. 29, No. 3, 1976, (C).

'Sex and race differences in non-academic wages in a university', *The Journal of Human Resources*, Vol. XI, No. 3, 1976, (C).
American evidence of post-employment (earnings) discrimination.

R.J. FLANAGAN

'Segmental market theories and racial discrimination', *Industrial Relations*, October, 1973, (C, D).
Radical account of contribution of racial discrimination to segmentation.

F. FIELD (ed.)

Low pay, London: Arrow Brooks, 1973.
Collection of essays on causes of low-paid or secondary sector employment, (C, D).

M.P. FOGARTY

The just wage, London: Allen and Unwin, 1961, (B, D).
Sets out to demonstrate that the historical stability of occupational earnings is related to a long-standing sense of hierarchical justice fostered and reinforced by social institutions such as the Church.

FORSCHUNGSBERICHT

Frauenarbeit und technischer Wandel. (Women's work and technical change) SOFI, Göttingen/Frankfurt a. Main: RKW, 1973, (C, D).
Empirical research into the relationship between qualification structure and technical change in industry. Sectors with a dominant female work force have a lower structure of qualifications than sectors that are predominantly male. Women are underrepresented in

better qualified and higher paying jobs. As a result women are more vulnerable to mechanisation and automation of their work, and they find re-entry after redundancy even more difficult than the men in similar circumstances.

J. FOSTER

Class struggle and the industrial revolution. Early industrial capitalism in three English towns, London: Methuen, 1977, (C, D).
Historical study of the labour problems during the industrial revolution in three English towns.

R.B. FREEMAN

Labour economics, Prentice-Hall, 1973, pp. 30-31, (A).
Textbook in the neo-classical tradition.

'Alternative theories of labour market discrimination: individual and collective behaviour' in van Furstenberg and others (eds.), *Patterns of racial discrimination*, Vol. 2, (B, C).

'Changes in the labour market for Black Americans 1948-72', *BPEA*, I: pp. 67-120, 1973 (B, C).
Few of several texts on labour economics which attempt to explain sources of segmentation in neo-classical terms.

M. FREEDMAN

'Getting hired, getting trained', Washington D.C.: Government Printing Office, 1965, (C, D).
Describes the hiring practices of employers in the context of the occupational structure of the firms: constructs a typology of firms with respect to the possibilities for training and promotion. Size, product, product market effected the probability of long tenure, skill acquisition and career prospects of entry workers.

The process of work establishment, New York: Columbia University, 1969, (C, D).
Traces the work histories of recruits in five different countries.

'Labour markets: segments and shelters', *Land Mark Studies*, New Jersey: Allanheld, Osmun and Co., 1976, (B, C).
Multi-factorial analysis of aggregated American data which distinguishes 'age' as the most significant discriminator.

D. FREIBURGHAUS

'Zentrale Kontroversen der neueren Arbeitsmarktpolitik.' (Central controversies of the new labour market policy) in M. Bolle (ed.), pp. 71-91, (B, C).
Develops the dual labour market theory and the job search and labour turnover theory and applies them to the German situation. Segmentation, the compartmentalisation of the labour market into sub-markets, is responsible for the clustering of unemployment in certain segments, while other segments have a stable employment pattern. Unemployment should be 'equally divided', that it should be spread more equally across the working population. In any case young people must be assured stable jobs, so that unstable behaviour does not spoil their chances early in their career, the number of primary jobs should be increased and should·be more open to discriminated groups.

D. Freiburghaus

'Dauer der Arbeitslosigkeit-Probleme der Messung und Interpretation', International Institute of Management, Berlin, August, 1977, d/p. 77-50, (C, D).
   The greater part of all research into unemployment, and the interpretations and political measures so derived, use as their empirical base stock analyses i.e. snapshots of a dynamic process. Such research can say little about the fluctuations in the labour market, which underly the actual stocks of unemployment. The duration of unemployment represents a link between the magnitude of the stocks and of the flows. The calculation of the distribution of duration throws up several methodological problems, which are discussed.
   The more 'elegant' and hitherto most-used approaches assume a static employment, unemployment and economic inactivity remain unchanged over long time-periods. Evidently this assumption is not appropriate for the most recent particularly interesting years in the Federal Republic. For this reason a method has been developed that drops this assumption and uses instead data about flows into unemployment. Since, however, these are not available for age groups, an estimation procedure had to be additionally developed for the age breakdown of the inflows.

D. Freiburghaus and G. Schmid

'Theorie der Segmentierung von Arbeitsmarkten', in *Leviathan*, Vol. 3, 1975, (B, C).
   An account of the researches done by the Munich Institute for Social Research, which leans heavily on human capital assumptions.

J. K. Galbraith

The new industrial state, London: Hamish Hamilton, 1967, Penguin edition 1969, (A).
   Warns of development of corporate state comprised of monopoly institutions.

J. L. Gastwirth and S. E. Haber

'Defining the labour market for equal employment standards', *Monthly Labour Review*, Vol. 29, No. 3, 1976, (C, D).
   Indicates the empirical problem of definition presented by the implementation of anti-discriminative legislation within boundaries that require such definition.

S. Gensior and B. Krais

'Gesellschaftstheoretische Erklärungsmuster von Arbeitsmarkten' (Macrotheoretical explanation of labour markets), in M. Bolle (ed.), pp. 92-114, (C, D).
   Objective of labour market research should be to link societal processes with labour market processes. In this respect the research done at the Institute for Social Research at Munich is exemplary. One of the most important problems is whether it is possible to direct technological development in accordance with consciously chosen societal and economic objectives.

A. Giddens

The class structure of the advanced societies, London: Hutchinson, 1973, (D).
   Classes treated as the most important vehicles of the reproduction of certain modes of production and thence of the 'structuration' of society. Classes are defined according to their market capacity in the Weberian sense.

E. Ginsberg (ed.)

Jobs for Americans, New York: American Assembly, 1976, (C).
  Selection of essays of an eclective nature.

H. Ginsberg

The myth of the deprived child, New York: Prentice-Hall, 1972, (D).
  Critique of educational approach to teaching working class children.

R. Glass

Newcomers, London: Allen and Unwin for the Centre for Urban Studies, 1960, (D).
  Study of downward social mobility among recent black immigrants to the U.K.

J.H. Goldthorpe, D. Lockwood, F. Bechhofer, and J. Platt

The affluent worker: industrial attitudes and behaviour, Cambridge University Press, 1968,
(D).
  With its companion volumes on political and social attitudes one of the most influential of
  recent sociological works. It is an attempt to examine the widely accepted thesis of
  working-class embourgeoisement through a study of a small sample of manual and
  clerical workers in Luton. Its findings deny that affluent workers have accepted
  middle-class beliefs or life-styles except in a most superficial way. Perhaps more
  important, however, was the finding that unskilled manual workers displayed few of the
  classical symptoms of alienation from work due to their largely instrumental or
  calculative view of their job and the discomforts that attended it. (For further comparisons see S. Mallet *La nouvelle classe ouvrière*, Paris: Éditions du Seuil, 1969, and A.
  Touraine et al. 1964, below).

J.H. Goldthorpe and K. Hope

The social grading of occupations: a new approach and scale, Oxford: Clarendon Press,
1974, (D).
  An attempt to widen the weak attitudinal basis upon which occupational hierarchies have
  been constructed by both sociologists and government statisticians. A variety of
  measures are used including value to society, standard of living, power, influence, and
  level of qualification.
  (For a general discussion of this issue see Phelps Brown, 1977 cited below pp. 111-118)

J.F.B. Goodman

'The definition and analysis of local labour markets: some empirical problems', *British
Journal of Industrial Relations*, Vol. VIII, No. 2, 1970, (B, C).
  A comprehensive review of the neo-classical literature on local labour market segmenta-
  tion and the definitional and conceptual problems and omissions.

L. Goodwin

Do the poor want to work? A social-psychological study of work orientation, Washington
D.C.: Brookings Institution, 1972, (B, D).
  An economist's assessment of the socio-psychological elements present in the propensity
  for work/non-work based on regression analysis of aggregated data.

E. GOFFMAN

Stigma, London: Pelican Books, 1968, (D).
    Analysis of the way stigmata are used in day to day interpersonal transactions.

D. M. GORDON

Theories of poverty and underemployment: orthodox, radical and dual labour market perspectives, Lexington (Mass.)/Toronto/London: Heath, 1972, (B, C).
    This book attempts to review and to clarify three alternative explanations of the employment situation in the United States.
    Gives an especially good introduction to the problems touched on by the radicals and the dualists and their analysis of the causes of the current employment crisis.

R. A. GORDON

'Some macroeconomic aspects of manpower policy', in Lloyd Ulman (ed.), *Manpower programs in policy mix*, Baltimore: Johns Hopkins University Press, 1973, (A).
    One of the few radical contributions to an otherwise institutionalist and neo-classical collection of essays.

A. GORZ

'Preface' in A. Gorz (ed.) *Critique de la division du travail*, Paris: Seuil, 1973, (B, D).
    Critical analysis of the destructuration of the labour market from a Marxist point of view.

Z. GRILICHES and W. M. MASON

'Education, income and ability', *Journal of Political Economy*, May/June, 1972, Part II, pp. 74-103, (C, D).
    Example of multi-factorial analysis supporting human-capital hypothesis.

H. G. GRIBEL, D. MAKEI and S. SAX

'Real and insurance induced unemployment in Canada', *Canadian Journal of Economics*, Vol. III, 2 May 1975, pp. 174-191, (B, C).
    A regression model which estimates that unemployment in Canada increased by 1.4% because of the introduction of minimum out-of-work benefits.

D. GUJARATI

'The behaviour of unemployment and unfilled vacancies: Great Britain 1958-71', *Economic Journal*, March, 1972, (B, C).
    Attempt to explain the declining relationship between the rate of change in the level of unemployment and the rate of change in earning levels.

J. HABERMAS

Technik und Wissenschaft als Ideologie, Frankfurt a. Main: Suhrkamp, 1968, (D).

J. HAEX, A. MARTENS and S. WOLF

Arbeidsmarkt, discriminatie, gastarbeid (Labour market, discrimination, immigrant labour), Leuven: S.O.I., 1976, (C, D).
    Marginal workers are an essential element in a capitalist economy. Immigrant workers are confined to a secondary segment of the labour market, and have an important function in the process of control of the entrepreneur of the labour market. For the

immigrant worker this means that he is caught in a cumulative process of inferiority from which he can escape neither economically nor culturally.

E. HALÉVY

The Growth of Philosophic Radicalism, Boston: Beacon Press, 1955.

R.E. HALL

'Why is the unemployment rate so high at full employment?', *Brookings Papers on Economic Activity*, 3, 1970, pp. 369-402, (B, C).

'Prospects for shifting the Phillips curve through manpower policy', *Brookings Papers on Economic Activity*, 3, 1977, pp. 659-701, (B, C).
Segmental explanation of long-term unemployment.

R.E. HALL and A. KASTON

'The relative occupational success of blacks and whites', *Brookings Papers on Economic Activity*, 1973, pp. 791-92, (B, C).
Empirical study of career histories of white and black populations with similar qualifications.

H.G. HAMAKER

Arbeidsmarkt en personeelvoorziening (Labour market and manpower allocation), Alphen a.d. Rijn/Brussel: Samsom, 1976, (C, D).
An analysis of manpower allocation processes in industry. Four stages in this process are distinguished: recruitment, selection, placement and internal mobility of workers. An important factor in recruitment is the extent to which the workers' attachment can be secured and whether the employee is willing to accept the tasks and working conditions. Some sort of grip on the external local labour market is conducive to attracting the right kind of workers. Selection procedures depend largely on the size of the firm and on personnel policies, which are in turn influenced by the fact whether or not labour shortages exist. So firms must adapt their manpower policies to labour market conditions, instead of being able to actively plan and direct those policies. Only big firms (electricity, oil) can afford to 'control' their personnel policies.

G.S. HAMILTON and J.D. ROESSNER

'How employers screen disadvantaged job applicants', *Monthly Labour Review*, September 1972, (C).
Empirical investigation of recruitment and induction practices in American companies.

K. HANF, B. HJERN, D.O. PORTER

'Implementation of manpower training: local administrative networks in the Federal Republic of Germany and Sweden', Berlin: International Institute of Management, d/p 77-112, December, 1977, (C, D).
The paper describes the multi-organisational networks of administration and implementation of labour market training in the Federal Republic of Germany and Sweden. Special attention is given to a description of the regional and local components in these networks. A comparison is made of training programs in the two countries, and recommendations are made for improving the performance of each of them. General strategies for the macro-organizational management of programs which work through multi-organizational networks, particularly social service programs, are suggested.

K. HANF and D.O. PORTER

'The administration and implementation of labour market policy at the local level in Sweden and the Federal Republic of Germany', Berlin: International Institute of Management, d/p 77-31, April, 1977, (C, D).
A project currently underway is described, which examines the implementation of active labour market policy at the local level in Sweden and the Federal Republic of Germany. Taking as its point of departure the importance of 'local presence' in the realization of national policy in these countries and some of the factors affecting their behaviour are to be examined. The report presents, from the perspective of the research design some preliminary information on labour market problems, policy instruments and formal labour administration institutions in Sweden and the Federal Republic of Germany.

G. HANOCH

'An economic analysis of earnings and schooling', *Journal of Human Resources*, Summer, 1967, pp. 310-29, (C).
Study of school-leavers' earners in the human-capital manner.

B. HARRISON

Education, training and the urban ghetto, Baltimore: Johns Hopkins University Press, 1972, (C).
Empirical verification of the positive feed-back effect of social milieu.

B. HEPPLE

Race, jobs and the law in Great Britain, London: Penguin Books, 1970, (D).
A lawyer's critique of then prevailing racial legislation and its ineffectiveness in preventing job discrimination in the U.K.

J.R. HICKS

The theory of wages, London: Macmillan, 1932, (A).
The first comprehensive neo-classical treatment of wages as a factor of production.

'A reconsideration of the theory of value', *Economica*, New Series, Vol. I, February 1934, pp. 52-76.

'Bilateral monopoly in the annual survey of economic theory: the theory of monopoly', *Econometrica*, Vol. 3, No. 1, pp. 1-20, 1935 (A).
One of the original neo-classical statements of bargaining theory.

Value and capital, London, 1939, (A).
A re-statement of marginal utility theory in terms of Paretan ordinality, e.g. the diminishing marginal utility is replaced by the diminishing rate of substitution, thus allowing different rates and directions of preference to be expressed. The constant utility of money assumed to exist in earlier theories and other aspects of comparative static exchange theory are also challenged.

G.H. HILDEBRAND et al.

'A symposium: evaluating the impact of affirmative action: a look at the federal contract compliance program', *Industrial and Labour Relations Review*, Vol. 29, No. 4, July 1976, (B, C).

Comprehensive summary of the effectiveness of government and judicial intervention based on a dualist interpretation of the market.

M. HILL et al.

Men out of work, Cambridge University Press, 1973, (C, D).
Study of the effects of long-term unemployment on the individual and the community.

J.S. HIMES

'Some work-related cultural deprivations of the lower-class Negro youth', *J. Marr. Fam.*, 26, 1964, pp. 447-449, (D).
Traces differences in work situation between white and black school leavers.

R. HOLMAN

Poverty: explanation of social deprivation, Oxford: Martin Robertson, 1978, (D).
A review of the current and historical explanations of poverty which ends with a number of suggestions for the radical restructuring of state agencies designed to combat social deprivation.

C.C. HOLT and M.H. DAVID

'The concept of job vacancies in a dynamic theory of the labour market', in *The measurement and interpretation of job vacancies*, NBER, 1966, (B, C).
Attempt at an aggregative model of the effects of unemployment which sets out neo-classical assumptions of the role of job vacancies.

C. HOLT et al.

'The unemployment-inflation dilemma: a manpower solution', Urban Institute 1971, (B, C).
Structural employment seen to be the result of the lack of macro-level manpower planning.

L.C. HUNTER

'Costs and benefits in the operation of a public employment service', OECD International Management Seminar on the Public Employment Services and Management, Supplement to Final Report, 1966, (C, D).
Critique of Employment Service in the United Kingdom.

L.C. HUNTER and G.L. REID

Urban worker mobility, Organisation for Economic Co-operation and Development, Paris, 1968, (C, D).
A summary of all the descriptive literature on this subject within a framework of neo-classical economic analysis combined with selected sociological and institutional material. Still the most thorough treatment of the problem available at present and essential reading for the labour market economist or occupational sociologist.

R. HYMAN

'Economic motivation and labour stability', *British Journal of Industrial Relations*, Vol. VIII, No. 2, July 1970, pp. 159-78, (D).

Critique of contingency theory approach (see Bowey 1969 above) from an 'action frame of reference' view-point, that is from the point of view of the different perspectives of the actors.

D. JACKSON

Poverty, London: Macmillan, 1972, (B, C, D).
An attempt to build a feed-back model of social deprivation and to match it against an input/output matrix of social welfare.

J.A. JACKSON (ed.)

Professions and professionalization, London: Cambridge University Press, 1970, (D).
A collection of articles around the theme of professionalisation that is the strategies pursued by occupational groups to close their labour market through the use of qualification and the individualised and esoteric nature of the service on offer.
(See also Jamous and Peliolle below).

E. JACQUES

Time-span handbook, London: Heinemann, 1964, (C, D).
A useful elaboration on Jacques' view that remuneration should (and actually does) accord with the span of time that elapses before an employee's task is checked by a superior or other 'built-in' controls.

M. JAHODA, P.F. LAZARSFELD and H. ZEISEL

Marienthal: the sociography of an unemployed community, Chicago/New York: Aldine/Atherton, 1971, (D).
Austrian unemployment in the 1930s: a classical study recently republished in English.

H.C. JAIN and P.J. SLOANE

'The disadvantaged in the labour market in the context of North America and selected European Countries', Research and Working Paper Series No. 128, Hamilton, Ontario: McMaster University Faculty of Business, March, 1977, (B, C).
A survey of anti-discrimination measures in Britain, Canada and America using a neo-classical economic framework.

E.R. JAKUBAUSKAS and N.A. PALOMBA

Manpower economics, Reading (Mass.): Addison-Wesley, 1973, (B).
A neo-classical approach to manpower problems with interesting suggestions for solutions applying to the American context.

H. JAMOUS and B. PELOILLE

'Changes in the French university-hospital system', in J.A. Jackson (ed.), *Professions and professionalisation*, 1970, pp. 111-152, (D).
A model of occupational crystallisation around the control of technological innovation over time using the French medical profession and its control over university faculties of medicine as an example. (See also Jackson, 1970 above.)

C. Jercko

Inequality: a reassessment of the effect of family and schooling in America, New York: Basic Books, 1972, (C, D).
    Collection of data demonstrating hierarchical order of early socialisation in U.S.A.

W. S. Jevons

Theory of political economy, London: Macmillan, 1924, first published 1871, (A).
    Important contribution to systematisation and quantification of economic relationships in the form of exchange equations. A 'commodity capable of satisfying wants in a number of different uses, such a labour, will', Jevons states, 'be distributed over all those uses in such a way that its final degree of utility is the same in every use. Equilibrium occurs when neither party can obtain any further advantages through exchange, at that point marginal utility will be proportionate to the price. The value of an input commodity such as labour will be proportionate to the value derived from the revenue product of its labour.'

K. Jones and A. D. Smith

The economic impact of commonwealth immigration, London: National Institute of Economic and Social Research and Cambridge University Press, 1970, pp. 29-84, (B, C).
    Aggregative assessment of the effects of black immigration in the U.K.

L. J. de Jonge

'Arbeidsbureau nieuwe stijl. Adviserend verslag van een experiment. Rapport opgesteld in opdracht van het Directoraat-Generaal voor de Arbeidsvoorziening.' (Public employment service new style. Report of an experiment, commissioned by the Directorate-General for the Manpower Services in the Netherlands.), Berg en Dal: GITP, 1978, (B, C).
    Contains the report of action research into new ways of mediating labour supply and demand in the Netherlands. The question of the optimal functioning of the public employment service is tackled from the motivational as well as from the organizational angle. Motivational, in so far as client's own wishes are a fundamental variable in the job/person selection process, organisational in so far as the Service is to be organised according to the problem with which clients (employers as well as employees) come into the market, into an 'open' and a 'closed' section. Central to this is the intake procedure, with its concomitant necessity to recognise the nature of the client's problems and the possibilities to solve them. Whether this setup will combat existing tendencies remains to be seen. Much depends on the material and professional abilities of the members of the employment service.

Heather Joslin

'Cyclical variations in the employment of opted-out married women and pensioners in G.B., 1961-1974.' Proceedings of the International Conference on Industrial and Labour Relations, The International Institute of Labour, Geneva, October, 1976, (C).
    Attempt to construct a statistical model of the manner in which the system of rewards and state-benefits affects the propensity to work among women. Of interest because of its use of previously unrevealed data collected by the State.

Sir K. Joseph

'Speech to the Preschool Playgroups Association', 29 June, 1972 reported in *Times*, June 30, 1972, (D).

Outline of the self-reinforcive 'cycle' of deprivation thesis of poverty.

E. KALACHEK

'Determinants of teenage employment', *American Journal of Human Resources*, Vol. IV, Winter, 1969, pp. 3-21, (C).
The study is based on 1960 American census data. Kalachek's most interesting finding comes from comparison of the 75 largest metropolitan areas in U.S.A. in cities where youth jobs (i.e. those in 'key' occupations or industries) are underrepresented in comparison with national distributions, young workers do not significantly increase their penetration of adult-type job activity; rather they assume more of the employment in these 'key' youth jobs. One may infer, although Kalachek does not, that men are less likely to be found in 'boys' jobs when 'men's' jobs are available.

H. KALLWEIT and G. SCHMID

'Arbeitslosenexport: Ausmass, Struktur und Folgen für die Arbeitsmarktpolitik der Bundesrepublik Deutschland', Berlin: International Institute of Management, dp/77-19, March 1977, (C).
This paper outlines the regional distribution of unemployment rates in the Federal Republic of Germany and describes the impact of recent economic developments on their variation. In particular it examines the disparity in the regional distribution of unemployment rates when the expulsion of foreign workers from the labour market is taken into account.

H.R. KAHN

Repercussions of redundancy, London: Allen and Unwin, 1964, (C).
A study of the process and outcomes of large-scale lay-offs of manual workers. (See also D. Wedderburn 1964, 1965, 1968, cited below)

F.E. KATZ

Autonomy and organization. The limits of social control, New York: Random House, 1968, (D).
One of several studies of the strategies pursued by medical practitioners in hospitals to establish and retain an occupational autonomy.

H. KERN and M. SCHUMANN

Industriearbeit und Arbeiterbewusstsein, Parts I and 2, Frankfurt a. Main/Köln: E.V.A, 1970, (C, D).
Relationships between technological development and the work situation.

C. KERR

'Labour markets: their character and consequences', *American Economic Review*, Papers and Proceedings, Vol. 40, 1950, May, pp. 278-291, (B).

'The Balkanisation of labour markets' in E. Wight Bakke et al. (eds.), *Labour mobility and economic opportunity*, MIT Press, 1954, (D, A).
The original statement of 'internal labour market' theory in which the author suggests that labour market boundaries are now established and identified by political-institutional pressures rather than as an aggregation of personal preferences expressed in a free market context.

J.M. KEYNES

General theory of employment, interest and money, London: Macmillan, first published 1936, (A).
A return to consideration of the economy at the macro level which relates investment to consumption and to saving, through (a) the propensity to consume, (b) the propensity to invest/remain liquid, (c) the marginal efficiency of capital. Demonstrates the ability of the economy to equilibrate at high level of unemployment. Most influential modern economist in shifting policy towards interventionism in Western liberal democracies.

P.R. KLEINDORFER and A. SERTEL-KUDAT

Economic and managerial aspects of foreign labour in West Germany, Berlin: International Institute of Management, dp/1-74-7, January 1974, (B,C).
A study of some of the causes and macro-effects of the migration of foreign labour into Western Germany.

R.A. KLITGAARD

'The dual labour market and manpower policy, *Monthly Labour Review*, November, 1971, (D).
Suggestions for changes in American manpower and minority groups policy towards a more active state intervention.

K.G.J.C. KNOWLES and D. ROBINSON

'Wage movements in Coventry', *Bulletin of the Oxford University Institute of Statistics*, Vol. 31, No. 1, February, 1969, (B,C).
One of a series of articles demonstrating the institutional boundaries existing within geographically defined 'local labour markets'.

A.I. KOBEN and H.S. PARNES

'Career thresholds', *U.S. Departement of Labour Manpower Research Monograph*, Vol. 3, No. 16, Washington: Government Printing Office, 1971, 43 p., (D).
Summary of American literature on career opportunities for school and college leavers.

E. KOOPMANS et al.

'Onderzoek onder werklozen, deel 1: moeilijkheden bij (her)intreding' (Investigation among jobless, part 1: problems at (re-)entry), Tilburg: IVA, 1976, (D).
An investigation among long-term unemployed, commissioned by the Dutch ministry of Social Affairs in 1974. Re-entry chances are distributed unequally: unemployed with favourable personal characteristics (that is those who are considered 'normal' in the eyes of employment officers) and who accept jobs which are less intrinsically rewarding are more likely to find jobs than those with unfavourable personal characteristics (e.g. over 50 years of age) and higher intrinsic aspirations. There seems to be an unemployment 'career', the situation of the unemployed getting increasingly unfavourable, in which the duration of the unemployed situation is an ever more negative factor in the selection process by the employer.

G.E. KRIMPAS

Labour input and the theory of the labour market, London: Duckworth, 1975, (B, C).

An attempt to validate the Jacques' 'time-span of discretion' theory against empirical data and to provide an economic explanation for the phenomenon.

A. KUDAT and M.R. SERTEL

'An exploration into the measurement of discrimination' in *Employment: foreign labour in West Germany*, Berlin: International Institute of Management Preprint Series 1/74-30, 1974, (C, D).
Study of effect of economic cycle on employment opportunities for foreign workers in Germany (see text).

F. LAMMERTIJN

'Arbeidsbemiddeling en werkloosheid' (Employment mediation and unemployment), Leuven: SOI, 1976, (C, D).
Empirical investigation of the function of the public employment service in Belgium shows that only a very small part of the labour market (10%) is penetrated by the public employment service and that this part is almost wholly confined to the 'secondary' segments of the market.

R. LAYARD

'On measuring the redistribution of lifetime income', in M.S. Feldstein and R.P. Inman, (eds.), *The economics of public services*. Proceedings of a Conference held by the International Economic Association at Turin, Italy, Macmillan, 1976, (B, C).
Interesting attempt to model the career income of various occupations.

R. LEDRUT

Sociologie du chômage, Paris: Presse Universitaire de France, 1966, (B, C).
Unemployment is a selective process in which persons possessing inferiority traits are particularly vulnerable. Such traits are age (very young, very old), aptitude (mentally and physically handicapped), sex (women are particularly vulnerable), migrant origin, etc.

D. LEES and B. CHIPLIN

'The economics of industrial training', *Lloyds Bank Review*, April 1970, p. 29, (B, C).
Critique of 'levy-dues' system of financing industrial training under the Industrial Training Act 1964. It uses Becker's distinction between specific and general training.

D.E. LEIGH

'Occupational advancement in the late 1960s: an indirect test of the dual labour market hypothesis', *The Journal of Human Resources*, Vol. XI, No. 2, Spring 1976, (C, D).
Empirical evidence of lack of mobility between primary and secondary markets in America.

G.G. LENSKI

'Status crystallisation: a non-vertical dimension of social statistics', *American Sociological Review*, Vol. 19, August 1954, (D).
The author sees status as being definable in a number of different spheres of activity. These 'situses' may be congruent or incongruent, low or high, resulting in different role expectations and aspirations.

R. LEROY

'De vrouwenlonen. Duizenden vormen van discriminatie.' (Women's wages. A thousand forms of discrimination.) *ACV-vakbeweging*, Nr. 69, 15 July, 1975, (C, D).
   Women's wages in Belgium are much lower than men's. The author points at the fact that 19% of these differences cannot be accounted for (nationally).

S.W. LERNER, J.R. CABLE and S. GUPTA (eds.)

Workshop wage discrimination, Oxford: Pergamon, 1969, (B, C).
   Collection of evidence on effects of fractional wage bargaining in the United Kingdom.

R.A. LESTER

'Shortcomings of marginal analysis for wage-employment problems', *American Economic Review*, Vol. 36, March, 1946, pp. 63-82, (A, C).
   Part of a more general critique of marginalist theory in analysing the workings of the firm which took the form of a dialogue between Lester and F. Machlup, 1946, (below).

S.A. LEVITAN and R. TAGGART

Employment and earnings inadequacy: a new social indicator, Baltimore: Johns Hopkins University Press, 1974, (B, C).
   A critique of the existing statistical basis for labour market analysis.

S.A. LEVITAN, G.L. MANGUM and R. MARSHALL

Human resources and labour market. Labour and manpower in the American economy, New York: Harper and Row, 1972, (A, B).
   One of the most comprehensive neo-classical handbooks on labour market processes.

H.M. LEVINSON

'Unionism, concentration and the wage changes: towards unified theory', *Industrial and Labour Relations Review*, Vol. 20, January 1976, pp. 108-205, (B, C).
   Examines evidence for market share giving employer greater bargaining power vis-à-vis unions through the existence of monopoly rents, control over entrance to the labour market and over wage rates, greater resources to restrict a union etc. Concludes that dispersion of industrial location may be as important as these other factors in determining bargaining strategies.

H.G. LEWIS

Unionism and relative wages in the United States: an empirical study, University of Chicago Press, 1963, (B, C).
   An institutionalist analysis of wage-movements.

O. LEWIS

'The culture of poverty' in D.P. Moynihan (ed.), *On understanding poverty*, New York: Basic Books, 1968, (D).
   Advances the thesis of a self-sustaining communal culture which impedes progress to a higher level of economic livelihood as well as maintaining the existing standard of living. Based on separately published empirical studies (1959, 1961, 1966).

R. M. LINDLEY

'Manpower movements and the supply of labour', Chapter 8 in *P oblems in manpower forecasting*, in J. S. Wabe, (ed.), Farnborough: Saxon House, 1974, (B, C).
    One of a number of pieces tracing importance of training to job-mobility.

S. LIPSET and G. SMITH

'Strategies of compensation: a review of educational projects for the disadvantaged in the United States', Paris: Report for the O.E.C.D., 1971, (D).

R. J. LOVERIDGE

'Commuting to work among office workers: a comparative study of commuting in London, the South East and Liverpool', Location of Offices Bureau, 1967, (C, D).
    Survey of attitudes among white-collar employees on their reasons for commuting to work.

'Occupational change and the development of interest groups among white-collar workers in the U.K.: a long-term model'. *British Journal of Industrial Relations*, Vol. X, No. 3, 1972, pp. 340-365, (D).
    An attempt to relate the process of occupational formation to the increased use of formal control systems by 'professionalised' management in large-scale bureaucracies.

J. G. LULOFS

De Amerikaanse arbeidsmarkt. Een onderzoek naar de arbeidsmobiliteit in de Verenigde Staten (The American labour market), Meppel: Boom, 1960, (B, D).
    Lulofs introduced the institutionalist analysis of the labour market to Dutch sociologists.

T. LUPTON

On the shop-floor, Oxford: Pergamon, 1963, (D).
    The most notable of a series of workplace studies emanating from the University of Liverpool Industrial Sociology Department which established a multi-factorial approach to the analysis of the economic and work situation of participants. This approach has subsequently become increasingly normative and management oriented.

T. LUPTON and A. BOWEY

Wages and salaries, Harmondsworth: Penguin Books, 1974, (C, D).
    An assessment of the relationship between job structure and wage structure within and across firms.

B. LUTZ

'Produktionsprozess und Berufsqualifikation.' (Process of production and occupational qualification) in Th. W. Adorno (ed.), *Spätkapitalismus oder Industriegesellschaft? Verhandlungen des sechzehnten Deutschen Soziologentages*, Stuttgart: Enke, 1969, (C, D).
    Lutz tackles the important question of the interaction between qualification as it emerges from demands of the production process, and qualification as personal and educable characteristics of people. Occupational classifications seldom take the characteristics of the production process and technological advances as the point of departure, and work is mostly defined as a human category, not as a category emerging from the production

process. There is thus a permanent gap between the formally defined work situation and personally perceived job situation.

'Bildungssystem und Beschäftigungsstruktur in Deitschland und Frankreich. Zum Einfluss des Bildungssystems auf die Gestaltung betrieblicher Arbeitskräftestrukturen.' (Educational and employment systems in Germany and France. On the influence of the educational system on the formation of manpower policies of the firm). in H.G. Mendius et al., 1976, pp. 83-151, (C).
Differences between labour market policies of firms in Germany and France are attributed to differences between the national educational systems in each country. For example, the German system requires fewer supervisors and has more craft-trained operators than the French one.

B. LUTZ and W. SENGENBERGER

Arbeitsmarktstrukturen und öffentliche Arbeitsmarktpolitik. (Labour market structures and public labour market policy), Göttingen: Verlag O. Schwartz, 1974, (B, C).
In the institutionalist tradition the authors distinguish three labour submarkets: unspecific submarkets, craft submarkets and firm specific submarkets. These three markets are the result of investment or non-investment in specific human capital in the form of qualifications. The authors criticize the Federal German labour market policy for paying too much attention to the craft submarket without noticing the changes which are taking place in the firm specific markets and the increasing importance of unspecific submarkets.

H. LYDALL

The structure of earnings, Oxford University Press, 1968, (A, B).
Important descriptive text in the neo-classical tradition.

B.D. MABRY

Economics of manpower and the labour market, New York and London: Intext Educational Publishers, 1973, (A, B).
A comprehensive handbook in the neo-classical tradition, treating the labour market on the micro-level, the institutional level as well as the macro-level.

G.L. MAGNUM

'Manpower research and manpower policy', in *Industrial Relations Research Association Series: A Review of Industrial Relations Research,* Vol. 2, University of Wisconsin: IRRA, 1971, pp. 109-10, (A, D).
Radical critique of orthodox manpower policy.

J.J. MC CALL

'Income mobility, racial discrimination and economic growth', Lexington: Heath, 1973, (B, C).
Attempt to trace the effects of discrimination on national economic efficiency.

B.J. MC CORMICK and E. OWEN SMITH

The labour market, London: Penguin Modern Economics, 1968, (A, B).
One of the best collections of neo-classical and institutionalist articles.

B.J. Mc Cormick and P.S. Manley

'The industrial training act', *Westminster Bank Review*, p. 44, February 1967, (B, C).
  Explanation of the British Industrial Training Act 1964 using the Becker framework of
  analysis.

F. Machlup

'Marginal analysis and empirical research', *American Economic Review*, Vol. 36, Sep-
tember 1946, pp. 819-84, (A).
  Defence of neo-classical position against critique of institutionalists and others (see
  Lester 1946 above).

R.W. Mack

'Occupational determinateness: a problem and hypothesis in role theory', *Social Forces*,
Vol. 35, 1956,(D).
  Puts forward a typology of occupations in terms of those in which the rights and duties
  are well defined and the expectation of role behaviour is fairly general and specific
  (determinate) and those of an opposite type (indeterminate).

D.I. Mackay

'Internal wage structures' in D. Robinson (ed.), *Local labour markets and wage structures*,
London: Gower Press, 1970, (B, C).
  Empirical study of internal labour market in regionally-based sample of British com-
  panies: largely concerned with explanation of earnings differentials.

D.I. Mackay, D. Boddy, J. Brack, J.A. Diack and N. Jones

Labour markets under different employment conditions, London: George Allen and
Unwin, 1971, (B, D).
  Empirical study of employment conditions in individual plants in five geographical areas
  in England and Scotland by a team of researchers from the University of Glasgow, from
  the external as well as from the internal labour market point of view.

D.I. Mackay and G.L. Reid

'Redundancy, unemployment and manpower policy', *Economic Journal*, December, 1972,
(B, C).
  Pleas for a more positive policy in relation to labour market information.

L. Mackie and P. Pattullo

Women at work, London: Tavistock, 1977, (C, D).
  The segmentation of women portrayed in vivid terms: women are paid less than men,
  work in smaller range of occupations, hardly ever ascend the company hierarchy and do
  not get the same education as the men.

D.R. Maki and Z.A. Spindler

'The effect of unemployment compensation on the rate of unemployment in Great Britain',
Oxford Economic Papers, 1975, (B, C).
  Neo-classical explanation of increases in unemployment compensation on job-search and
  long-term unemployment.

G.B. MALKIEL and J.A. MALKIEL

'Male-female pay differentials in professional employment', *American Economic Review*, September 1973, (B, C).
Empirical study supporting post-employment (earnings) discrimination thesis.

T.R. MALTHUS

Principles of political economy, London, 1820, (A).
Challenges Jean Baptiste Say's view that there can be no general over-production or glut of capital in an economy because the producers themselves provide the market for the goods produced. Malthus regarded effective demand for a commodity as that level which would ensure its continuous supply. This is fixed at a level which enables the entrepreneur to cover his costs including material and capital. Within a closed economy aggregate wages will therefore always tend to provide less by way of consumption than the level required to sustain effective demand.

M. MANN

Workers on the move: the sociology of relocation, Cambridge University Press, 1973, (D).
An empirical analysis of the relocation of a complete factory in the Midlands of England. This important book gives an interesting account of how employment dependencies enter into the decision of individual employees to move or not to move.

C. MANN and K. LAWRENCE WILLIAMS

'Organization impact of automation in white-collar industrial units', in Simon Marcson, (ed.), *Automation, alienation and anomie*, New York: Harper and Row, 1970, p. 194, (D).
Supports the view that white-collar tasks are becoming increasingly narrow in range and depth of content as a result of automation.

MANPOWER REPORT OF THE PRESIDENT AND REPORT ON MANPOWER REQUIREMENT, RESOURCES, UTILIZATION AND TRAINING

Washington DC: U.S. Department of Labor, 1966, (C).
General statement of the policy and strategy intended for the 'Great Society' programme of aid for deprived minorities in America.

JUDITH MARQUAND

'Which are the lower paid workers?', *British Journal of Industrial Relations*, November, 1967, pp. 359-74, (B, C).
Early criticism of statistical presentation of aggregate earnings figures in the U.K.

A. MARSHALL

Principles of economics, London, 1927, first published 1890, (A).
Perhaps the foundation of modern British economic thinking. Its central doctrine of value is that it is useless to ask whether demand or supply determine price since they act 'like blades of a scissor'. The marginal utility of the commodity is reflected in the demand process of the buyer while the marginal disutility of providing it is reflected in the price. Both the buyer and seller will be comparing prices in order to gain the best 'balance of net advantages' from the particular transaction they are engaged in.

A. Martens

'25 jaar wegwerparbeiders. Het Belgisch immigratiebeleid na 1945.' (25 years of waste workers. Belgian immigration policy since 1945) Leuven: KUL-SOI, 1973, (C, D).
   A critical analysis of the Belgian government's policy towards foreign workers, which has in many ways been conducive to the segmentation of the labour market in Belgium.

A.J. Mantel

'Bouwarbeid en arbeidsmarkt. Splitst zich de arbeidsmarkt?' (Building industry and labour market. Is there a fragmentation process?) in: *Bouw/Werk* 8 (2), no. 4, 1977, pp. 239-259, (B, C).
   Segmentation tendencies in the building industry.

A. Mantel, J. van Wezel and H. Zanders

'Bouwarbeidsmarkt–politiek op middellange termijn: bouwarbeiders of bouwvakarbeiders?' (Labour market of the building industry–long term policy, building workers or building craftsmen?) *Bouw*, 14, June, 1975, (B, C).
   Discussion of the extent to which segmentation in the building industry labour market is a function of institutions consciously created for the purpose.

S. Marglin

'Origines et fonctions de la parcellisation des taches' in A. Gorz (ed.), *Critique de la division du travail*, Paris: Seuil, 1973, (D).
   Tries to answer the question 'What are bosses for?'.

'What do bosses do?' in A. Gorz (ed.), *The division of labour*. The labour process and class struggle in modern capitalism, Atlantic Highlands, N. Y.: Humanities Press, 1976, (D).
   The division of labour in the capitalist mode of production exists purely to garantee the capitalist his essential role in the production process.

A. Marin and G. Psacharopoulos

'Schooling and income distribution', *Review of Economics and Statistics*, August, 1976, (B, C).
   Empirical study using analysis of aggregated data to demonstrate pre-employment (career) discrimination.

R. Martin and R.H. Fryer

Redundancy and paternalist capitalism. A study in the sociology of work, London: George Allen and Unwin, 1973, (C,D).
   Tries to integrate a sociology of the labour market and a sociology of work. To this end they view the labour market from an arena perspective: the labour market is in their view 'an arena within which individuals attempt to satisfy material, psychological, social and cultural needs, and achieve personal goals, within the perceived limits of a specifiable occupational structure'.

D. Marsden and E. Duff

Workless. Some unemployed men and their families, Harmondsworth: Penguin Books, 1975, (D).

Account of in-depth interviews with a score of unemployed people in the prime of their life. Need for government policy not only for the material aspects of unemployment, but also for the retention of occupational skills and identity.

S.T. MARSTON

'The impact of unemployment insurance on job search', *Brookings Papers on Economic Activity*, Vol. 1, 1975, pp. 13-60, (B, C).
Although there is some evidence to suggest that unemployment benefits influence the duration of unemployment, workers are unlikely to quit their jobs in order to collect such benefits. There is a small work disincentive exerted by unemployment insurance.

K. MARX

Capital, Vol. 1, 1867. Published in Penguin Books, 1976, (A, D).

Value, price and profit, 1865, (A, D).
Extracts from both produced in *The essential left*, London: Unwin Books, 1960.

Grundrisse. Foundation of the critique of political economy, (rough draft), Harmondsworth: Penguin Books, 1973, (A, D).
Offers theoretical framework to explain segmentation as part of a more general theory of dialectic materialism.

J.L. MEIJ

'Wage-structure and organization-structure' in J.L. Meij (ed.), *Internal wage structure*, Amsterdam: North Holland, 1963, (B, D).
Interesting attempt to relate the earnings structure of the enterprise with its structure or organisational roles.

H.G. MENDIUS et al.

Betrieb-Arbeitsmarkt-Qualifikation I (Firm-labour market-qualification I), Frankfurt a. Main: Aspekte, 1976, (A, B, C).
A collection of original articles on the relationship between among others: economic development, schooling, bureacratic structure, and labour market segmentation.

H.G. MENDIUS and W. SENGENBERGER

'Konjunkturschwankungen und betriebliche Politik. Zur Entstehung und Verfestigung von Arbeitsmarkt-segmentation' (The business cycle and policy of the firm. On the genesis and structuration of labour market segmentation), in H.G. Mendius et al. 1976, pp. 15-81, (B).
Two main reactions to fluctuations in a firm's product demand are distinguished, 'adaptation' and 'stabilisation'. The first strategy demands flexibility in productive capacity and manpower supply; the second requires executive management to 'neutralise' the more hostile elements in the firms' environment.

J.R. MERCER

Labelling the mentally retarded, Los Angeles: University of California Press, 1973, (D).
A study of the process by which individuals become 'labelled' and treated according to a stereotype of the 'mentally incapable'.

D. METCALF

'Pay dispersion, information and returns to search in a professional labour market', *Review of Economic Studies*, October, 1973, (B, C).

'Book review of *Equal pay for women: progress and problems in seven countries*', edited by B. Pettman, *British Journal of Industrial Relations*, Vol. XIV, No. 2, 1976, (B, C).
 Strong argument for the existence of pre-entry discrimination (careers) rather than the post-entry form (earnings) displayed in the Pettman book.

F. MEYERS

The ownership of jobs: a comparative study, Los Angeles Institute of Industrial Relations: University of California, 1964, (C, D).
 Meyers stresses that while British unions may not have taken an official interest in such questions, shop-stewards do negotiate informally about job security.

W. H. MIERNYK

The economics of labour and collective bargaining, Lexington, Mass.: D.C. Heath, 1973, (B. C).
 An excellent textbook in the institutionalist tradition, with an eye for the importance of historical factors in union-management relations.

R. L. MILLER and J. A. JACKSON

'Determinants of occupational status and mobility in Northern Ireland and the Irish Republic: the size and determinants of the marginal labour force', preliminary report to the European Economic Community, July 1977, (D).
 A multi-factorial analysis of demographic and attitudinal data classified by (1) part-time workers, (2) in-family employment, (3) retired, (4) unemployed, (5) second-job holders, (6) overqualified by education, (7) over-qualified by apprenticeship, (8) downwardly mobile.

J. S. MILL

Essay on Liberty, Oxford: Blackwell, 1942 ed., (A, D).
 Not one of Mill's economic theses but the work in which he expresses most succinctly his rejection of the 'balancing of net advantages' leading to an optimum distribution of labour.

J. MINCER

'Investment in human capital and personal income distribution', *Journal of Political Economy*, August 1958, pp. 281-302, (A).
 One of the earliest attempts to apply human capital theory to the distribution of personal incomes in America.

'On-the-job training: return and some implications', *Investment in Human Beings*, NBER Conference 15, supplement to *Journal of Political Economy*, October 1962. Also in J. F. Burton, et al. (eds.) *Readings in labor market analysis*, New York: Holt, Rinehart and Winston, 1971, pp. 201-230, (A, B).
 Tentatively concludes that investment in on-the-job training is a very large component of total American investment in education (as important as formal education for male labour

force): that expenditure on on-the-job training has been *increasing* since 1939 particularly among *higher* skill levels: that the return to the employer from on-the-job training was as high as that from formal education but that it was lower for the recipient: that on-the-job training is highly correlated to stable employment conditions and to those higher skilled manual workers who enjoy these conditions.

'Labor force participation of married women: a study of labor supply' in *Aspects of labor economics*, Princeton University Press for National Bureau of Economic Research, 1962, (B, C).
Study of part-time and temporary work by women.

'Property and unemployment', in R. A. Gordon and M. S. Gordon (eds.), New York: Wiley and Son, 1966, pp. 73-112, (B, C).
Mincer's study is a comprehensive analysis of movements into and out of employment in the United States which concludes that a great deal of 'hidden unemployment' occurs because of the long-term 'dropping out' of marginal labour.

'Youth, education and work', *Teachers College Record*, Vol. 74, February 1973, p. 312, (B, C).
An analysis of school-leaver unemployment.

'Schooling, experience and earnings', N.B.E.R., New York: Columbia University Press, 1974, (B, C).
An application of human capital theory to data on general and specific qualification.

J. Mincer and S. Polachek

'Earnings of women', *Journal of Political Economy*, Part II, March/April 1974, (B, C).
A restatement of human capital theory to include discrimination against women.

Minority Rights Group

Western Europe's migrant workers, London: M.R.P., 1977, (C, D).
A pressure-group critique of the policies of European states towards foreign workers.

A. L. Mok ,

'Professie en arbeidsvoldoening', in J. Berting and L. U. de Sitter (eds.), *Arbeidsvoldoening en arbeidsbeleid*, Utrecht-Antwerp: Het Spectrum, 1968, 139-162, (D).
Analysis of closure of professional labour markets.

'Is er een dubbele arbeidsmarkt in Nederland?' (Is there a dual labour market in the Netherlands?), in *Werkloosheid. Aard, omvang, structurele oorzaken en beleidsalternatieven. Pre-adviezen van de Vereniging voor de Staathuishoudkunde*. The Hague: Martinus Nijhoff, 1975, (B, D).
Departing from a four-segment model of the labour market (see text) the answer to the question posed in the title is that not enough research has been done in the Netherlands to give a verdict, but that some developments point in the direction of a dual labour market existing in the Netherlands. Three such developments are discussed, as well as the ongoing restructuring of the Dutch employment service.

'De marginaliteit van tijdelijke arbeid. Een sociologische beschouwing' (The marginality of temporary work. A sociological view), in *Vijf preadviezen over tijdelijk werk*. Amsterdam: ABU, 1976, pp. 56-69, (B, D).

Temporary work can be called marginal work for three reasons: (1) because employers and unions alike want to safeguard the hard core of the employment structure: (2) because temporary work agencies occupy only a minor role among the mediating agencies in the labour market and (3) because within the work situation the temporary worker wants to belong to the work group, he is denied a permanent place because of his connections with an external source of stigmatisation and because of the limited time perspective employed by all concerned with the assessment of his work and career prospects.

A. L. MOK and J. BRACKE

'De arbeidsmarkt: een poging tot integratie van economische en sociologische gezichtspunten' (The labour market: an attempt to integrate economic and sociological points of view), *Economisch en Sociaal Tijdschrift*, 30, No. 4, 1976 pp. 551-626, (B, D).
Four clusters of labour market theories are distinguished: neoclassical, Marxist, institutional and dual theories. The development of these theories is seen as an historical process from collectively oriented to more individualistic theories, and from objective to more subjective theories. Theories that are both individualistically and subjectively oriented are almost totally lacking. This could perhaps be a fruitful area in which economic and sociological points of view can be integrated. The authors mention the «arena theories» as an example (see, for instance, Martin and Fryer, 1973, cited above).

D. MORSE

The peripheral worker, New York/London: Columbia University Press, 1969, (B, C).
The author suggests that the American labour force is becoming ever more bifurcated. There is one half of the market where employment is full time over the full year, with high rewards and important fringe benefits and good working conditions. In the other segment workers must accept employment with relatively low wages, low fringe benefits, often part-time and intermittent. However, the concept of peripherality does not distinguish between those who want to work part-time or intermittently and those who do so by default, between those who want to be mobile and those who are forced to by the circumstances of the market. Morse's analysis concentrates on the latter.

D. P. MOYNIHAN (ed.)

On understanding poverty: perspectives from the social sciences, New York: Basic Books, 1968, (D).
A collection of anthropological studies around the theme of the 'culture of poverty'.

S. K. MUKHERJEE

'The job creation programme in the United Kingdom', Berlin: International Institute of Management, dp 77-30, May 1977, (B, C).
An account of the establishment of the Job Creation Programme (operated by Britain's Manpower Services Commission) is given and the economic and general policy issues which formed the background to the initiation of that Programme are analysed. A case is argued for the view that economic recovery in Western industrial countries generally and Britain in particular, will do little to reduce the prevailing, post-war record, high levels of unemployment. The author points out that specific measures for 'non-market-generated' employment creation are necessary as an antidote to the present excessive unemployment; and, that such measures are likely to create no greater costs in terms of public expenditure than are incurred in the existence of present level of unemployment. That

argument is made by reference to the losses to the advanced industrial countries' economies incurred in the financing of high unemployment compensation to those who are out of work; from the loss of revenue to the exchequer from taxes foregone on incomes and consumption; and from losses of inflows of contributions to the social security funds. An attempt is made to calculate these losses in broad terms for nine countries, and in more detail for Britain and Germany.

S.K. MUKHERJEE

'Unemployment: a note on current view', Berlin: International Institute of Management, dp 77-107, November 1977, (C, D).
  A reconsideration of unemployment as a concept, with regard to the methods used for measuring it, and in terms of the costs of it for those who are out of work, and for the community as a whole is the purpose of this paper. The first part reviews and comments on the past and present discussions involving the concept and measurement of unemployment.

NATIONAL BOARD OF PRICES AND INCOMES

'General problems of low pay', Report No. 169, London: H.M.S.O. April, 1971, (B, C).
  Study of causes of low pay in Britain and possible means to their alleviation.

J. VON NEUMANN and O. MORGENSTEIN

Theory of games and economic behaviour, Princeton University Press, 1948, (A).
  Original statement of 'games theory' as applied to dual monopoly bargaining.

O.E.C.D.

'Manpower policy in the member countries', Organisation for Economic Co-operation and Development, Paris, 1970, (B, C).
  Series of resumes of manpower policies in Europe and North America.

W.OI

'Labor as a quasi-fixed factor', *Journal of Political Economy*, 1962, (A, B).
  One of the first neo-classical treatments of labour as capital of specific skills and experience.

A.M. OLUN

'Upward mobility in a high pressure economy', *Proceedings of the Economic Association*, Vol. 1, 1973, pp. 207-52, (A, C).
  Traces movement of labour from secondary to primary jobs in periods of high demand.

M. OLSON Jr.

The logic of collective action: public goods and the theory of groups, New York: Schocken Books, 1968, (A, D).
  An economic theory of interest groups using the concept of 'public goods', that is advantages that can only be obtained and consumed on a collective basis.

V.K. OPPENHEIMER

'The female labor force in the United States', *Population Monograph Series No. 5.*, Berkeley: Institute of International Studies, University of California, 1970, (B, C, D).
  Comprehensive review of female employment in the United States.

P. OSTERMAN

'The empirical study of labour market segmentation', *Industrial and Labour Relations Review*, Vol. 28, July 1975, pp. 508-523, (B, C).
  Aggregative study of labour market segmentation in the United States.

G.L. PALMER

Labor mobility in six cities, New York: Social Sience Research Council, 1954, (B, C).
  One of the earliest studies of attachment to work and occupation which sought to explain the *immobility* of certain groups.

V. PARETO

Manuel d'economie politique 2nd.ed, French translation 1927, (first published in Italian 1906), (A).
  Most famous for its elaboration of the *ordinal* concept of utility and its development of consumer preference curves. It is also the best statement of the objectively neutral science of economics sought after by the Lausanne economists. Earlier (*Cours d'economie politique* 1897) Pareto had demonstrated the constant distribution of income levels for different times and countries. He saw this distribution as complementing a similar distribution in the unequal distribution of human ability (an early example of human capital theory). Pareto's further conclusion was that a reduction in inequality could only be achieved through a rise in average income, that is by production growing faster than population.

A.H. PACKER

'Categorical public employment guarantees: a proposed solution to the poverty problem' in *Studies in Public Welfare*, Paper 9 (pt. 1), pp. 68-127, (B, C).
  Radical suggestion for job-creation in the primary sector.

F. PARKIN

Class inequality and political order: social stratification in capitalist and communist societies'. London: Paladin, 1972, (D).
  An interesting development of Gramsci's theory of capitalist class hegemony through the fragmentation of working class interest and the acceptance of the 'dominant' ideology existing within a social system. This exists alongside an opposing but accomodative belief system among workers and working class institutions and a 'radical' tradition that rejects the bases of both sets of prevailing beliefs.

H.S. PARNES

'Research on labor mobility: an appraisal of research findings in the United States', Bulletin 65, Social Science Research Council 1954, (B).
  Excellent statement of the neo-classical approach to the labour market.

D.O. PARSONS

'Specific human capital: an application to quit rates and lay off rates', *Journal of political Economy*, Vol. 80, November/December 1972, pp. 120, (B, C).
Use of internal labour market theory to explain longevity of 'core' workforce.

A.M. PETTIGREW

The politics of organizational decision-making, London/Assen: Tavistock/Van Gorcum, 1973, (D).
An analysis of the processes of decision-making accompanying technological innovation: focussing on the generation of pressure group power in organisations.

B. PETTMAN (ed.)

Equal pay for women: progress and problems in seven countries, MCB Books, 1975, (B, C).
A collection of evidence of a quantitative and largely econometric kind.

E.H. PHELPS BROWN

'Minutes of evidence to the Royal Commission on Trade Unions and Employers' Associations', London: HMSO, 1966, (B, C, D).
See especially the author's remarks on the effects of plant bargaining in Britain.

'Report of the Committee of Enquiry under Professor E.H. Phelps Brown into certain matters concerning labour in building and civil engineering', CMND 3714, London: HMSO 1968, (B, C, D).
A report of the economic and social effects of 'labour-only' sub-contracting in the British building industry which concluded that subject to certain safe-guards it should not be regulated by the State.

The inequality of pay, Oxford: Oxford University Press, 1977, (B, C, D).
Probably the most comprehensive review of the literature and evidence on this subject. Inspite of its width of sources its conclusions are somewhat indeterminate and heavily shaped by the author's bias towards a neo-classical frame of analysis.

P.J.C. PERRY

'The evolution of British manpower policy–from the Statute of Artificers 1563 to the Industrial Training Act, 1964', London: British Association for Commercial and Industrial Education 1976, (C, D).
Describes break-down of centralised Elizabethan system of labour market regulation under the impact of industrialisation and the reemergence of central direction in recent times.

M.J. PIORE

'The impact of the labour market upon the design and selection of productive techniques within the manufacturing plant', *Quarterly Journal of Economics*, Vol. 82, 1968, pp. 602-20, (A, B, C).

'Jobs and training' in S.H. Beer and R.E. Berringer (eds.), *The state and the poor*, Winthrop, 1970, (B, C).

'Fragments of a 'sociological' theory of wages' in *American Economic Association,* Papers and proceedings of eighty-fifth annual meeting, 1972 (*American Economic Review*, Vol. 63, May 1973, pp. 377-84), (B, C, D).

Three articles developing Piore's thesis that the choice of manufacturing technology is heavily structured by institutionalised interests.

'Notes for a theory of labor market stratification' in R.C. Edwards, M. Reich and D.M. Gordon (eds.), *Labor market segmentation*, Lexington (Mass.) / Toronto / London: Heath, 1975, (A, B, C).

Piore develops a threefold model of labour market segmentation, corresponding to a threeclass view of social stratification. Segments are largely determined by the structure of technology and by the extent of labour mobility, that is the location of capital investment. The supply of labour is determined by the sub-culture of workers' origin and by the structure of their qualifications. These shape their propensity to work and determine their place of entry into one segment or the other and their subsequent patterns of mobility. (See also R.C. Edwards et al. above.)

A.C. PIGOU

The economics of welfare 4th. edition, London: Macmillan, 1950, (A).

Most important influence on Keynes whom he predated in his concern for structural effects of laisser-faire capitalism. As well as contributing the basis for what is now known as 'welfare economics' he also suggested many of the macro-concepts later used by Keynes, e.g., investment accelerator.

D.O. PORTER

'Adapting the 'responsibility center' concept to government administration', February 1977, p. 34, (D).

The predominant pattern for administering governmental programs is through multi-organisational networks. Relying on a theory of resource mobilisation and an analysis of allocation processes within the public sector, the paper argues that individual units within the multi-organisational networks are increasingly beyond the traditional control mechanisms of the market or ballot box.

G. PSACHAROPOULOS

'Family background, education and achievement, *British Journal of Sociology*, December 1977, (C, D).

'Labour market duality and income distribution: the case of the U.K.', Presented to the S.S.R.C. Labour Economics Study Group, London School of Economics, March 1977, (C, D).

Multi-factorial analysis of aggregated data on income and career demonstrating a clear dichotomy between 'working class' and 'middle class' occupations with little evidence of other segmentation as significant as this one.

G. PSACHAROPOULOS and R. LAYARD

'Human capital and earnings: British evidence and a critique', unpublished manuscript, London School of Economics, 1976, (B, C).

Critique of the human capital hypothesis based on the distribution of earnings in the U.K.

ANNOTATED BIBLIOGRAPHY 227

S.A. RHEA

'Unemployment insurance and labour supply: a simulation of the 1971 Canadian Unemployment Insurance Act', *Proceedings of the Conference on Trends in Industrial and Labour Relations*, Montreal, May 1976, pp. 226-284, (B, C).
  An attempted simulation of the effects of the Unemployment Insurance Act introduced by the Canadian Federal Government 1971. It suggests an *increase* in the qualifying period of waiting in an unemployed state as a dis-incentive to seek leisure.

M.W. REDER

'The theory of occupational wage differential', *American Economic Review*, 1955, (A, B).

Wage differential: theory of measurement, aspects of labor economics, New York: National Bureau of Economic Research, 1962, pp. 257-299, (B, C).
  An attempt to explain short term and secular trends in occupational wage structures within a neo-classical framework. Useful for its integration of the theoretical and available empirical data.

'Job scarcity and the nature of union power', in McCormick and Smith (eds.), *The labour market*, London: Penguin Books, 1969, pp. 120-142, (B, C).
  Arguments for the dominance of market forces over those of exogenous trade union pressures in determining wage levels and wage differentials.

A. REES

The economics of trade unions, Oxford University Press, 1962, (A, B).

The economics of work and pay, New York: Harper and Row, 1973, (A, B).

'Information networks in labour markets', *American Economic Review*, May 1966, pp. 559-66, (B, C).

A. REES and G.P. SCHULTZ

'Workers and wages in an urban labor market', University of Chicago Press, 1970, (B, C).
  Empirical study of a metropolitan labour market covering seventy-five establishments. Analyses the factors that determine wage differentials among professional, clerical and manual workers.

M. REICH, D.M. GORDON and R.C. EDWARDS

'A theory of labour market segmentation', *American Economic Review*, Vol. 63, 2, 1973, pp. 359-365, (A, B).
  Radical statement of dual market theory (see text).

G.L. REID

'The role of the employment service in redeployment', paper presented to the Second World Congress of the International Industrial Relations Association, Geneva, 1-4 September 1970, (B, C, D).
  Study based on redeployment of redundant workers in Britain (see text).

D. RICARDO

Principles of the political economy. Works and correspondence of David Ricardo, Sraffa edn., Cambridge University Press, Vol. 1, 1951-73, (A).
   Original statement of the law of diminishing returns to inputs: basis for much of the Marxist theory of value.

R.R. RITTI

'Underemployment in engineers', *Industrial Relations*, 9, 1970, pp. 437-452, (C, D).
   One of a number of studies of this phenomenon which illustrate the specific and narrow use to which engineering skills are put within the enterprise.

B.C. ROBERTS and J.H. SMITH

Manpower policy and employment trends, G. Bell and Sons for London School of Economics, 1966, (B, C, D).
   A collection of (then) pioneering essays which have now largely been overtaken by subsequent developments. The occupational scheme quoted above has not however received any kind of conceptual attention.

B.C. ROBERTS, R. LOVERIDGE and J. GENNARD

Reluctant militants–a study of industrial technicians, London, Heinemann, pp. 3-55, 1972, (C, D).
   A study of the emergence of industrial technicians as an occupational group in Britain with its attendant industrial relations problems for management. It presents the process as the result of a series of incremental recruitment and induction decisions taken in a largely unconscious manner by many diverse managers concerned only to maintain their control over their *local* workplace situation.

C.J. ROBERTS

'The demand for manpower: employment functions', Chapter 6 in J.S. Wabe (ed.), *Problems in manpower forecasting*, Farnborough: Saxon House, 1974, (B, C).
   Review of current measures of occupational demand and their deficiencies.

D.J. ROBERTSON

'A market for labour', Hobart Paper, No. 12, Institute of Economic Affairs, 1961, p. 25, (A, B, C).
   Examines institutional blockages to labour mobility in Britain and consequent 'bottle necks' in the supply of labour.

D. ROBINSON

'Myths of the local labour market, *Personnel,* December 1967, p. 37, (A, B, C).

'Wage drift, fringe benefits and manpower distribution', O.E.C.D., Paris, 1968, p. 66 (B, C).

(ed.), *Local labour markets and wage structures*, London: Gower Press, 1970.
   Critique of neo-classical explanation of labour markets using an internal labour market approach in a broadly institutionalist manner.

J. ROBINSON

The economics of imperfect competition, London, 1933, (A).
A re-statement of marginalist theory in conditions in which the firm is able to bring about super-normal profits at less than full efficiency. Of special interest since Mrs. Robinson traces the effect of this condition on the reward to factors of production.

E. ROLL

A history of economic thought, London: Faber and Faber, 1957, (first published 1939), (A).
A history of main schools of economic thought from the Old Testament onwards. Still regarded by many economists as the most lucidly comprehensive exposition of the conceptual evolution of their field, it reveals the danger of attempting any easy categorisation. 'This absence of a neat chronological sequence in the evolution of economic doctrine is most striking when different countries are compared... Ideas, dead in one country, reappear in another if the economic environment is more suitable'. p. 15.

P. ROLLE

'Qualités de travail et hiérarchie des qualifications'. *Sociologie du Travail*, 15, 2, 1973, pp. 157-176, (A, D).
Interesting observations on the origin and development of labour markets.

E. J. B. ROSE et al.

Colour and citizenship, Oxford University Press for the Institute of Race Relations, 1969, (D).
Major study of employment and social position and context of immigrant workers in the UK.

H. ROSE

'Up against the welfare state: the claimants' unions', in R. Miliband and J. Saville (eds.), *The Socialist Register* 1973, London: Merlin Press, 1974, (D).
One of few descriptions of an attempt by secondary sector workers to organise in an attempt to gain more financial and other support from the State.

S. ROSEN

Book review of D. M. Gordon's *Theories of poverty and underemployment* in *Journal of Political Economy*, Vol. 82, March/April 1974, pp. 437-39, (B, C).

'A Review of Industrial Relations Research', Vol. 2, University of Wisconsin: IRRA, 1971, pp. 109-10, (B, C).
Discussion of the radical approach to dual market theory.

'Human capital: a survey of empirical research', Department of Economics, University of Rochester, Discussion Paper 76-2, January 1976, (B, C).
Useful summary and critique of the literature on the human capital hypothesis.

A. M. ROSS

Trade union wage policy, Berkeley: University of California Press, 1948, (A, B).
The author argues that collective bargaining is a political rather than economic process: part of a sustained dialogue with Dunlop (see Dunlop 1944 above).

W. W. Rostow

The stages of economic growth, Cambridge University Press, 1960, (A, D).
    An analysis of the macro-process of industrialisation which divides it into five stages of growth, (1) pre-conditions for take-off; (2) the take-off; (3) the drive to maturity; (4) the age of high mass-consumption; (5) beyond consumption.

G. Routh

Occupation and pay in Great Britain, 1906-1960, Cambridge: Cambridge University Press, 1965, (B, C).
    Comprehensive longitudinal study of occupational change in the United Kingdom.

M. Rutter and N. Madge

Cycles of disadvantage—a review of research, London: Heinemann, 1976, (D).
    A comprehensive summary of the evidence of the existence of a 'cycle of disadvantage' among deprived groups in Britain. Conclusions are that whilst several factors come together to make the position of the poorest workers one which is likely to be perpetuated from one generation to another, in over 40% of the families social mobility is experienced by one or more siblings.

P. Salama and J. Valier

Une introduction à l'économie politique, Paris: Maspero, 1973, (A, D).
    An attempt to interpret labour market segmentation in terms of social class.

G. Salaman

Community and occupation. An exploration of work/leisure relationships, Cambridge University Press, 1974, (D).
    One of several works by this author illustrating the importance of occupational identity to the occupants of certain jobs.

K. Saunders

'Occupational stigmatization in the British hotel and catering industry', M. Phil. Dissertation, University of Aston, 1976, (D).
    Attempt to explain the process of stigmatization by reference to the role of the kitchen porter.

F. W. Scharpf and F. Schnabel

'Steuerungsprobleme der Raumplaning', Berlin: International Institute of Management, November 1977, (C, D).
    The article offers an overview of the conditions requiring a systematic governmental planning of regional development and of the direct and indirect control instruments presently available to regional planners.

F. W. Scharpf, B. Reissert and F. Schnabel

'Policy effectiveness and conflict avoidance in intergovernmental policy formation', Berlin: International Institute of Management, December 1977, (C, D).

The paper presents the theoretical frame of reference and some of the empirical findings of an ongoing study of joint federal-state decision making in West Germany. At the theoretical level, an attempt is made to link the typology of problems which are systematically generated within decentralised decision structures with an analysis of potential control instruments that might correct these problems.

G. Schmid

'Zur Konzeption einer aktiven Arbeitsmarktpolitik' (The concept of an active labour market policy), in M. Bolle (ed.), pp. 165-185, (B, C).
An active labour market policy is concerned with balancing the labour market so that none of the parties involved will be able to play a power game. In this context the author does not want to limit such a policy to the external labour market, but includes internal labour markets in order to help prevent some disadvantaged groups from permanent marginalisation. He applies his concept of an active labour market policy to a comparison between Sweden and the German Federal Republic, from which Sweden does not emerge as the paradise some think it is.

Gesellschaftliche Entwicklung und Industriesoziologie in den USA, Eine historische Analyse, Frankfurt a.M./Koln: EVA, 1974, (B,D).
A discursive study of the American institutionalist school.

'Strukturelle Arbeitslosigkeit in der Bundesrepublik. Beitrage zur Problemanalyse der Unterbeschäftigung und Uberlegungen zu arbeitsmarktpolitischen Konsequenzen', Berlin: Industrial Institute of Management, IIM 77-6, August 1977, 85 pps, (B,D).
The first part of the paper presents an overview and an evaluation of the discussions about 'structural unemployment' in the Federal Republic of Germany. A structural approach is designed to take into account not only the external, visible interrelations, but also the internal dynamics and the functioning of the labour market. In the second, empirical part, the distribution of unemployment in West Germany is examined using time series analyses (a) of the regional distribution of unemployment from 1965-1976, and (b) of the redistribution of unemployment by age, status and sex from 1966-1976.

'Wage-cost subsidy programme in Germany 1974/75. Some circumstantial evidence of its impact and effect-a quantitative study'. Berlin: International Institute of Management, dp. 77-111, December 1977, 60 pp., (B, C).
A 'Programme for the Promotion of Employment and Growth during Stability' was decided in the Federal Republic at the end of 1974. The study describes the distribution of the expenditure in detail according to: type of industry, regions, labour offices and demographic characteristics. Three aspects of the effectiveness of the programme are differentiated: (a) Utilization of the Programme: i.e. how many unemployed who were potentially eligible for subsidy were affected by the programme. The average utilization figures were 22%; regionally the utilization figures varied between 3 and 75%. (b) Effectivity of the Programme: i.e. what real increase in employment the programme achieved? The outcome of the study shows that the net effectivity of the programme was about 25%. It was also attempted, with the help of multiple regression analysis, to find out the reasons for the different utilization and the low nett effectivity. (c) Cost-Benefit - Relationship of the Programme: On the grounds of the relative low nett effects a deficit of approximately DM. 70 million for the state and parafiscal organizations was calculated. A nett effect of 50% should indeed have been calculated. The study comes to the preliminary conclusion that wage-cost subsidies might have a place in an active labour market policy.

G. Schmid and D. Freiburghaus

'Active labour market policy with special reference to youth unemployment in the Federal Republic of Germany', International Institute of Management, Berlin, dp 77-1, January 1977, (B, C).

General criteria for an 'active labour market policy' at different 'system levels' are developed mainly with respect to dealing with the problem of combating youth unemployment. Ideas presently under discussion are taken up, in particular the concept of subsidising additional employment creation. Displacement effects and side effects of policies on the functioning of the overall labour market are emphasised.

'Arbeitsmarktpolitik in Schweden und in der Bundesrepublik: Überlegungen zu einer möglichen Wende arbeitsmarktpolitischer Konzeption', International Institute of Management, Berlin, dp/77-48, July 1977, (C, D).

Both the Federal Republic of Germany and Sweden claim to pursue 'active manpower policies'. All available data suggest however that, at least in the fight against unemployment, the Swedish policies have been and still are significantly more effective. The main explanation seems to lie in the existence of a labour administration structure and a method of implementing manpower policy which make it possible to pursue the objective of high employment in a much more direct way.

N. Schoemaker, A.M. de Jong-van der Poel and R.W. Hommes

De positie van de vrouw op de arbeidsmarkt (The position of women in the labour market), Amsterdam: SISWO, 1978, (B).

The inferior position of women in the labour market is described and analysed in a dualist perspective. Stress is laid on the structure of demand for female labour, and on the actual behaviour of women in the labour market. The authors give useful directions for further research into women's work situation.

R. Schultz-Wild

Betriebliche Beschäftigungspolitik in der Krise, (Manpower policy of the firm in (the) crisis), Frankfurt/New York: Campus, 1978, (C).

The recession of 1973-74 brought about changes in the manpower policy of many firms, but not in all of them. Some firms can pursue a policy of stabilising their work force in times of crises, others adapt to the rise and fall of demand for their product. The author investigates the conditions that make firms decide to follow the former course or the latter. The theoretical framework is applied to a specific industrial sector in a specific geographical context (the automobile industry in Germany).

T.W. Schultz

'The formation of human capital by education', *Journal of Political Economy*, December 1960, (A, C).

'Investment in human capital', *American Economic Review*, March 1961, pp. 1-17, (A, C).

Two of the earliest modern expositions of the view that differential returns in the form of income to different occupations can be explained in terms of the length of training, and level of qualification gained on entry or during the course of one's career.

Investment in human capital: the role of education and research, New York: Free Press, 1971, (A, C).

A development of the human capital interpretation of differences between countries in respect to Gross Domestic Product and economic growth rates.

U. Schumm-Garling

Herrschaft in der industriellen Arbeitsorganisation, Frankfurt a.M.: Suhrkamp, 1972, (D).
   Analysis of the internal labour market from a Marxist point of view.

T. Scitovsky

Welfare and competition, London: Unwin University Books, Allen and Unwin, 1952, (A).
   A closely argued attempt to bring together neo-classical price theory with the challenges presented under the heading of 'welfare economics'. (See also I.M.D. Little *A critique of welfare economics*, Oxford University Press, 1950).

S. Seidman

'The design of Federal employment programs: an economic analysis', Ph. D. dissertation, University of California, Berkeley, 1974, (B, C).
   Comprehensive and largely descriptive critique of labour market policy in USA.

W. Sengenberger

Die gegenwartige Arbeitslosigkeit auch ein Strukturproblem des Arbeitsmarkts, (The present unemployment situation as a structural labour market problem), Frankfurt: Campus, 1978, (B).
   The high rate of unemployment and underemployment in advanced industrial societies like the Federal Republic of Germany is analysed as a problem of the interaction and segmental tendencies in the labour market.

W. Sengenberger, (ed.)

Der gespaltene Arbeitsmarkt. Probleme der Arbeitsmarktsegmentation (The split-up labour market. Problems of labour market segmentation), Frankfurt/New York: Campus, 1978, (B).
   A reader of partly old, partly original articles, with specific reference to a comparison between developments in the United States, Germany and France.

G.L. Shackle

'The nature of the bargaining process' in J.T. Dunlop (ed.), *The theory of wage determination*, London: Macmillan, 1957, pp. 292-314, (A).
   Formal presentation of method of wage settlement by bargaining.

J.R. Shea et al.

Dual careers, Vol. 1, Columbus, Ohio: Center for Human Resources Research, Ohia State University, May 1970, p. 36, (C, D).
   Investigation of the working careers of women in America.

J.J. Silvestre

Les salaires ouvriers dans l'industrie française, Paris: Bordas, 1973, 416 pp., (B, C).
   The author discounts neo-classical explanations of mobility in the French labour market and in doing so proposes another explanation of the manner in which decisions are taken in the market.

R. D. Sleeper

'Labour mobility over the life cycle', *British Journal of Industriai Relations*, Vol. XIII, No. 2, 1975, (B, C).
   Interesting explanation of the functions of marginal employment for the individual set out in detail in the text.

M. de Smidt

⟨ Bedrijfsstructuur en arbeidsmarkt in een ruimtelijk kader. (Industrial structure and labour market in a regional context). Utrecht: Geografisch Instituut, 1975, (B, C).
   The labour market as influenced by the local and regional industrial structure.

R. C. Smith and C. C. Holt

'A job search-turnover analysis of the black-white unemployment ratiò', reprint 69-350-26, Washington: The Urban Institute, 1971, (B, C).
   Empirical evidence of transitory nature of employment in urban ghetto.

R. Shirwen

Book review of Gordon's *Theories of poverty and underemployment* in *Journal of Political Economy*, Vol. 82, March/April, 1974, pp. 437-39, (A, B).
   Critique of radical theory of dual markets.

S. H. Slichter et al.

'The impact of collective bargaining on management', Brookings Institution, Washington, 1960, (B, D).
   Important exposition of institutionalist approach to the forces acting on the demand for labour inside the firm.

P. J. Sloane and W. S. Siebert

'Hiring practices and the employment of women', Paisley College of Technology, (mimeo), 1977, (B, C).
   Study of overt and covert methods of discrimination employed within a sample of firms.

A. Smith

An inquiry into the nature and causes of the wealth of nations. Edinburgh: Thomas Nelson, 1845, (first published 1776), (A).
   This work marks the break with Mercantilism and Physiocratism in economic theory. The first volume discusses the division of labour as the basis for economic functioning, the theory of exchange, money and distribution. The second volume is devoted to the analysis of capital formation.

W. R. Smith

'Imperfect competition and marketing strategy', *Cost and Profit Outlook*, October 1955, (B, C).
   Article on theory of product market segmentation used here to illustrate the demand-orientation of neo-classical economics.

R. M. Solow

'Short-run adjustment of employment to output', in J. N. Wolfe (ed.), *Value, capital and growth*, Edinburgh: University Press, 1968, (A., C).
Contribution to long-standing debate on factors contributing to economic growth.

A. M. Spence

'Job market signalling', *Quarterly Journal of Economics*, Vol. 87, Aug. 1973, pp. 355-74, (B, C).

Market signalling: informational transfer in hiring and related screening processes, Harvard University Press, Cambridge, Mass., 1974, (B, C).
Study of 'statistical filtering' employed in the hiring practices of a sample of firms.

G. Standing

'The distribution of concealed unemployment in Great Britain', *British Journal of Industrial Relations*, Vol. X, No. 2, 1972, (B, C).
Critique of statistical use of unemployment records in the UK with an interesting break-down of evidence of unemployment in certain occupations and industries (see text).

C. Steinberg

Reply to Rea 'Unemployment Insurance and Labour Supply', *Proceedings of the Conference on Trends in Industrial and Labour Relations*, Montreal, May 1976, (B, C).
A technical and empirical critique of the concept of 'voluntary unemployment' as contained in Rea's model using the work of Swan (EEC Working Papers 31 and 32, May 1976).

J.E. Stiglitz

'Approaches to the economics of discrimination', *American Economic Review*, Papers and proceedings, May 1973, (A, B).

'Theories of discrimination and economic policy' in G. M. von Furstenberg, et al. *Patterns of racial discrimination*, Vol. 2, *Employment and income*, N.Y.: Heath, 1974, (A, B).
Discursive but illuminating pieces in the neo-classical manner.

F. Stoeckel-Fizaine

'Effet d'entreprise et structuration du marché du travail', *Annales de l'INSEE*, no 16-17, May-December, 1974, pp. 240-261, (B, D).
The article examines the role of the enterprise in structuring the labour market and presents a criticism of neo-classical theory in the manner of ILM theorists.

K. Taira

'Internal labour markets, human resource utilisation and economic growth', International Institute for Labour Studies, Research Conference on Urban Labour Markets, Geneva, 9-13th September 1976, (B, D).
Interesting attempt to relate ILM theory to the effective allocation of labour at the macro level.

F.W. TAYLOR

Scientific management, New York: Harper and Row, 1947, (D).
The best-known statement of the rational-logical means to controlling manufacturing production. The basis for the discipline of work-study and much of original content of production engineering.

J. TAYLOR

'Unemployment in Britain: an interpretation of the last twenty-five Years'. University of Lancaster, (mimeo), 1975, (B, C).
Post-Keynesian interpretation of unemployment.

A. TEULINGS

Philips: Geschiedenis en praktijk van een wereldconcern, (Philips: History and Practice of a global concern), Amsterdam: Van Gennep, 1976, (B, D).
Case study of the well-known Dutch electronics firm in which it is made quite clear that there are other forms of labour market behaviour than mobility (like sickness absenteeism). There is labour market segmentation within the firm, including 'external' segments, which provide for optimal flexibility in manning levels: the number of permanent production workers for core processes is kept small and many peripheral tasks are performed by foreign workers, students, temps and women.

C. THELOT

'Mobilité professionnelle plus forte entre 1965 et 1970 qu'entre 1959 et 1964', *Economie et Statistique*, no. 51, Decembre 1973, p. 3-32, (B, C).
The author demonstrates considerable job mobility exists within a comparatively stable structure of jobs.

'Le fonctionnement du marché de l'emploi: l'example des Pays de la Loire'. *Economie et Statistique*, no. 69, July-August 1975, p. 51-58, (B, C).
This study reveals the simultaneous growth of employment and unemployment within the Loire region. The author examines the nature and function of offers of employment and the sources of mobility and immobility among workers.

B. THOMAS and D. DEATON

Labour shortage and economic analysis: a study of occupational labour markets, Oxford: Blackwell, 1977, (B, C).
An interesting attempt at an empirical study of the occupational markets for bus-men, teachers and draughtsmen in Britain using the concept of 'structured' external and internal labour markets.

B. THOMAS, J. MOXHAM and J.A.G. JONES

'A cost-benefit analysis of industrial training', *British Journal of Industrial Relations*, Vol. VII, No. 2, pp. 231-264, 1969, (B, C).
A critique of the 'levy-grant' system set up by the Industrial Training Act 1964 (see text for detail).

B. Tizard et al.

'Environmental effects on language development: a study of young children in long-stay residential nurseries', *Child Development*, 43, 1972, pp. 337-358, (D).
One of a series of studies on the effects of narrow social environments on children of deprived groups.

J. Tizard

'Race and IQ: the limits of probability', *New Behaviour*, I, pp. 6-9, 1975, (D).
Suggests the dominance of environmental influences in the formation of measurable intelligence and academic achievement.

L. C. Thurow

'Redistributional aspects of manpower training programs' in L. Ulman (ed.), *Manpower programs in the policy mix*, 1965, pp. 84-89, (B, C).

'Education and economic equality', *The Public Interest*, No. 28, Summer 1972, pp. 66-81, (B, C).

'Measuring the economic benefits of education' in M. Gordon (ed.), *Higher education and the labour market*, New York: McGraw-Hill, 1973, (B, C).
A series of articles demonstrating the effects of training and education on segmentation in America.

C. Thurow and K. E. B. Lucas

'The American distribution of income: a structural problem', A study prepared for the use of the joint economic committee, 92nd Congressional Session, 1972, (B, C).
A most comprehensive collection of data on segmentation in the American labour market.

F. Tönnies

Community and society, Harper Torchbook edition, New York: Harper and Row, 1963, (D).
Early statement of sociological bases of discrimination.

A. Touraine et al.

Workers' attitudes to technical change, Paris: OECD, 1964, (B, D).
A discursive but comprehensive review of the literature on employee attitudes to their job to changes in the work environment.

H. A. Turner

'Inflation and wage differentials in Great Britain', in J. T. Dunlop (ed.), *The theory of wage determination*, London: Macmillan, 1957, pp. 123-135, (B, C).
Argues the view that wage-trends are generally due to the role of 'coercive comparisons' in collective bargaining and that the economy 'has tolerated' these institutional pressures because of its state of full employment and economic growth.

Trade union growth, structure and policy, London: Allen and Unwin, 1962, (B, D).
A theory of trade union structure based on the original analysis of policies of 'openness' and 'closure' developed by the Webbs (1897, see below).

P. Turnbull and G. Williams

'Sex differentials in teachers' pay', *Journal of the Royal Statistical Society*, Series A, Vol. 137, Part 2, 1974, (B, C).
Empirical demonstration of the effects of pre-entry (career) discrimination (see text).

L. Ulman

'Labour mobility and the industrial wage structure in the Post-war United States', *Quarterly Journal of Economics*, Vol. 79, Feb. 1965, pp. 73-97, (B, C).
Institutionalist analysis of relationship between wages and jobs in the U.S.A.

U.S. Bureau of Labour Statistics

'Major collective bargaining agreements: seniority in promotion and transfer provisions', Bulletin 142, 5-11, 1970, (B, C).
Example of manner in which centrally collected statistics may contribute to the understanding of micro-phenomena - given the existence of centralised enforcement procedures!

W. van Voorden

Institutionalisering en arbeidsmarkt. (Institutionalisation and the labour market), Alphen a.d. Rijn: Samsom, 1975, (D).
An analysis of Dutch labour market policies since World War Two from the institutionalist point of view. Only recently has the stage been reached in which one can speak of an active labour market policy, that is a policy which operates on both sides of the market. Under pressure from international developments, especially the OECD, this labour market policy has been closely bound up with the objective of economic growth. Notwithstanding the pressure towards activism in the labour market, policy is still concentrated too much on the supply side of the market and for example does not penetrate into the manpower management of the firm. For that reason the public employment service in the Netherlands has only a limited scope.

B. Vanderostyne-Buysse and C. Festjens- Van Raemdonck

'Arbeidsmarkt en achterblijvers. Loopbanen en levensomstandigheden van werklozen uit het Arrondissement Leuven', (Labour market and laggards. Careers and life chances of unemployed from the district of Louvain), Leuven: S.O.I., 1976, (B, C).
Taking the dual labour market theory as the point of departure the authors conclude that very often the jobs themselves are conducive to the instability which is taken as the central characteristic of secondary workers.

T. Vietorisz

'We need a $ 3.50 minimum wage', *Challenge*, Vol. 16, May/June 1973, pp. 49, pp. 60-61, (A).
Argument for minimum wage legislation (see Robinson, ed., 1970 for opposite argument).

A. Vissers et al.

'Sociale ongelijkheid op de arbeidsmarkt' (Social inequality in the labour market), in J.J. van Hoof and A. Martens (eds.), *Arbeidsmarkt en ongelijkheid. Sociologische Gids 24*, 1977, nos. 1-2,pp. 34-57, (B, D).

Blue collar workers and white-collar workers have both become dependent on the market position of their firm and/or their sector. The historical division between those two classes of workers is making place for a new division between those workers who are in the good jobs/firms/sectors of the economy, and those who are not. The rigidity of this segmentation tendency is shown in that some workers find it almost impossible to cross the barrier between the 'good' and the 'bad' segments (women, young people, immigrant workers, the inept and handicapped).

A.M.C. VISSERS

'Arbeidsmobiliteit en segmentering van de arbeidsmarkt' in J. van Wezel, (ed.), *Arbeidsmarkt in beweging*, The Hague: VUGA, 1977, (B).
Labour market segmentation as a result of a more detailed division of labour in the firms.

H.M. WACHTEL

'Capitalism and poverty in America: paradox or contradiction?' in B. Silverman and M. Yanowitch (eds.), *The worker in 'post-industrial' capitalism: Liberal and radical responses*, New York: The Free Press, 1974, pp. 288-299, (B, D).
The orthodox view sees poverty as individual failure, the radical views poverty as a result of the workings of capitalism, with its structural inequality in the labour market.

'Employment on low wages', *Review of Economics and Statistics*, Vol. 54, May 1972, pp. 121-29, (B, C).
One of the most quoted examples of the use of regression analysis on aggregated data to demonstrate the existence of a dual market.

H.M. WACHTEL and C. BETSEY

'Determinants of working poverty' in H.L. Sheppard, B. Harrison and W.J. Spring, (eds.), op. cit., pp. 77-84, (B, D).
Explanation of factors making for 'positive feedback' effect in American urban ghetto.

M.L. WACHTER

'A labour supply model for secondary workers', *Review of Economics and Statistics*, Vol. 54, May 1972, pp. 141-151, (B, C).

'Wage determination, inflation and the industrial structure', *American Economic Review*, Vol. 63, Sept. 1973, pp. 675-92, (B, C).

'Primary and secondary labour markets: a critique of the dual approach', *Brookings Papers on Economic Activity*, 3, 1974, (A, B).
A well-argued critique of the theory of dual labour markets in which the author sets out to explain the phenomena used as evidence by radical, segmentalist and institutionalist theorists in neo-classical terms.

L. WALRAS

Elements of pure economics, (Trans. by W. Jaffe), London: Macmillan 1954, (A).
Like Jevons, Walras interprets hedonism by means of mathematical method: he is indeed the man who may be said to have created 'hedonistic calculus' in its literal sense. By assuming a valuefree currency (numeraire) he is able to postulate a determinate solution for the problem of general equilibrium.

S. Webb and B. Webb

Industrial democracy, London: Longmans, Green and Co. 1919 edition, (C, D).
Generally regarded as the most profound analysis of the growth and structure of trade unions in Britain in the 19th century. As the authors have demonstrated in the present text its basic sociological analysis is equally applicable to pressure group activity at any period of history.

D. Wedderburn

White-collar redundancy: a case study, Cambridge: Cambridge University Press, 1964, (C, D).

Redundancy and the railwayman, Cambridge: Cambridge University Press, 1965, (C, D).
Two surveys of the effects of redundancy on the social and economic lives of the unemployed.

'Redundancy' in D. Pym (ed.), *Industrial society*, London: Penguin Books, 1968, (D).
Discursive piece on the effects of redundancy on white and blue collar workers.

(ed.) *Poverty, inequality and class structure*, Cambridge: Cambridge University Press, 1974, (C, D).
A collection of essays analysing the social structure of the United Kingdom from a largely radical viewpoint. Significant contributions include those by J. Goldthorpe ('Social inequality and social integration in modern Britain') and R. Milliband ('Politics and poverty').

L. W. Weiss

'Concentration and labour earnings', *American Economic Review*, March 1966, pp. 96-117, (B, C).
This paper tests two hypotheses: (1) that concentrated industries pay high annual rates for labour of 'particular occupations': (2) that these high earnings are more than accounted for by the personal characteristics of the labour employed. The first hypothesis holds up well but the second hypothesis is rejected because of the 'misallocative' effects of union and employer discrimination.

R. D. Weiss

'The effects of education on the earnings of blacks and whites', *Review of Economics and Statistics*, May 1970, (B, C).
Important evidence of post-entry discrimination against blacks; the 'anti-human capital' hypothesis is supported by this data.

F. Welch

'Education and racial discrimination' in O. Ashonfelter and A. Rees (eds.), *Discrimination in labour markets*, Princeton University Press, 1973, (C, D).

'Employment quotas for minorities', *Journal of Political Economy*, Vol. 84, No. 4, part 2, 1976, (C, D).
Discussions of the problems connected with 'reverse-discrimination measures' in the U.S.A.

WETENSCHAPPELIJKE RAAD VOOR HET REGERINGSBELEID (W.R.R.)

Maken wij er werk van? (Let's make a job of it), The Hague: Staatsuitgeverij, 1977, (C, D).
  The Dutch 'think tank's' report on the relationship between active and non-active people in the working population. The proportion of non-actives is growing. Non-actives are those persons who do not actually participate in the labour force and do not receive a wage for doing so (like the jobless, the inept, the sick). To an ever greater extent the actives work to keep the non-actives alive. This poses the difficult question for policy makers whether to accept the increasing inactivity or to try to stem the tide and to try to reduce the number of inactives. The report suggests the latter choice, and proposes measures to reach the goal of a reduction of the number of inactive persons in the population.

J. A. M. VAN WEZEL

Herintreding in het arbeidsproces. Een onderzoek onder werklozen. (Re-entry into the labour force. An investigation among unemployed people), Tilburg: Gianotten, 1972, (C, D).
  Re-entry into the labour force is determined by the objective possibilities of the unemployed person, especially his or her 'personal inferiority', his or her willingness to work and his or her willingness to make sacrifices for re-entrance. In this investigation of a sample of 1700 Dutch unemployed people it is clearly shown that many unemployed stay unemployed because of their inferior market value. Negative willingness to work is more often than not the result of previous experiences of a deprived work situation. Labour market policy does very little to remedy this, partly because it is often exclusively government policy and seldom part of negotiations for collective contracts.

J. VAN WEZEL et al.

De verdeling en waardering van de arbeid. Een studie over ongelijkheid in het arbeidsbestel. (The distribution and evaluation of labour. A study of inequality in work), Tilburg: IVA, 1976, (B, C).
  A review of predominantly Dutch literature on the problems of work and non-work. The attitudes of unions, employer organisations and professional groups are explicitly dealt with. Work and duty of work are still central societal values, but these are differentially evaluated by different societal groups, according to sex, education and age. The authors advocate the decrease of the number of inactive people in the working population and a more active labour market policy on the regional and local level especially by unions and employer organisations.

E. WIGHT BAKKE (ed.)

'Labour mobility and economic opportunity', Technology Press of MIT and Wiley, 1954, (B, C).
  An early attempt to explain mobility/immobility from the viewpoint of the prospective worker.

G. WILLIAMS

Recruitment to skilled trades, London: Routledge and Kegan Paul, 1957, (B, C).
  Early study of occupational choice and socialisation of a largely descriptive nature.

O. E. WILLIAMSON, M. L. WACHTER and J. E. HARRIS

'Understanding the employment relation: the analysis of idiosyncratic exchange'. University of Pennsylvania, 1974, Proceedings, *Bell Journal of Economics and Management Science*, 1975, (B, D).
  Presents an ILM analysis of employment practices.

P. de WOLFF et al.

Wages and labour mobility, Paris: OECD, 1965, (B, C).
  Summary of the neo-classical work on this subject with policy implications.

B. WOOTTON

The social foundations of wage policy, London: Heineman, 1955, (B, D).
  Draws attention to the far-reaching social meanings given to the structure and continuity of earnings in society.

G. D. N. WORSWICK (ed.)

The concept and measurement of involuntary unemployment, London, 1976, (B, C).
  Collection of neo-classical articles covering recent problems of structural unemployment.

P. L. WRIGHT

The coloured worker in British industry, London: Oxford University Press, 1968, pp. 153-8, (D).
  In Wright's survey, 22 respondents (48 %) stated that turnover was lower among coloured workers and only 9 said it was higher.

M. YOUNG and P. WILLMOTT

Family and kinship in East London, Institute of Community Studies, London: Routledge and Kegan Paul, 1957, (D).
  An important study of a working class community which demonstrated its self-supporting nature and the dangers of destroying the extended family basis for this support through the dispersal of such communities in re-housing schemes.

H. L. G. ZANDERS et al.

Kwaliteit van de arbeid, 1977, (Quality of Work, 1977), Tilburg: IVA, 1977, (D).
  Empirical research into the quality of work of a representative sample of people in the Netherlands, based on studies done in the US (Institute for Social Research, Ann Arbor, Michigan)

D. ZISKIND

'Affirmative action vs. seniority, retro-active seniority: a remedy for hiring discrimination', Industrial Relations Research Association, Proceedings of the 1976 Annual Spring Meeting, Denver, Colorado, May 6-8th, 1976, (C, D).
  Example of the concern of dualists for the effects of specific hiring and promotion blockages in an American firm.

Supplementary bibliography

AMERICAN BUREAU OF CENSUS

Census of population. Occupation by earnings and education, Washington: Government Printing Office, 1973, (C).
  Ten yearly survey which provides the basis for most American statistical and econometric studies in this area.

Ann Arbor Studies

Institute of Labour and Industrial Relations Research Group, Ann Arbor, Michigan, 1976, (C, D).
  A verbal account of research on the economic activity of poor whites and blacks in Detroit ghettoes given to Professor Loveridge in May 1976.

P. ANTHONY

The ideology of work, London: Tavistock, 1977, (D).
  Alienating effects of the mechanisms of the labour market from a Marxian perspective.

Arbeidsblad, Vol. 78, June-July 1977, Nos. 6-7, 'De tewerkstelling en de werkloosheid van de vrouwen in België' (Employment and unemployment of women in Belgium). Brussels: Ministry of Employment and Labour of Belgium, (B,C).
  Statistical evidence of the existence of labour market segmentation and of mainly post-entry discrimination of women in Belgium.

G.S. BAIN

'Trade union growth and recognition with special reference to white collar unions in private industry', *British Journal of Industrial Relations,* Vol. IV, November 1966, pp. 304-335. See also: Royal Commission on Trade Unions and Employer Associations, Research Paper No. 6, H.M.S.O., 1967, and *The growth of white collar unionism,* Oxford: Oxford University Press, 1970, (C,D).
  A historical account of the growth of white collar unionism in the U.K. The author develops a model in which the density of unionism is seen to be a function of the level of bureaucratisation in the work-place, the degree to which employers are prepared to recognise unions and the extent of governmental action supporting union recognition.

F.J. BAYLISS

British wages councils, London: Heinemann, 1964, (C,D).
  A review of the work of statutory minimum wage councils in Britain. The author concludes that their effect on the level of earnings in low-wage sectors of employment was minimal.

H. Behrend

'The effort bargain', *Industrial and Labor Relations Review,* Vol. 10, No. 4, 1957, (C,D).
   One of the first attempts to conceptualise the manner in which earnings levels are set
   through fractional bargaining in the work place.

J. Berting

Paradigmata, sociaal-wetenschappelijk onderzoek en engagement van de onderzoeker
(Paradigms, sociological research and involvement of the researcher), Rotterdam: Erasmus
'University, 1976, (D).
   A very useful taxonomy of sociological theories.

P.M. Blau and O.D. Duncan

The American occupational structure, New York/London: John Wiley, 1967, (C,D).
   An ambitious attempt to model the American occupational structure on the basis of
   sample surveys.

B.R. Blishen

'The construction and use of an occupationel class scale', *Canadian Journal of Economics
and Political Science*, Vol. XXIV, No. 4, November 1958, pp. 520-535, (C).
   An early attempt to classify occupations in terms of their input of training and the formal
   qualification required for entry.

N. Bosanquet and G. Standing

'Government and unemployment 1966-1970: a study of policy and evidence', *British
Journal of Industrial Relations*, Vol. X, No. 2, July 1972, pp. 180-192, (D).
   A critique of government statistics on employment and unemployment. Suggests the
   introduction of a 'permanent' occupational level based on jobs held by unemployed
   workers over the previous five years of work.

E. Bott

Family and social network, London: Tavistock, 1957, (D).
   A study of personal frames of reference which demonstrates the reliance that individual
   actors have on immediate social contacts in building their general images of society at
   large.

J. Bracke

'Werkeloosheid', *De nieuwe maand*, Vol. 20, 1977, No. 5, pp. 247-306, (C).
   A series of three articles on unemployment in one issue of the journal, with empirical
   evidence of the existence of a dual labour market in Belgium.

D. Braybrook and C.E. Lindblom

A strategy for decision, New York: Free Press of Glencoe, 1969, (D).
   An explanation of business decisions as an incremental process related to the contingencies of the organisational environment.

C. Brinton

The anatomy of revolution, New York: Vintage Books, 1958, (D).
Sets out a 'J-curve' theory of revolutions in which collective aspirations are seen to move ahead of realised expectations at a point where the latter cease to rise in pace with the former.

W. Brown

'Piecework wage determination in Coventry', *Scottish Journal of Political Science*, Vol. XVIII, No. 1, February, 1971, (C,D).
This study shows piecework earnings to be insensitive to changes in the external labour market and to fluctuations in profits. Much of the 'wage-drift' within companies is also unassociated with increases in productivity. Earnings levels relate to workers expectations established by 'custom and practice'.

Lord Bullock

Report of the Committee of Inquiry on Industrial Democracy, London H.M.S.O. (Cmnd 6706), January, 1977, (D).
Report of the committee set up by Harold Wilson in 1975 to enquire into the possibilities of shop floor representation at the board of director level of private and public companies and corporations in the United Kingdom.

John Child

'Organisational structure, environment and performance: the role of strategic choice', *Sociology*, Vol. 6, No. 1, January 1972, pp. 1-22, (D).
The author argues against a simple deterministic theory of organizational structure. He suggests that 'strategic choice' extends to the context within which an organisation is operating, to the standards of performance against which the pressure of economic constraints has to be evaluated, as well as to the structure itself.

H. Clay

The problems of industrial relations, London: Macmillan, 1929, pp. 213-30, (C).
A restatement of neo-classical wage-theory in institutional (described here as 'dynamic') terms.

Department of Employment

'Unemployment in the United Kingdom', *Department of Employment Gazette*, September 1977, p. 964, (C).
A breakdown of statistics of registered unemployed in the United Kingdom showing Commonwealth 'coloured' immigrants suffer a proportionate amount of unemployment similar to that of the population as a whole. Occupation, duration of previous unemployment, age (at both extremes) and the assessment of the applicants' chances by the government employment official handling the case, were all better predictors of the applicants' chances of stable employment.

L.A. Dicks-Mireaux and J.C.R. Dow

'The determinants of wage inflation - United Kingdom 1945-1956', *Journal of the Royal Statistical Society*, Series A, Vol. 122, part 2, page 145, 1959, (C,D).
Puts forward a statistical index for the effect of trade union 'pushfulness' on the rate of inflation in the UK economy.

246   SUPPLEMENTARY BIBLIOGRAPHY

R. DORE

British factory - Japanese factory. The origins of national diversity in industrial relations,
London: George Allen and Unwin, 1973, (D).
  An attempt to compare the culture and internal labour market of an English factory with
  that of a Japanese establishment. The comparison is used to develop a theory of
  industrialisation based on the belief that the 'late developer' learns from the experiences
  of industrialisation in other countries.

J. DUNLOP

Wage determination under trade unions, (New York: Augustus Kelley,) 1944, Oxford:
Blackwell, 1950, (A,D).
  An 'economic' interpretation of trade union strategy in which similarities in wage-levels
  (wage-contours) emerge from the 'satisficing' behaviour of union leaders. Resulted in a
  remarkable dialogue with A. Ross whose 'political' explanations placed more emphasis
  on the 'orbits of coercive comparisons' resulting from member expectations.

W.R. DYMOND

'Impact of wider educational opportunities on labour markets: a life-long educational
experience', Proceedings of the 4th World Congress of the International Industrial
Relations Association, Geneva, September 1976, (D).
  Assessment of influence of educational access on the careers of women and other
  minority groups.

S. ERBES-SEGUIN, C. CASSASSUS and O. KOURCHID

Les conditions de développement du conflict industriel, Report to the Ministry of Labour by
the Groupe de Sociologie du Travail, Paris, 1977, (D).
  Reports on industrial conflict in several industries and within a number of French
  companies which provide evidence of the nature of segmental markets.

L. FAASE

Arbeid en mobiliteit - de verdeling en waardering (Labour and mobility - distribution and
evaluation,) Rotterdam, Erasmus University, 1977, (C).
  Report of a research project on optimal allocation of labour comparing the attitudes to
  work and mobility of movers and non-movers in the Netherlands.

A. FLANDERS

The internal social responsibilities of industry, in A. Flanders: *Management and unions*,
London: Faber and Faber, 1970, pp. 129-153 (first published 1966), (D).
  A moralistic essay on the manner in which managerial responsibilities should be
  exercised in changing the existing basis of the 'psychological contract' of employment.

M.P. FOGARTY, R. RAPOPORT and R.M. RAPOPORT

Sex, career and family, London: George Allen and Unwin, 1971, (C).
  An anthropological approach to segmentation based on an analysis of social prejudice in
  its socio-historical context.

M. FRIEDMAN

A theory of the consumption function, Washington: National Bureau of Economic Research, 1957, (A).
> An explanation of changes in propensity to consume according to anticipations of long term or 'normative' income on the part of the consumer.

H. FRIEDRICH et. al.

Frauenarbeit und technischer Wandel, (Women's work and technical change), Frankfurt a. Main: RKW, 1973, (C).
> Technology brings about a polarisation in the structure of the labour market whereby women generally take the unqualified jobs, while men take the qualified ones.

V. FUCHS

Differentials in hourly earnings by region and city size, Occasional Paper 101, New York: National Bureau for Economic Research, 1967, (C).
> The author uses statistical standardisation procedures to explain differences in earnings levels between North and South in the USA. He finds that one third of regional differences are due to differences in 'human-capital', one third to the smaller average size of city (employer monopsony of labour) and much of the remainder to discrimination against the black population.

J. GAITSKELL

'Study of employment', Unpublished survey used by E.J.B. Roxe et al., *Colour and Citizenship*, Oxford: Oxford University Press, 1969, (C).
> A local study demonstrating pre-entry job discrimination.

M. GAY and W.L. TONGE

'The late effects of loss of parents in childhood', *British Journal of Psychiatry*, Vol. 113, 1967, pp. 753-759, (D).
> A study demonstrating an association between social inadequacy and parental loss in childhood.

E. GOFFMAN

Interaction ritual - essays on face-to-face behavior, New York: Anchor Books, 1967, (D).
> An account of the ways in which social interaction has become stylized in American society in a manner which alienates individuals from its former meaning and basis of reciprocity. Rules may however be changed by action and response within 'serious' situations.

E. HALÉVY

The growth of philosophic radicalism, Boston: Beacon Press, 1955 (Orig. 1928), (A).
> A philosophical critique of utilitarianism.

K. HALL and I. MILLER

'Industrial attitudes to skills dilution.', *British Journal of Industrial Relations*, Vol. IX, No. 1, March, 1971, pp. 1-20, (C,D).
    An assessment of union attitudes to skills dilution based on a survey of the experiences of 184 men trained on short courses in Government Training Centres in the U.K.

P. HALL and W.L. TONGE

'Long-standing continuous unemployment in male patients with psychiatric symptoms', *British Journal of Preventive Social Medecine*, Vol. 17, 1963, pp. 191-196, (D).
    A study associating poor employment record with psychiatric symptoms.

A.I. HARRIS

Labour mobility in Great Britain, 1953-1963, London: H.M.S.O. 1966, (C).
    An empirical study containing a critique of labour-turnover as an index of social or economic stability: points out need for indices which reflect other aspects of the workplace and labour market situation.

F. HERRON

Labour market in crisis. Redundancy at Upper Clyde Shipbuilders, London and Basingstoke: Macmillan, 1975, (C).
    Examines the behaviour of redundant workers and the effectiveness of the public employment office in combating unemployment.

P. HESSELING

'The institutional structuring of the labour market', Unpublished paper from a conference on *The future of industrial relations*, Santa Marguerita, Italy, April 1978, (D).
    An illustration of the manner in which labour market expectations are shaped by governmental and other institutionalised agencies.

J.R. HICKS and R.G.D. ALLEN

'A consideration of the theory of value', *Economica*, 1934, (A).
    A questioning of the nominal function of utility.

J.J. VAN HOOF

'Arbeidsmarktonderzoek op een keerpunt' (Labour market research at a turning point), in Arbeidsmarkt en ongelijkheid, J.J. van Hoof and A. Martens (eds), *Sociologische Gids*, Vol. 24, 1977, nos. 1-2, pp. 5-33, (D).
    Segmental theory has gradually changed the focus of labour market research in Belgium and the Netherlands to the labour market as the most important source of unequal distribution of income, power and privileges in societies and to the demand side of that market.

J.J. HUGHES

'The role of manpower training programmes: a critical look at re-training in the United

Kingdom', *British Journal of Industrial Relations*, Vol. X, No. 2, July, 1972, pp. 206-223, (C).
> This paper examines the benefits that are likely to result from investment in manpower re-training. In particular the author stresses the need for flexibility and adaptability in the management of re-training.

P. A. KOEFOED

Een schets van een onderzoeksmodel van de arbeidsmarkt, (Outline of a research model for the labour market), Amsterdam: SISWO, 1972, (D).
> Argues among others that the malfunctioning of the labour market is mainly a problem of information flows. Uses Dutch and other material.

J. W. KUHN

Grievance settlement, New York: Columbia University Press, 1961, (C,D).
> An early study of fractional bargaining between work groups in the workplace.

S.M. LIPSET and R. BENDIX

Social mobility in industrial society, Berkeley: University of California Press, 1959, (D).
> One of the pioneering studies of these authors on the effects of social unequality on social, political and economic behaviour in advanced industrialised societies.

I.M.D. LITTLE

A critique of welfare economics, Oxford: Oxford University Press, 1950, (A).
> A lucid critique of the formal new-classical exposition of welfare, or community, economics using the same, neo-classical, frame of reference.

R. LOVERIDGE

'Decision making as a participative process', Unpublished working paper. University of Aston, 1978, (D).
> An attempt to categorise decision making activities in relation to modes of subordinate participation.

'Bureaucratisation and the Occupational Interest Association: alternative approaches to white collar unionisation', Unpublished working paper, University of Aston, 1978, (D).
> An attempt to extend the positivistic association of factors found to be related to unionisation in Bains analysis.

MANPOWER SERVICES COMMISSION

Report on adolescent unemployment, London: HMSO, May, 1977, (C).
> A study of the effects of unemployment on young people based on aggregated data combined with qualitative judgements.

M. MARKOWE, W.L. TONGE and L.E.D. BARBER
'Psychiatric disability and employment: a survey of 222 registered disabled persons', *British Journal of Preventive Social Medicine*, Vol. 9, 1955, pp. 39-45, (D).
> A study showing an empirical association between poor employment record and early experience of psychiatric disability within the family.

A. MARTENS

'De destructuratie van de arbeidsmarkt' (The destructuration of the labour market), in
Arbeidsmarkt en ongelijkheid, J.J. van Hoof and A. Martens (eds); *Sociologische Gids*,
Vol. 24, 1977, nos. 1-2, pp. 118-136, (B,C).
 Dualist treatment of the labour market from a Marxian perspective which points at the
 gradual destructuration of the primary segment as a source of dynamics in the labour
 market. Contains empirical evidence from Belgium.

U. MEHRLÄNDER

*Beschäftigung ausländischer Arbeitnehmer in der Bundesrepublik Deutschland unter
spezieller Berücksichtigung von Nordrhein-Westfalen.* (Employment of foreign workers in
Germany, especially in Nordrhein-Westfalen), Köln: Westdeutscher Verlag, 1969, (C,D).
 An empirical study of the employment conditions apertaining to foreign workers in West
 Germany.

R. MEIDNER

Employee investment funds: an approach to collective capital formation, London: George
Allen and Unwin, 1978, (British edn. translated by Dr. T.L. Johnston), (C,D).
 Radical proposal for capital ownership by trade unions in Sweden.

R.K. MERTON

Social theory and social structure, New York: Free Press, 1949, (D). See also A.K.
Cohen, The study of social disorganisation and deviant behavior, in R.K. Merton et al.
(eds), *Sociology today - Problems and prospects*, Vol. II, New York: Harper Torchbook,
1965, pp. 461-484, (D).
 Deviant behaviour is seen as a response to strain. The latter is defined as individual
 ambivalence relative to the institutionalised expectations of the group when the subject is
 positively motivated to respond to these expectations but is frustrated by overriding
 constraints and obligations. Merton sets out several adaptive responses which range
 from confrontation to ritualistic conformity.

H. MINTSBERG

The nature of managerial work, New York: Harper and Row, 1973, (D).
 An analysis of managerial decision-making as a process involving a number of
 categorised activities.

NETHERLANDS MINISTRY OF EDUCATION AND SCIENCES

National programme of labour market research, The Hague, 1978, (C).

Hoofdlijnen van het nationaal programma arbeidsmarktonderzoek, The Hague: Staatsuitgeverij, 1978, (C).
 These brochures contain the main elements of the long term planning of labour market
 research with an eye to an effective labour market policy of the Dutch government.

G.M. NORRIS

'Unemployment, subemployment and personal characteristics', (A) the inadequacies of
traditional approaches to unemployment; (B) job separation and work histories: the

alternative approach, *Sociological Review*, Vol. 26, 1978, nos. 1 and 2, pp. 89-108 and pp. 327-347, (B,C).

    Forcefully argues the case for taking account of job characteristics (as opposed to personal characteristics) in causing unemployment and subemployment.

OFFICE OF POPULATION CENSUSES AND SURVEYS

Young peoples employment study: preliminary report, No. 1, London, OCPS, social survey division, 1973, (C).

    With a second report published in 1974 the first real attempts to analyse this segment of the labour market in the United Kingdom.

J. PEN

Income distribution, London: Allen Lane, 1971, (A).

    Important neo-classical textbook on theories of incomes distribution as related to the labour market.

S. PERLMAN

A theory of the labor movement, New York: Kelley, 1949 edn, (first published 1922), (B,D).

    A theory of unionism based on 'job-consciousness' and an awareness of the scarcity of employment opportunities among workers.

PROJEKTGRUPPE ARBEITSMARKTPOLITIK/CLAUS OFFE (eds)

Opfer des Arbeitsmarktes. Zur Theorie der strukturierten Arbeitslosigkeit (Sacrifices in the labour market. Towards a theory of structured unemployment), Neuwied/Darmstadt: Luchterhand, 1977, (B,C,D).

    A forcefully argued collection of articles on the theme of the increasing 'polarisation' of the labour market between good and bad jobs and the increasing part played by disadvantaged workers in a capitalist economy.

D.S. PUGH, D.J. HICKSON, and C. TURNER

'Dimensions of organisation structure', *Administrative Science Quarterly*, Vol. 13, 1968, pp. 65-105, (C,D).

    A pioneering attempt to operationalise the six primary dimensions of organisational structure in a manner which allowed their measurement.

B. RADIN

'Coloured workers and Britain trade unions', *Race*, Vol. 8, 1966, pp. 157-173, (D).

    A study of the enforcement of racial discrimination in the United Kingdom.

A.H. RICHMOND

Migration and race relations in a English city: a study in Bristol, Oxford: Oxford University Press, 1973, (D).

    A well-drawn picture of pre-entry job discrimination on racial grounds in one English city.

O. ROELS, I. VANOVERBEKE and P. VAN ROMPUY

Theorie en empirie van de arbeidsmobiliteit in België (Theory and empiry of labour mobility in Belgium), Leuven: Acco, 1975, (C).
   Empirical evidence of labour mobility in Belgium from a neo-classical point of view.

ROYAL COMMISSION (LORD DONOVAN)

Report on trades unions and employer associations 1965-1968, London, HMSO, Cmnd 3623, 1968, (C,D).
   A lucid description and analysis of British industrial relations in the 1960's with a particular focus on the engineering industry.

J. RUBERY

'Structured labour markets, worker organisation and low pay', *Cambridge Journal of Economics*, 1978, pp. 17-36, (B).
   The role of trade unions in bringing about or maintaining labour market segmentation.

M.H. RUTTER, B. GULE, J.F. MORTON and C. BAGLEY

'Children of West Indian immigrants. Home circumstances and family patterns', *Journal of Child Psychology and Psychiatry*, Vol. 16, 1975, pp. 105-124, (D).

M.H. RUTTER, J. TIZARD and K. WHITMORE (eds)

Education, health and behaviour, London: Longman, 1970, (D).
   One of several psychological studies of intergenerational continuities in the effects of social environment on families.

SALMON COMMITTEE

Report of the commitee on Senior Nursing Staff, Ministry of Health, London: HMSO, 1970, (D).
   One of the several administrative reforms to the British National Health Service suggested and enacted during the 1960's and early 1970's. This report gave qualified (Registered) nurses the opportunity for promotion to senior managerial positions in the N.H.S.

L. SAYLES

Behavior of industrial work groups: prediction and control, New York: John Wiley, 1958, (C,D).
   An influential analysis of the negotiating strategies of industrial work groups according to their prior orientations to their work, occupation and their position within the technology and work flow of the organisation.

E.H. SCHEIN

Organisational socialisation and the profession of management, in D. Koll et al. (eds), *Organisational psychology: a book of readings*, Englewood Cliffs: Prentice Hall, 1974 (2nd ed.), (D).
   A higly normative but insightful analysis of organisational socialisation as a phased process.

W.H. Scott, J.A. Banks, A.H. Halsey and T. Lupton

Technical change and industrial relations - a study of the relations between technical change and the social structure of a large steelworks, Liverpool: Liverpool University Press, 1956, (B,D).
   A pioneering study of the workings of a company-based internal labour market.

N.J. Smelser

Theory of collective behaviour, London: Routledge and Kegan Paul, 1976 edn. (first published 1962), (D).
   A structuralist's explanation of collective behaviour moving through a series of staged processes from the source of experienced 'strain' to the choice of collective action to be taken in response to it.

O. Stevenson

From the general to the specific, Report to the UK Dept. of Health and Social Security, London, 1975, (D).
   A review of empirical studies demonstrating an association between childhood experiences and social inadequacy in later life.

A.F. Sturmthal (ed.)

Contemporary collective bargaining in seven countries, Ithaca, New York: Institute of International Industrial and Labor Relations, Cornell University Press, 1957, (D).
   One of the early collections of comparative descriptions of industrial relations systems.

H.A. Turner

Trade union growth, structure, and policy, London: George Allen and Unwin, 1962, (D).
   An extension of the Webbs-morphology of trade union structure into a concept of 'openness' or closure in the unions' recruitment policy.

T. Vietorrz and B. Harrison

'Labor market segmentation: positive feedback and divergent development', *American Economic Review - Papers and proceedings*, Vol. 63, 1973, 366-376, (B,C).
   Neo-classical labour market theory is characterized by 'negative feedback mechanisms': high wages lead to substitution leads to a fall in demand for labour and subsequently lower wages. V. and H., however, discern a stronger 'positive feedback' mechanism: investment in capital leads to higher productivity and subsequently to higher wages, while in labour intensive production processes productivity, and hence wages, remain low.

A. Vissers and T. Heinen

Werkloosheid en herintreding. Een secundaire analyse. Deel 1: Informatiekanalen en sollicitatieprocedures, (Unemployment and re-entry. A secondary analysis), Tilburg: IVA, 1976, (C).
   Relationship between job search and duration of unemployment using Dutch empirical material.

J.A.M. Van Wezel (ed.)

Arbeidsmarkt in beweging. Analyse, planning en beleid (The dynamics of the labour market. Analysis, planning and policy), The Hague: VUGA, 1977, (D).
    A collection of articles on the relationship between job structure and labour market policy in the Netherlands.

B. Wootton

Social science and social pathology, London: George Allen and Unwin, 1959, (D).
    One of the earliest attempts to conceptualize a theory of 'labelling' to explain social deviancy.

A. Ziderman and C. Driver

'A Markov chain model of the benefits of participating in government training schemes', *The Manchester School*, December 1973. See also A. Siderman and A. Walder, 'Trade unions and the acceptability of G.T.C. trainees: some survey results', *British Journal of Industrial Relations*, Vol. XIII, No. 1, 1975, (C,D).
    Two of several empirically based papers from a project designed to assess the usefulness of statutorily provided government skills training: the general judgement is favourable.

Index